The making of a counsellor

... essays in *The Making of a Counsellor* offer a
... rature on counselling. In the first place, they
demonstrate the versatility of psychoanalytically based counselling, as they
... which on the face
of ... illustrate
worl ... ans and
debt ... aticians,
and ... groups
of p ... rk with
neur ... amilies,
and ... on of a
coun ... of the
prob ... second
aspe ... he two-
year ... nd they
port ... gling to
beco ... eir new
learn

In ... hat the
expe ... g it an
excel ... me, the
wide ... s on the
appli ... rienced
coun

Ellen ... nselling
Tuto ... dies at
Birkb ...

The original and thoughtful essays in *The Making of a Counsellor* [illegible] double contribution to the literature on counselling. In [illegible] demonstrate the versatility of psychodynamically based [illegible] describe how the ideas and techniques are used in settings [illegible] seem to offer little scope for a counsellor. Two case studies [illegible] done with 'impossible' clients; other essays about orphaned [illegible] accountancy trainees and expatriate employees, mathematics [illegible] musicians take the reader into new ways of thinking about these [illegible] people. More traditional, perhaps, are the essays about work [illegible] physical patients, [illegible] youth club members, traumatised [illegible] the chronically mentally ill, but each one speaks from the position of [illegible] counsellor, breaking fresh ground in understanding the complexities [illegible] problems and the richness of the counselling relationship. This is the [illegible] of the book. The authors of the essays were all at the end of [illegible] course leading to a Diploma in Adult or Student Counselling, [illegible] essay in the writing something of the personal process of struggling [illegible] become a professional counsellor and delighting in the efficacy of [illegible] [illegible]

[illegible] vivid narrative, *The Making of a Counsellor* conveys what [illegible] experience of thinking and working as a counsellor is like, making it [illegible] excellent introductory text for would-be counsellors. At the same time, [illegible] range of situations covered in the essays offers new perspectives on [illegible] versatility of counselling which will be of interest to more experienced [illegible] psychotherapists and allied professionals.

[illegible] Noonan is Head of Counselling and Lawrence Spurling a Counsellor [illegible] at the University of London Centre for Extra-Mural Studies, [illegible] College. They are both practising counsellors and psychotherapists.

The making of a counsellor

Edited by
Ellen Noonan
and
Laurence Spurling

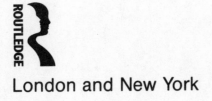

ROUTLEDGE
London and New York

First published in 1992
by Routledge
11 New Fetter Lane, London EC4P 4EE

Simultaneously published in the USA and Canada
by Routledge
29 West 35th Street, New York, NY 10001

Reprinted 1993

Typeset in Times by EXCEPT*detail* Ltd, Southport
Printed and bound in Great Britain by
Mackays of Chatham plc, Chatham, Kent

A Tavistock/Routledge publication

British Library Cataloguing in Publication Data
A catalogue record for this book is available from the British Library.

Library of Congress Cataloging in Publication Data
The Making of a Counsellor/edited by Ellen Noonan and Lawrence Spurling.
p. cm.
Includes bibliographical references and index.
1. Counseling–Case studies. 2. Psychodynamic psychotherapy–Case studies. I. Noonan, Ellen.
II. Spurling , Lawrence, 1950–
BF637.C6M285 1992 91–43167
158′.3–dc20 CIP

ISBN 0–415–06768–5

Where there is no guidance, a people falls; but in an abundance of counsellors there is safety.

Proverbs 11:14

Contents

Contributors

Diana Bass has a background in general nursing in South Africa. She has worked in both adult and student counselling in individual and group work, and is presently working as a student and staff counsellor in the United Medical and Dental School of St Thomas' and Guy's Hospitals in London.

Anne Bell, after twenty years in teaching, now works as a counsellor at Open House and at the College of Law in Guildford, Surrey.

Ena Blyth was a teacher of mathematics at a girls' comprehensive school when she wrote her paper. Subsequently she has trained as a psychotherapist and is now in private practice.

Julia Bridgment was the Student Examination Manager of a large international accountancy firm when she wrote her paper. She is currently pursuing her training as a counsellor.

Julia Buckroyd was Director of Hollins College, London, at the time of writing her paper and is now a psychotherapist in private practice and co-therapist at the Vector Centre for Eating Disorders, London.

Trudy Chapman, after ten years in the youth service, is now a staff counsellor for the Guy's and Lewisham National Health Service Trust.

Sally Holder was working in the headquarters of a large international organization in the public sector at the time of writing. At present she is at home, bringing up her son.

Maya Jarrett worked in an agency for the chronically mentally ill. Her main interest is in short-term counselling and she is currently starting her private practice in London.

Angela Mann is currently working as a welfare rights adviser in a New Town Advice Centre. She has recently been involved in the setting up of a redundancy counselling service.

Elizabeth Nabarro worked as a research psychologist on projects dealing with adolescent and family problems before training as a psychodynamic counsellor. She now works as a student counsellor and is training as a psychotherapist.

John Nicholas trained while counselling the long-term mentally ill, as described in his paper. Currently he is employed by South Warwickshire Health Authority in a community centre that offers psychodynamic counselling individually or in groups.

Barbara Rickinson trained and practised as a student counsellor before becoming the head of the newly established Support and Counselling Service at Birmingham University.

Preface

The essays in this book were written by students of the *Diploma in Student Counselling* and *Diploma in Adult Counselling* courses run by the University of London Centre for Extra-Mural Studies at Birkbeck College. They were originally submitted as dissertations (except for Chapters 11 and 12, which were written as case studies), the final piece of work to be done before graduation.

The dissertation is designed to show how the student has brought together theoretical understanding and counselling practice. The courses teach a common theoretical framework, derived from the tradition of psycho-dynamic therapy and counselling. But it is for each student to interpret this tradition in the light of their new experience and integrate it with the demands of their work role. The theory has to become their own, so that it gives shape and expression to a way of working which is truly personal.

This is an important part of how a professional identity as a counsellor comes to be assumed or constructed by each student, and these essays illustrate this process in a particularly compelling way. Whether they are engaged in explicit counselling, or in work with a counselling component, or applying a counselling perspective in a particular setting, the authors recount their experiences with that mixture of candour, humour, anguish, bemusement and exuberance which often characterizes this stage of gaining a qualification but losing one's innocence.

In preparing this book for publication we have asked each author to undertake some necessary revision and editing. Details of clients, interviewees, and institutions have been changed or omitted in order to preserve confidentiality. Some authors have taken the opportunity of inserting a few comments in the present tense, looking back over a piece of work which might have been written several years ago. Considerations of space have meant that some parts of the original dissertations have been abridged or left out. But in all cases we have ensured that, both in substance and in spirit, these essays are a record of each student's *rite de passage* from novice to counsellor.

We would like to acknowledge permission from the *Bulletin of the British Association of Psychotherapists* to reprint the paper 'Mirrors on girls and maths' by Ena Blyth, which appeared in the issue of July 1985, pp. 73–98, and is an edited version of her original dissertation.

The papers in this book came out of each author's individual experience, which was shaped by being part of a particular group of students and staff, and it is to all of those involved in the Diploma Counselling Courses of the Centre for Extra-Mural Studies that this book is dedicated.

Ellen Noonan, *Head of Counselling Section, University of London Centre for Extra-Mural Studies at Birkbeck College*

Laurence Spurling, *Course Tutor, Diploma in Adult Counselling Course, University of London Centre for Extra-Mural Studies at Birkbeck College*

September 1991

Introduction

> Our civilization imposes an almost intolerable pressure on us and it calls for a corrective. Is it too fantastic to expect that psycho-analysis in spite of its difficulties may be destined to the task of preparing mankind for such a corrective? Perhaps once more an American may hit on the idea of spending a little money to get the 'social workers' of his country trained analytically and to turn them into a band of helpers for combating the neuroses of civilization.[1]

Courses in psychodynamic counselling have been offered by the University of London Centre for Extra-Mural Studies since 1972. The first one, the Certificate in Student Counselling, was the product of a confluence of two 'missions'. From the one direction came the recognition that the traditional medical services in educational institutions were inadequate to the demands being made on them, and they might not, in any case, provide the best response to the kinds of problems students have. In the main, these problems are developmental hitches rather than physical or psychiatric illnesses, and they take a form which implicates the academic tasks and setting. From the other direction came a commitment to the dissemination of the ideas and techniques of psychoanalysis, taking them out of the consulting room into the work-place and applying their insights to the particular needs and problems of various everyday situations – in this case, to the business of teaching and learning in educational organizations. Perhaps, as Freud had hoped, non-medical people with a professional understanding of the psychological aspects and hazards of learning could be trained so that they could look after the personal well-being as well as the academic achievement of students?

The challenge of creating this hybrid creature and promoting the integration of a counselling perspective into the educational process led to the design of the first course. In subsequent years, that course was expanded and refined, eventually becoming a diploma; and the same values and principles underlying it were replicated in the more recent Diploma in Adult Counselling which embraces just about every occupation which has an integral element of responsibility and concern for the emotional health and development of people. (There are other shorter courses offered for specific professional groups and as tasters of what counselling involves, but those are not central to this book.)

The two 'missions' could join relatively easily because they were both looking to the same horizon. A second confluence of forces was rather more turbulent and potentially troublesome. We needed to attend to the voices of two masters who had significantly different requirements. One was the university which set standards of academic and intellectual achievement; the other was the profession of counselling, which was developing formally at the same time and was setting standards of practical competence and personal maturity. These four forces acting together provided the 'problem' which had to be resolved through the design of the course.

We began with the view that the two 'voices' may be different but not incompatible. In fact, a debilitating gap between intellectual and emotional capabilities was exactly the kind of problem frequently presented to student counsellors, so the course itself could become a model of how to work on the relationship between them. This set the framework for the design: the course is conceived of as a learning institution, and the participants' immediate experience of being students on the course and members of this temporary institution is used as material for studying learning-based problems (exam anxiety, rivalry and envy in the classroom, authority and dependency issues around the rules of the university and the staff as teachers and managers), 'ordinary' human problems as they arise in the lives of the members while they are on the course (making and breaking of relationships, birth and death, separation and reunion, love and hate, career decisions and work stress, and so on), and the dynamics of organizations.

To do this we maintain the expectation throughout that the content and the shared events in the lifetime of the course will be personally meaningful for everyone, and we set aside regular time and space for the students and staff to consider together those meanings at a personal and group level and in particular how they affect our ability to teach and learn. We anticipate that these discussions will promote personal insight and development as well as greater understanding of the theory and technique being taught. For instance, in the first meeting of the course we make a space for people to speak about their anticipatory hopes and fears as they enter into a new experience and try to find their place in a new group of people. They link these to other personal experiences of beginning and joining and, as they conceptualize these feelings, they also relate them to issues in counselling when, say, the client arrives for a first session, speaks apprehensively about taking up a new job, or anxiously avoids meeting the 'in-laws' for the first time. We are aware that we are treading a fine line between therapy and education in promoting this degree of explicit self-reflection, but the feelings and interactions are continually linked with work and work problems. Furthermore, learning to contain and control the personal responses which have been aroused by the work is part of acquiring the professional stance of a counsellor.

Although the focus on student problems is not so germane to the Adult Counselling course, the pursuit of professional development through personal learning is equally relevant. Here, too, what the students are learning will evoke a response from their own experiences of similar situations, they will find points of contact with their own fears, recollections, yearnings, worries, and dreams, and through analysing these and relating them to their work the learning becomes alive and significant.

The structure of the courses is based on the premise that counsellors need a good grasp of theory, a repertoire of skills, well-developed self understanding, and a broad awareness of organizational and professional factors in order to practise effectively and ethically. Each course meets for a day a week over two academic years, and each day is structured to work on these four basic elements. It has a theoretical component where, through lectures, seminars, and guided reading, the members can gain a solid grounding in psychoanalytic ideas about human growth and development and the nature of emotional problems; practical components where, through case discussion and practical workshops, they can learn counselling techniques and processes and can explore the complexity of the counselling relationship or the application of these ideas and principles to other working relationships and their organizations; and a personal component where, in the groups as described above and in individual tutorials, they can reflect on the emotional impact of what they are learning. The institutional element consists mainly of a residential week in the summer between the two years where through intensive group work they can become aware of the conscious and unconscious forces at work in organizations which affect how people function in their roles and teams.

The assessment follows this structure closely: students are examined in a traditional way on the academic syllabus to demonstrate their grasp of the theory; they present a case study to demonstrate their proficiency in counselling and their capacity to reflect on their work; they are continually assessed on their progress on the course and in their work; and they write a dissertation which demonstrates their ability to relate theory to practice by developing a theme arising from their work.

Not everyone on the courses is, intends to become, or even wishes to become a counsellor (nor do we encourage that, given the basic philosophy of the course), but they do wish to discover the potential for using counselling processes in one-to-one or group relationships, whether the purpose is therapeutic, educational, supportive, managerial, or developmental. The single formal requirement for entry to the course is that applicants are engaged in counselling (full-time or part-time, as the whole or part of their work), and the students come from a broad range of settings: education, religion, hospitals and community health care, youth work, the social services, legal centres, commercial businesses, local authority and government services, careers offices, and specialist counselling and advice agencies. On the whole they hold a degree, may well have a postgraduate academic or vocational qualification, and are likely to have already completed a basic course in counselling. Most have had or can contemplate personal counselling or psychotherapy for themselves.

Because we believe that a major tool of counselling is the individual's capacity to use his/her own self in the work, we attend carefully to that in the rigorous selection procedure. Applicants have an in-depth interview which aims to assess their motivation for undertaking counselling work and their comfort with the psychoanalytic framework, whether they are mature enough to learn from the experiential nature of the course, and whether they have the internal resilience and external support for sustaining them through the stresses of the course. There is also a group interview structured as a case discussion where they can show a sample of their way of approaching a counselling problem and where their capacity to work in this paradoxically co-operative and competitive setting can be assessed. A third short interview tidies up loose ends and asks the applicant to reflect on the process of being selected. Together these three events give the applicants a taste of what is to come and what is expected of them. A group of about twenty students is put together from these interviews, so there are additional considerations about forming a group which has a mixture of background without too much disparity of experience.

We do not underplay the stresses of the course: as explained here, the content of the course is, by definition, emotional, and the students' feelings and anxieties are deliberately held in a searching light as a means of learning. The course is also very intensive as the group attempts to cover a lot of ground in very little time, and individuals form strong positive and negative bonds with each other. Above all, however, many students come on the course when they do because, knowingly or not, they are ready for a transforming experience. They may be reconsidering their career, their family relationships may be in transitional states, they may be of an age when changes in their internal worlds are rumbling and coming to fruition. The course can help them with these transformations, but inevitably the students who commit themselves wholeheartedly to the experiential learning undergo a personal crisis of some magnitude.

While preparing the dissertation and case study for the final assessment, the students bring this transformation to some kind of conclusion. This work is part of the internalization of the ideas and principles which has been going on through the two years; and the submissions are opportunities to present convincing evidence of their theoretical and professional identification with the work which the staff stand for and which they aspire to in their own way. Consequently as they write they are encouraged to offer the reader glimpses of the pain and excitement which have accompanied their efforts to get to grips with the material and its impact on them. The results are frequently powerfully personal and, as the deadline closes in, the whole course has the feel of a labour ward. Students hand over the papers explicitly or implicitly seeking some reassurance that their creations – and their embryonic identity – will be handled with respect and even tenderness. In both a real and symbolic sense, the process of preparing these papers is the making of the counsellor.

The papers selected for this collection are, we think, evidence of a creative outcome of the tensions generated by the confluences explained at the outset of this introduction. The original and thoughtful essays show how psychoanalytic thinking has been integrated into work which is not necessarily immediately associated with counselling. They are testaments to the power of bringing intellectual and emotional resources to bear on the problems experienced by the clients and counsellors alike. They reveal something of the strength and struggle of people who work in the often daunting front line with clients suffering from the 'neuroses of civilization'.

NOTE

1 S. Freud, *The Question of Lay Analysis*, *Standard Edition* XX (London: Hogarth Press and the Institute of Psycho-Analysis, 1927), pp. 249–50.

Chapter 1

Debt counselling

The unfortunate, the incompetent, and the profligate

Angela Mann

INTRODUCTION

There is a scene in *David Copperfield* where Mr Micawber offers some advice on how to be happy:

> Annual income twenty pounds, annual expenditure nineteen nineteen and six, result happiness. Annual income twenty pounds, annual expenditure twenty pounds ought and six, result misery. The blossom is blighted, the leaf is withered, the god of day goes down upon the weary scene, and – and in short you are for ever floored.[1]

This study is an attempt to examine debt and its effect on the individual, using as a basis the debt counselling service currently offered in a New Town Advice Centre, which is run by the local authority. Although debtors' prisons such as featured in *David Copperfield* are thankfully a thing of the past, it is still generally agreed that debt and misery go hand in hand. Clients using the debt counselling service are often severely depressed and describe fears of imprisonment and destitution. Sometimes suicidal thoughts are expressed. Counsellors working in the service often feel that in taking on debt counselling they are presented with problems that cannot be resolved simply by money management exercises. They discover a prevalence of Mr Micawber's attitude of linking money to happiness, and find that money problems often arise because of deeper unresolved conflicts in people's lives.

Debt can be the trigger which brings about a request for help. The client/debt counsellor relationship, in my opinion, provides a potential framework for a therapeutic working-through of problems which have surfaced.

CREATING ORDER OUT OF CHAOS

Serious debt has become a major social problem in recent years. In the 1980s, lending to individuals doubled. By the end of the decade more than £130 billion was owed in mortgages and £36 billion in consumer purchases. The number of mortgage repossessions has risen eightfold since 1980. In

1986 8 per cent of council tenants were in serious rent arrears. Ninety thousand households a year had their electricity disconnected and 60,000 lost their gas supply in 1987. Between 100,000 and 200,000 families are thought to have multiple debt problems.[2]

It was in response to the problems created by multiple debt that a debt counselling service was established in a New Town Advice Centre in 1986. The service offers clients counselling and support, representation at court and enhancement of relationships between debtors and creditors. After 'maximizing' the client's income, a repayment programme is worked out with the client, using disposable income (however small) to distribute proportionate payments to creditors which are within the client's ability to maintain. Debts are 'prioritized' according to the sanctions available to creditors if they are not paid, and priority debts are dealt with first. Clients are supported and encouraged in the process of negotiation and repayment. The aim, as one counsellor put it, is to create order out of chaos, to change a crisis into a manageable problem, and to convert a mood of confusion and despair into one of understanding and light at the end of the tunnel.

Each case takes considerable time to resolve; some are never resolved. Some clients have been receiving help since the service first started in 1986. This is often not because of the technical complexities of debt problems but because of the emotional difficulties which accompany debt. Counsellors, however, find themselves working under immense pressure to close cases. Results are measured by the agency in terms of statistics. There is also pressure from people needing the service; there is a long waiting list for initial appointments. The effect of these pressures on the debt counsellor cannot be ignored. All too often a client is 'patched up' for the moment and no attention is paid to the long-term effect. This is counterproductive in the long run, as the client who receives this type of assistance almost inevitably reappears at a later date requesting further help.

Counsellors within the service see emotional support as crucial to helping a client, quickly establishing relationships with their clients and becoming treated as confidants. The starting point for assessment of a client's needs may be to consider the meaning of indebtedness for the individual.

THE UNFORTUNATE, THE INCOMPETENT, AND THE PROFLIGATE – THE ORIGINS OF DEBT

The way in which a client got into debt, however long ago, is of primary importance to establish, as for me it determines the whole focus and shape of the work to come. In my opinion, the client's account of his or her situation is the key to understanding them. I find that I never have to ask how they got into debt; the information is always volunteered. This seems to indicate that at some level the client is also aware of its significance.

Mark, aged 36, came to see me because he was at risk of losing his flat due to rent arrears. He also had a number of bills which he couldn't pay. He said that he had been very depressed since the breakdown of his marriage and subsequent divorce nine months ago. Things came to a head when he was sacked from his job six months ago because he didn't bother to turn up for work. Since then he had lived on a loan and his bank account, gradually sinking into debt and deeper depression.

Mark had an apparent need to talk to me about his marriage and subsequent deterioration. His ex-wife had recently moved out of the area, with their three children, telling him that she needed a break and was feeling pressurized by his demand that they get back together. She would not give him a forwarding address, but said she would get in touch, and Mark was feeling quite desperate about this. Of all his debts, the telephone bill was the one he was most anxious about. If his telephone was disconnected, he said, she would be unable to contact him.

During the session he was able to talk about all of this and experienced obvious relief. I had the impression that the problem with his wife had taken him over and become the focus of his life, and that underneath there was a man who was perfectly able to manage and organize himself, and I conveyed this to him. He reacted positively and agreed that he had been functioning in the hope that his wife would take pity on him and return. Before he left he acknowledged that he had some responsibility to himself. He rang me the following week to cancel his second appointment because he had found a job; he was feeling a bit better and had already managed to pay some bills with his first wages.

This is an example of someone who, on the face of it, has plunged into debt because of marriage breakdown and unemployment. However, plenty of people survive such crises without going into debt. This encounter shows that it is important to give the client the opportunity to tell his story. Mark responded to the opportunity swiftly and was able to use the experience of one session to start thinking more positively about himself. My minimal intervention was all that was necessary, for Mark then found the resources to go from that point to negotiate repayments himself. If I had taken a more active role immediately, or denied Mark the opportunity to discuss his feelings, the outcome might have been different, the danger being that he might have become dependent on me to sort out his problems, as he was hoping his ex-wife would, and his feelings of depression and inadequacy would have continued.

Andrew (aged 34) and his wife, in contrast, have been receiving help from the debt counselling service for three years. The original debt trigger was attributed, as was Mark's, to unemployment. Andrew has been in and out of jobs, none of them lasting for longer than a few months. He approaches each new situation hopefully, but inevitably each employer complains about his incompetence or lack of adaptability. Andrew has fallen victim to the lure of consumerism and the easy availability of credit. He manages to get credit for the purchase of items whenever he starts a new job. Optimistically, he will manage the first few payments and then lose his job and the problems start again. He goes in and out of court as his creditors lose patience with him and invoke sanctions. Because his income fluctuates so much he cannot manage repayment programmes. When it appeared at one stage that things were stabilizing, his wife became pregnant. The extra expense of the child caused further problems. His indebtedness could be linked to his instability and difficulty in sustaining a situation, and it is only now that this basic problem is being addressed that there are some signs of progress.

Contrary to popular belief, the person who gets into debt because of calculated, irresponsible spending is in the minority, but such people do exist and it is important to address this issue. In my experience, the person who milks the system is usually doing so to cover up some pain or failure which is unacceptable to them. Rosemary, a single woman aged 32, built up a huge scale of debt. She owed a total of over £24,000 in consumer credit, and her monthly repayments at one time totalled as much as her salary. She attributed the origins of her indebtedness to taking on too much credit over a period of years, without fully realizing how it was accumulating. She had for some time been managing an incredibly intricate balancing act of setting one creditor off against another, paying just enough to prevent them from taking further action, a sophisticated way of 'robbing Peter to pay Paul'. When she was made redundant her system collapsed. She experienced no apparent worry or guilt about her situation and insisted that creditors treat her with respect. Within a few weeks of initially seeing me she found herself alternative lower-paid employment and started borrowing again. She told me that she felt she had to maintain her standard of living and surround herself with good things. Rosemary was virtually unable to tolerate any frustration of her desires.

Rosemary's indebtedness and pattern of borrowing can be linked to very infantile feelings and fears. In Melanie Klein's view, the prenatal state and being part of the mother contributes to the innate feeling that there is an object which will fulfil all needs and desires. This feeling is first directed towards the breast and persists in the unconscious throughout life.

> The infant's longing for an inexhaustible and ever present breast stems by no means only from a craving for food and from libidinal desires. For the urge even in the earliest stages to get constant evidence of the mother's love is fundamentally rooted in anxiety . . . his desires imply that the breast, and soon the mother, should do away with these destructive impulses and the pain of persecutory anxiety.[3]

Some frustration in relation to the breast and to the mother is inevitable and necessary for healthy development. Rosemary found it very difficult to tolerate frustration. Rosemary's relationship with her mother had apparently always been fraught with difficulty. She described her mother as a very cold woman and refused to tell her mother about her debts because she felt her mother would morally judge and condemn her behaviour as unacceptable. She related this to feelings she experienced as a child, when her mother would lecture her on her poor manners. Her failure to build up an early secure relationship with her mother meant that she now denied her own capacity to give or receive love and gratitude which could have enabled her to stand some frustration. Money, for her, was a way of magically bypassing anxieties: a feed from a bountiful breast. After many sessions with me she admitted that she was experiencing great distress about her boyfriend's infidelity, which she had chosen to ignore, and she surrounded herself with expensive material possessions in order to compensate for the love which she felt he was withholding from her.

Although aware of her level of debt, it was very difficult for Rosemary to face her own destructive use of credit, the destructiveness of her own nature. She became very critical of me and devalued the help I offered as insufficient or inadequate. She would undermine my work with her by making her own arrangements with creditors, based on her own criterion of paying those who were most likely to lend her more in the future. She was unable to confront her partner with her knowledge of his affairs and carried on defending herself against frustration and anxiety.

Rosemary's use of credit had a compulsive quality about it, elements of which, in a less extreme form, are often experienced by clients who have accumulated debts. Teresa, aged 25, is another example of someone who used credit in a complusive way. After a miscarriage and divorce Teresa went on a spending spree using 'every plastic card I could get my hands on'. She described the episode as 'legitimized shoplifting' and was afterwards shocked by the loss of control she had experienced. She felt that she had got away with stealing. Winnicott's work on the urge to steal which can occur in young children has been helpful to me in understanding the compulsive element in the use of credit by clients like Rosemary and Teresa. Winnicott uses the example of a child who will compulsively steal apples, without knowing why he has done so,[4] and he explains the urge in terms of maternal deprivation:

> The antisocial tendency always arises out of a deprivation and represents the child's claim to get back behind the deprivation to the state of affairs that obtained when all was well.[5]

The apples, or the stolen items, are not the important things in Winnicott's view; it is the urge which the child experiences to re-establish contact with the mother which motivates the stealing:

> the mother in her adaptation to the small child's needs enables the child creatively to find objects. She initiates the creative use of the world. When this fails, the child has lost contact with objects, has lost the

> capacity creatively to find anything. At the moment of hope the child reaches out and steals an object.[6]

Both Rosemary and Teresa agreed that the material items they surrounded themselves with were ultimately of little value to them. Both had experienced a partner who was withholding the love and affection they craved. Teresa had also experienced the loss of a child. Their debts were undoubtedly related to these experiences, which in turn related to memories of early childhood deprivation and frustrations.

For me, these clients show that it is crucial to look at the origins of an individual's indebtedness as it almost always leads me to an understanding of their difficulties. From this point it is then possible to analyse the defences which they bring into the situation.

REACTIONS TO THE DEBT EXPERIENCE

Once someone has crossed the line from being a socially accepted credit user into being a debtor they experience considerable anxiety. How they cope with this anxiety depends to a large extent on inner resources and their availability. A person may rise to a crisis with unexpected strengths or become so strained that the burden is too much to bear. There is often a strong sense of crisis when a client first approaches the debt counselling service. Some clients have been attempting to deal with a downward spiral of multiple debt for months or years but have reached a point when they feel they cannot go on any longer, or have realized, after much denial, that things are getting worse. Sometimes pressure from creditors has reached the point where an urgent response is needed. A sense of crisis brings with it heightened anxieties, and clients are frequently more defended against anxiety than normal.

Ann Andrews and Peter Houghton, who pioneered work in this country with debtors in the Birmingham Settlement, have likened the stages in the debt experience to steps down a staircase into financial despair.[7] They list the following:

- Denial
- Realization/shock
- Guilt – anger – aggression
- Search for a solution
- Hopelessness
- Loss of house/goods/services
- Loss of self-respect/partner/friends/children

From my own experience of dealing with clients in debt I find that they do not necessarily proceed down the steps in this order; they may be working through any of the stages, or a combination of them, at any one time.

It can be seen that the first five stages correspond to a large extent with stages of grief examined in studies of bereavement and reactions to loss.[8] Loss plays an important part in debt; loss of a job, or loss of a home, sometimes loss of a partner. Marris says:

> The analysis of grief and mourning has been concerned with situations of loss which we recognize as painful. But by the same argument, a similar process of adjustment should work itself out whenever the familiar pattern of life has been disrupted.[9]

It follows, therefore, that we can learn a great deal about the nature of anxieties experienced by debtors by studying reactions to loss.

Denial

Denial is a common reaction to the debt experience. Bills are left to pile up and life carries on as normal. Irene and Paul, aged 38 and 39, had let their debts accumulate for some time following the collapse of Paul's small business. During their first session with me they said they had a good feeling that something better was around the corner. They were having difficulty managing the mortgage repayments but did not think it was necessary yet to contact the building society. They ignored creditors but paid those who called at the door. They cheered each other up with encouraging thoughts that things would get better; Paul was looking for a better job, Irene was good at economizing. They thought there were many people who were worse off than them and they hoped they weren't wasting my time. When the building society took action to repossess their home they wanted me to offer unrealistically large monthly repayments, and became upset when I insisted that they would be unable to keep to these. Irene and Paul were attempting to deal with their problems by denial and when they were forced to think about their situation they became overwhelmed by a sense of panic, which prompted the urge to make unrealistic offers.

Parkes, in his studies of widows, noted that it was common for widows to react to bereavement by withdrawing or denying their grief:

> The theory of psychic defence rests on the assumption that there is a limit to the amount of anxiety an individual can tolerate and that when this limit is reached individuals will defend themselves by withdrawing, psychologically, from the situation that evokes the anxiety.[10]

Melanie Klein links denial with idealization.[11] Idealization and denial are invoked, she says, when the threat of persecution is too uncomfortable or too much to bear. Irene and Paul not only idealized their own situation, by continually stressing their advantages, but also reacted to me as an idealized helper. I was their rescuer and I surely wouldn't let them come to any harm. They worked through an intensely painful period of coming to terms with their debts, which involved the loss of their house and their subsequent rehousing, with their children, in a homeless persons' hostel.

Realization/shock

Realization and shock are often accompanied by symptoms of strain. Loss of appetite, or weight, difficulty sleeping and headaches, are all reported by debtors when their situation is acknowledged. Parkes says:

> When the strain exceeds a certain threshold of severity (which varies from one individual to another), learning capacity falls off and individuals find themselves unable to cope with the situation and are overwhelmed by it. They may persevere in useless activities which are inappropriate to the present situation but may have been successful in the past, or they may panic and behave in a thoroughly disorganized and fragmented manner.[12]

Elizabeth, aged 50, was plagued by fears that her creditors would turn up on her doorstep and threaten her. She was terrified about confronting them in court and would have agreed to anything rather than go through that experience. She realized that her fears were irrational but felt helpless and would shake uncontrollably or weep floods of tears. Elizabeth's way of coping with the strain she experienced was by exhibiting vice-like control over her finances and, in a similar way, over her husband. She talked of giving her husband 'pocket money' and would not allow him to behave in certain ways. She would spend hours working out her finances and would be thrown into a panic when the figures wouldn't balance. The need to control others is often a way of controlling parts of the self which have been projected. Elizabeth's tight controls on her husband represented her attempt to control her own feelings of disintegration. She was exasperated with her husband, telling me that he was helpless and weak and was failing to help with their finances. In this I believe she was also expressing her frustration with her own weakness. Throughout, she kept her husband apart from me and the whole process of negotiation with creditors and subsequent repayment. She was, I believe, acting out a strong urge to keep the 'bad' husband away from the 'good' counsellor, so that he wouldn't upset me as he had upset her. Similarly, she wanted to keep herself away from her 'bad' creditors, shown by her terror that she would have to meet her persecutors in court. In this way Elizabeth was using the mechanism of splitting as a defence to cushion herself from the pain which her situation caused her.

Guilt - anger - aggression

Parkes' studies showed that many widows experienced irritability and bitterness following a bereavement. Anger brought about guilt, self-reproaches, and blame. This is very similar to reactions to debt. Being in debt causes feelings of insecurity and the anger is associated with the feeling that the world has become an insecure and dangerous place.

Anger often becomes misdirected, and quarrels with partners and general tension in the family are common. Those who express anger run the risk of becoming isolated as friends and relatives shy away, thereby increasing the debtor's sense of loneliness and guilt. There is frequently a search for someone to blame and a tendency to go over the events leading up to the indebtedness. Parkes says:

> The tendency to go over the events leading up to the loss and to find someone to blame even if it means accepting blame oneself is a less disturbing alternative than accepting that life is uncertain. If we can find someone to blame or some explanation . . . then we have a chance of controlling things.[13]

Feelings of shame and guilt are especially acute in breadwinners. They quickly lose confidence in their ability to do things, and feel disgraced or degraded. What is the nature of the guilt being experienced in this situation?

Melanie Klein places the experience of guilt at a very early stage in development, and links it to depressive anxiety and the tendency to make reparation, to repair the damage done to loved objects.[14] She says that, although guilt may be experienced in the paranoid-schizoid position, it is generally a characteristic of the depressive position, with concern being felt about having harmed loved objects. Alternatively, an immature ego can resort to manic defences and attempts are made to repair the damage in a manic or omnipotent way. In Elizabeth's case, for example, I believe that her guilt was related to her persecutory fears, and her attempts to repair the damage were rather, as Klein puts it, attempts to pacify her persecutors.

Winnicott stresses the importance of guilt as a developmental process and a sign of emotional growth.[15] He also introduces the term 'concern' which, he says, has positive connotations, unlike 'guilt' which implies anxiety linked with ambivalence. Concern implies growth, integration, and responsibility in relationships. He sees one of the early functions of the mother as providing general management of the infant and being available to receive the child's reparative gestures. If she fails to do this, then guilt becomes intolerable and concern cannot be felt. Failure to make reparation leads to a loss of the capacity for concern, and it is replaced by a more primitive form of guilt and anxiety.

This seems, for me, to point to the need for the counsellor to be available and to provide consistent management of the case, as well as to be aware when a reparative gesture is being offered, and to acknowledge this offer. Similarly, the counsellor must beware of trying to impose a sense of guilt when this seems to be lacking. It is tempting to be drawn into pointing out an absence of guilt with clients like Rosemary. However, this would be of limited value. In Winnicott's terms, given the right environment the sense of concern will develop naturally, and does not have to be inculcated.

Search for a solution

Parkes says that 'a great deal of human and animal behaviour contains elements of searching. Searching fills the gap between aims and object.'[16]

The act of approaching the debt counselling service may in itself be part of a search for a solution. However, one of the reasons debtors often wait so long before asking for help is that they do not think the service is what they need. Understandably, they feel that a solution to their problems requires money, rather than less concrete assistance. There is commonly a period of 'waiting for a miracle' – promotion, winning the pools, inheriting money – to lift them out of their problems.

There follows the search for a solution in terms of further borrowing, often from relatives, to attempt to ease the situation, which increases the burden of guilt. Attempts to communicate with creditors often end in failure, as debtors struggle to acknowledge their difficulties in the face of the computerized machinery of debt recovery.

Approaching the debt counselling service as part of a search for a solution brings with it a variety of expectations. For some people it is a last attempt at a solution and they are unconvinced that they will be able to be helped if all their previous attempts at solutions have failed. Others immediately hand the problem over to the counsellor, giving up all responsibility. Shaun, aged 24, became over-dependent on me as his counsellor from an early stage. A former alcoholic, he was very sensitive to any hint of criticism and reminded me of a child in the way he would seek out my approval. He would bring reports of his progress and took care to present himself as a 'good' client. He managed to arouse protective feelings in all those around him, including myself, but particularly in his older sister, who took on almost total responsibility for him during his recovery from alcoholism, enabling him to regress to a very infantile position. Unfortunately, his sister was unable to tolerate the ugly, aggressive side of his nature and would punish him when this showed signs of emerging. She established a system of rewards for his good behaviour. For example, she would cook him a favourite meal or buy him a record, and would withhold these treats if he had behaved badly. Shaun, while enjoying her attentions and having his own infantile state acknowledged, was also prevented from allowing a more mature self to emerge. He transferred similar feelings on to me as he had about his sister, and would become very lost and confused if I resisted taking responsibility for him. With clients like Shaun the pressure is to perceive oneself, the counsellor, as the solution and it is vital to keep this in perspective if clients are to be helped to take responsibility for themselves.

Hopelessness

Parkes found that as time passed after a bereavement anger grew less and periods of apathy and depression took over. Debtors often present with a submissive, defeated attitude, claiming that they have 'lost hope'. Confidence in the ability to deal with financial affairs has often been severely shaken, and some people feel that they are no longer able to function in society. The stigma which is attached to being in debt further exacerbates this feeling. Parkes says: 'If I lose my ability to predict and to act appropriately, my world begins to crumble, and since my view of myself is inextricably bound up with my view of the world, that too will begin to crumble.'[17] Family breakdown is common at this stage, as old ties and patterns of sharing are abandoned.

However, some re-establishment of self is possible as part of the process. Anne, aged 35, whose husband left her with four children and many debts, went through a period of deep depression and withdrew almost completely, finding it extremely difficult to get up in the morning or leave the house. However, she gradually found herself able to take on more, and her confidence increased when she found part-time work and started repaying the debts. She said that she emerged as a more competent woman than her husband had ever imagined she could be, and her new-found confidence pleased her. She felt that, having survived the pain and indignity of desertion and debt, she gained strength and was not as plagued by anxieties and fears as she had been during her marriage. Marris says:

> Change appears as fulfilment or loss to different people, and to the same person at different times. In either aspect it presents some common features: the need to re-establish continuity, to work out an interpretation of oneself and the world which preserves, despite estrangement, the thread of meaning . . . the outcome therefore depends on the ability to face the conflict and find a way through it.[18]

I believe that an important part of the role of the debt counsellor is to help clients to do this.

THE THERAPEUTIC RELATIONSHIP

Holding

As mentioned previously, there is often a strong sense of crisis when a client comes to debt counselling, and this means that anxiety is at a peak and the client is more disturbed than normal. Intervention at this stage can be therapeutic if the counsellor is available to receive the anxiety without being overwhelmed by it. Winnicott puts this concept well when he talks in terms of the parental model.[19] The mother responds to her crying baby by picking him up and cradling him. She is not only holding him physically, but also emotionally, communicating to him that he is not falling to bits, but is being held together and contained. The mother's understanding of his fear and also her response meet his needs.

In counselling there is a need to be available to listen to anxiety and fear, and not to be frightened by it. The client who finds a responsive person who is able to bear what seems unbearable is given some sense of hope. An additional factor in debt counselling is that some action is often taken by the counsellor: creditors may be contacted, procedures delayed.

This alleviates anxiety by giving the client the hope that a solution is possible. It is also a demonstration of the counsellor's ability to keep calm under the pressure of a crisis and handle the situation without becoming overwhelmed. This may in turn lead to the client taking back some sense of things being held and controlled.

Because of the stigma attached to being in debt, people around the debtor are often unwilling to get involved and listen to communications of worry or despair. Similarly, debtors are often ashamed and do not want to talk to others about their financial problems. Partners frequently keep their anxieties about money hidden from each other. Therefore, for many people the debt counsellor is the first person who has been available to receive their distress. Relief after the initial consultation is usually expressed. Clients say things like 'It's such a relief to talk to someone about it' or 'How can you bear to listen?'. The phantasy which exists before counselling is that the counsellor will become just as despairing as the client or find the situation totally out of control. In addition, there is much misunderstanding about sanctions available to creditors, so fears of imprisonment or destitution are often plaguing the client but have never been communicated. If these fears can be openly addressed it brings tremendous relief.

Fears

A person comes to debt counselling because there has been a failure in his or her life: an inability to pay. Fear of criticism from the counsellor is usually a factor in the counselling even if it is not stated explicitly. Geoff, aged 35, was 'sent' for debt counselling by his wife, who booked his first appointment with me. He was doubtful whether it would be useful. Initially he was belligerent, challenging me and then treating my suggestions with scorn. He attributed blame for his situation to other people. I felt that he was doing this to avoid having to experience guilt, and that telling me things were not his fault indicated he was expecting me to blame him. As time went by he became more difficult, not keeping to arrangements, missing appointments, and appearing uncooperative. I felt that he was inviting me to take a punitive stance, provoking me into becoming angry by his actions in order to fulfil his phantasy of being judged and blamed. When confronted with this, he agreed that this was what he was doing. If I became angry with him or deserted him he would feel punished, which was exactly what he felt he deserved. The work with Geoff improved after this problem was addressed. When he could appreciate that I was truly non-judgemental about his debts, we could further explore the reasons for his phantasy.

Active intervention

Because of the nature of the work, the debt counsellor frequently has to take an active role. It is important to look at the effect this has on the dynamics of the counselling relationship.

Action often has to be taken at an early stage if there is a crisis: court procedures halted, creditors contacted, sometimes money obtained. If things are at a very late stage, intervention by an agency such as the Advice Centre is often all that is acceptable to creditors, as they then know it is possible to negotiate repayment. The effect of such intervention is to relieve anxiety fairly quickly. The debt counsellor is often perceived by the client as someone both powerful and helpful, and an idealizing transference is often established.

Ellen Noonan, in talking about a directive approach to counselling, says:

> Clients do want something that will put an end to their need, just as a trip to the doctor meets their need for relief from physical distress. The problem, however, is that so long as one individual wants or needs the goods provided by another and cannot imagine that he could provide them for himself, he is tied into that relationship and is forced to perpetuate it. Dynamically, he has projected the helping part of himself into the counsellor and therefore has to stay with her, in order to stay in contact with that part of himself.[20]

She goes on to point out that the aim of counselling is to enable the client to help himself, and the danger of active intervention is that it can increase the client's dependence and sense of helplessness.

There is also the danger that the intervention is so reassuring that it damages the client's determination to work at a solution. One debt counsellor working in the service described to me how, after taking the pressure off people, she often saw them default on agreements. With Shaun, it was very easy to be drawn into taking an active role, 'taking care' of him. However, this encouraged his dependence and prevented him from using his own resources.

However, there are also problems surrounding the non-directive stance, particularly when an urgent response is called for. Ellen Noonan says:

> for clients who are up against some real or emotional deadline, this approach runs the risk of not respecting their immediate difficulties. If

> already feeling shamefully inadequate, and faced by the silent and remote counsellor who is apparently so unhelpful and so vastly different from what he expected, the client can feel overwhelmed by a sense of helplessness and isolation and may retreat into depression or angry, spurious independence.[21]

In debt counselling there is a need not to deny the problems faced by clients on a low, inadequate income and the social set-up in which they find themselves. The environment is often causing a great deal of suffering or is inhibiting emotional growth.

Douglas, aged 40, was referred for debt counselling by the social services department, who said that he had been trying to persuade them to take his children into care, but that they did not feel it was appropriate. He was due to have both his gas and electricity disconnected and by the time he got to see me he was feeling quite desperate. I obtained a charity payment which prevented disconnection, but Douglas was still able to work on his long-term situation with me without becoming over-dependent.

It seems to me that the difficulty in debt counselling lies in knowing when to resist active intervention. Too active intervention runs the risk of infantalizing the client, leading to inertia, resentment, or persecutory feelings, as well as provoking despair in the client about not being able to cope without the counsellor. However, at times clients are genuinely overwhelmed and unable to cope, or are at risk, so that it is important to intervene. Occasionally clients have had little experience of concern, and the first demonstration of this is through practical assistance. It does not necessarily follow that this cannot be used constructively.

The counsellor's active intervention will inevitably affect the client's phantasies about himself and the counsellor so I feel the primary concern is to be able to address this together. The particular skill of the debt counsellor seems to me to lie in the combination of taking action with exploring feelings, but the aim in debt counselling does not conflict with the aims of other forms of counselling. The debt counsellor is similar to other counsellors in that she is aiming to encourage the mature part of the client to come to the fore, and to encourage growth, understanding, and responsibility.

Transference

Transference is commonly regarded as the centre of the therapeutic interaction and also as the instrument by which the counsellor arrives at an understanding of the client. It is therefore important to examine whether transferences arising in debt counselling situations have any common or recurring features which help us understand and make progress with this client group.

Freud first observed that transference feelings came about as the result of a 'false connection' between a person who was the object of earlier feelings in his patients and himself, the doctor.[22] These feelings had been excluded from consciousness and emerged as a result of the 'false connection'. He referred on the whole to the emergence of infantile feelings which became directed towards the analyst.

Being in debt can place the client in a rather infantile, dependent state. As we have seen, the client often relies on the counsellor to negotiate and make certain decisions for him. Hence the transference often contains traces of the client's relationship to his parents. Rosemary experienced a cold, withholding mother whom she felt would be excessively moralistic if she knew the extent of her indebtedness. She transferred these feelings to me to a large extent. She kept some debts hidden from my knowledge for some time, despite my stress on the importance of knowing the full picture.

Sandler, Dare, and Holder[23] refer to transference not just as the client's perception of the analyst as another person, but also as the client's attempts to manipulate or provoke situations which are a repetition of earlier experiences.

The pattern of repetition can be seen in many clients who initially have a positive transference reaction to the debt counsellor as someone helpful who brings relief. After a number of sessions they become disillusioned and the counsellor becomes another creditor, making demands. This was apparent with Irene and Paul, who initially established an idealizing transference but later became resentful. After experiencing many other similar reactions I was for a while confused, having my own image of myself as a non-judgemental, caring person apparently contradicted by my clients, who were seeing me as someone who was making demands and threatening punishment. When I was able to see this as part of a process I was better able to address it with my clients and it became a powerful experience, enabling changes to be made.

Long-term work

Debts do not disappear overnight and clients' abilities to cope with debt over a period of time vary. Long-term work often involves slow change and many relapses and can be frustrating for both client and counsellor. Both may be tempted to give up. In long-term work the strength of the counselling relationship is tested.

Ellen Noonan talks of the therapeutic alliance stemming from trust[24] and I find from my experience that long-term counselling is not a possibility unless a basic trust is established between client and counsellor. They must experience some sense of responsibility towards each other in order for the relationship to survive and have meaning. For the client's part this means accepting the help offered and being prepared to work within the framework the counsellor provides. On the counsellor's side it involves having the emotional strength to hold the situation for some time. The client who is coping with debt over a period of years is going to face material deprivation and will direct a great deal of frustration towards the counsellor. The client will often behave in a way which brings about helplessness in the counsellor. The counsellor will feel rejected when efforts to help are not taken up, or may have to withstand onslaughts of anger for not solving the problem. It is vital that the counsellor is able to withstand this, survive it, and make sense of it for the client. The relationship should be the place where the client can safely express feelings of anger and frustration without damaging the relationship.

It is important, in long-term work, not to encourage dependency. In some cases it appears to be easier to ask the client to hand all the debts over and let the experienced counsellor sort them out. But it is important to remember whose debts they are. Clients like Shaun need encouragement to find a more mature part of themselves, and they will do this only if the counsellor recognizes them as people capable of responsibility, however limited this may be. A counsellor who is able to be in touch with the more mature part of the client enables this to come forward. Isca Salzberger-Wittenberg describes the counsellor well, I feel, as 'a kind of mother who takes away the mess that the child produces, and cleans it up and helps him to do so gradually himself'.[25] This, I believe, is the essence of the successful debt counselling experience.

CONCLUSION

When approaching this study, my first concern was with the apparent lack of literature on which I could base my own experience of counselling debtors. Debt is an increasing problem in modern society, but it is by no means a new problem. Services offering debt counselling are relatively new and are still few and far between, but by the same argument, so are services offering AIDS counselling, and yet many studies are being undertaken in this field. My conclusion was that money problems are often seen as something for which counselling is not appropriate, and the term 'debt counsellor' means, all too often, someone who will just offer advice on debts. In the same way as some of my clients feel that the only thing which will put an end to their money problems is more money, so counsellors can feel that what debtors need is money, rather than less concrete assistance.

My aim has been to show that psychoanalytic counselling can be a way of helping people who are experiencing problems with debts, and can be combined with practical advice and assistance. I feel that debt is not an isolated problem, but is something which is inextricably linked to other things going on in a client's life.

Attitudes towards debt are slowly changing, and debtors are no longer outcasts from society. I believe that the growth of services offering debt counselling is some measure of society's recognition that this client group deserves help. Large finance companies are beginning to provide funding for debt counselling services, in recognition of their responsibility to help those who have difficulty paying. There are moves to reform the legal machinery of debt recovery, to provide simpler procedures which give the debtor a chance.

These moves, combined with the exploration and evaluation of help offered to people overwhelmed by debt, will hopefully provide a framework within which people can find the confidence and help to overcome problems and deal with their debts.

NOTES

1 C. Dickens, *David Copperfield* (London: Penguin Classics, 1985), p. 231.
2 R. Berthould, *Credit, Debt and Poverty* (London: Policy Studies Institute, 1989).
3 M. Klein, *Envy and Gratitude and Other Works, 1946–1963* (London: Virago Press, 1988), p. 179.
4 D. W. Winnicott, *Home Is Where We Start From* (London: Penguin, 1987), pp. 90–100.
5 D. W. Winnicott, *The Maturational Processes and the Facilitating Environment*, p. 204.
6 D. W. Winnicott, *Home is Where We Start From*, p. 93.
7 A. Andrews and P. Houghton, *How to Cope with Credit and Deal with Debt* (London: Unwin Paperbacks, 1986), p. 9.
8 C. M. Parkes, *Bereavement* (London: Penguin, 1988).
9 P. Marris, *Loss and Change* (London: Routledge & Kegan Paul, 1986), p. 41.
10 C. M. Parkes, op. cit., p. 58.
11 M. Klein, op. cit., pp. 6–8.
12 C. M. Parkes, op. cit., p. 57.
13 Ibid., p. 103.
14 M. Klein, op. cit., p. 37.
15 D. W. Winnicott, *The Maturational Processes and the Facilitating Environment*, pp. 73–82.
16 C. M. Parkes, op. cit., p. 74.
17 Ibid., p. 114.
18 P. Marris, op. cit., p. 42.
19 D. W. Winnicott, *The Child, the Family and the Outside World* (London: Penguin, 1987), p. 86.
20 E. Noonan, *Counselling Young People* (London: Methuen, 1984), p. 113.
21 Ibid., p. 115.
22 S. Freud, *Introductory Lectures in Psychoanalysis* (London: Penguin, 1986), pp. 482–500.
23 J. Sandler, C. Dare and A. Holder, *The Patient and the Analyst* (London: Karnac, 1979), p. 48.
24 E. Noonan, op. cit., p. 79.
25 I. Salzberger-Wittenberg, *Psycho-Analytic Insight and Relationships* (London: Routledge & Kegan Paul, 1986), p. 155.

Chapter 2

The inside story

On seeing clients in their own homes

John Nicholas

This chapter looks at a form of psychodynamic counselling which is applied in an unusual setting: the client's own living environment. The counselling described here seeks to apply insights that have by and large originated from work done in the consulting room (the usual setting for psychodynamic counselling) to a setting that is in many respects quite different. The counsellor attempts to bring him- or herself, together with the method or technique, into the home of the client.

I was involved in this work for three years while employed in Central London by MIND, a voluntary organization serving the needs of the mentally ill. People seen by the project were unable or unwilling (because of the severity of their emotional problems) to make use of the existing services, such as day centres. Many were psychotic or borderline, and they were often elderly.

In this unusual and often changing setting, the counsellor will have more information to try to make sense of; therefore the focus of the work and of one's attention is much broader, as there is literally much more to take in.

In her paper 'The psycho-analytic play technique', Melanie Klein states that:

> I came to the conclusion that psycho-analysis should not be carried out in the child's home. . . . More important still, I found that the transference situation – the backbone of the psycho-analytic procedure – can only be established and maintained if the patient is able to feel that the consulting-room or the play-room, indeed the whole analysis, is something separate from his ordinary home life.[1]

In her paper entitled 'Some aspects of the analysis of a schizophrenic', Hanna Segal described the analysis of Edward conducted in a number of different settings. The initial interview took place in a hospital and after a few days the patient was transferred to a nursing home where she conducted a regular analysis of five hours a week. The man was sufficiently improved after three months to be able to return home where the analysis continued and, 'after about three months treatment at home, we decided that he should start coming to me for the analytic sessions'.[2] Segal's paper indicates that a transference was set up and maintained despite the changes. It was an acknowledgement of the fact that in some cases it would not be possible to conduct the work in the consulting room and that much can be achieved in a different setting.

She stated that, in the months before a standard treatment could be tried, her aim:

> was to retain the attitude of the analyst even without the co-operation of the patient. To achieve this, I had, first of all, to make him accept interpretations instead of the various gratifications he wanted, and to do it without appearing needlessly rude or cruel. I tried to show him in every interpretation what he wanted from me, why he wanted it at any particular moment, and why he wanted it so desperately.[3]

Winnicott, familiar with the practice of making home visits, puts an emphasis on environment and its consequences for early infant development. He states that it is healthy and normal for the individual to be able to defend the self against specific environmental failure by a freezing of the failure situation. This freezing is accompanied, according to Winnicott, by an unconscious hope that one day it will be possible to re-experience the failure situation but in an environment that is making adequate provision. But he also makes clear that 'in the extreme case the therapist would need to go to the patient and actively present good mothering, an experience that could not have been expected by the patient'.[4] But will the client be there when you arrive? Will you be let in? Will the person remain with you in the same room? Will someone else be there when you arrive?

Making home visits to disturbed individuals brings the counsellor face to face with the confusion, fixity, ambivalence, and hostility of the client, together with their vulnerability and tremendous dependency. Working with such a client group is often very demanding and is rarely rewarded by tangible evidence of change. Winnicott states that 'you tolerate the client's illogicality, unreliability, suspicion, muddle, fecklessness, meanness, etc. etc. and recognize all these unpleasantnesses as symptoms of distress (in private life these same things would make you keep at a distance)'.[5] He continues by saying how one should not be frightened by the client going mad, or feel guilty because of this or the client's disintegration, extreme behaviour, or attempts at suicide, successful or otherwise. All these are signs of despair because of loss of hope for help. This laudable and compassionate attitude in the face of often extremely taxing behaviour from the client is an ideal attitude and one that is difficult to sustain.

Clear guidelines based upon psychodynamic principles were followed when making home visits. This was an acknowledgement of the fact that the very disturbed individual responds positively to reliability and consistency of relationship: i.e., keeping to time boundaries, letting the clients determine the pace and content of the dialogue, not bringing one's own personal issues into the relationship, interpreting the client's more immediate anxieties wherever possible, not retaliating as a response to the client's material, not exchanging or receiving gifts or acting out on one's own or the client's behalf. Such boundaries are also important for the counsellor to help maintain an appropriate distance from what can be extremely confusing and contagious behaviour.

The value of proper support and supervision cannot be overestimated. Supervision can help to find the signs of small changes, and it is also important in helping the counsellor to work through feelings of omnipotence and indispensability. Otherwise, as Winnicott describes in the paper 'Hate in the counter-transference',[6] the counsellor's hate will get couched in ever more subtle 'therapeutic' disguises. I was often surprised how a belief that I had developed about a client's isolation would turn out to be a fantasy, and that, in fact, other agencies or family members were also on the scene.

SOME OF THE ISSUES THAT MAY BE ENCOUNTERED WHEN MAKING HOME VISITS

Institutional factors can play a part, particularly when considering whom the referral is really intended to benefit.

A social worker assigned to a man named Paul contacted the project for which I worked to ask for a counsellor to visit his client. Paul was an ex-offender imprisoned for incest. He was living in a hostel and the social worker visited him regularly. Paul's family had disowned him except for his son who maintained fairly regular contact. The manager of the institution was very pessimistic about Paul, saying that he was either very withdrawn or alternatively rather manic and at such times used to make unrealistic plans for the future. Essentially the staff at the institution were thoroughly baffled by his behaviour and dismayed at not being able to do anything to integrate him into the community. Following assessment it was decided to start a counselling relationship and I visited him. But when I went to his room he was not there. The manager, however, asked me into her office and expressed to me her feelings of concern and confusion with respect to Paul, and also that she felt it was very important that I should meet regularly with her to share the content of the meetings. I said it was important that Paul could come to feel that the meetings were confidential, but that if I felt he was suicidal I would certainly inform her. She said that it wasn't the way they worked there and was surprised to hear of this attitude, but rather grudgingly went along with it. The contact broke down after a dozen or so very short visits in which Paul treated me like somebody who knew everybody that he spoke of and who was checking up on him. He revealed that he had been encouraged very strongly to talk to me, and in response to this I stated the voluntary nature of the contact. During the next visit he took down the answering machine number and used it the following day to instruct me to end the visits. This referral seemed largely to have been made to try to deal with the frustrations and anxieties of the people involved with Paul.

The client's motivation for counselling is a very important issue and is well understood with regard to counselling conducted in the more usual setting. When conducting domiciliary counselling it is a far less clear matter. The substantial majority of clients are seen via referrals from professionals. The individual demonstrates behaviour that gains the attention of the various professionals who themselves are motivated to respond in some way. The organizing energy and planning come from the various agencies involved and generally not from the client, and effectively all mobility resides in the counsellor. Even were it possible to change the setting there would always be a large proportion of people for whom such an arrangement would be too distressing. The obvious danger is that the client gets the message that only if they stay put will they get the attention that they want. It is important, therefore, to be aware of developments arising which indicate that a client can take on more initiative.

It is common for the counsellor's role to be confused with those of other professionals such as the general practitioner or community psychiatric nurse. Most clients get to see only other professionals and fellow sufferers and in many instances there is no one who willingly goes to visit. There is often an anticipation that the counsellor will provide something more tangible, such as advice, treatment, help with various tasks, or that the client will want something from the counsellor such as answers to particular questions.

Any form of aggressive behaviour, be it sexual or violent, is an issue for all counsellors and therapists. The very fact of being two people in private in a room can automatically set up sexual fantasies of a heterosexual or homosexual nature. Careful client assessment is essential to determine the likelihood of such fantasies being acted out. There is the extra difficulty related to being in the client's home and away from any of the usual professional safeguards. Also, it is generally felt that one can do as one pleases inside one's own home. The counsellor is therefore isolated and vulnerable to unpredictable behaviour. Being able to keep in touch with the anxieties both of oneself and of the client is essential because in some cases being out of touch can have worrying consequences. The power dynamic can switch and one can start to feel very much like an unwanted intruder or, more benignly, like an ineffectual person with nothing of value to offer. Feelings resulting from not being, as it were, on one's own territory can compound this. It is taken for granted in most, if not all, cultures that certain behaviour is expected from someone who enters another person's home, that one is a guest and should behave accordingly, with deference to the host.

These concepts are deeply felt and they are related to the principle that a person is more vulnerable and exposed when at home. There is a paradox around when a counsellor makes a home visit. If, for example, clients say that they want you to leave, judging and evaluating this communication can be very tricky. Acting on this literally could be unhelpful, just as staying put could be felt as intrusive and hostile.

When entering the client's external physical space the counsellor also enters his or her internal world. The client's state of mind at that time will determine whether the counsellor's appearance is felt to be desirable or not. The counsellor has a responsibility to try to assess these situations as far as possible and in particular to determine the possibility of working with negative transference. The boundary, however, is never clear. Isolated persons are often very bound to their environment and so the inclusion of another person in their space can easily be felt as something threatening; home is both sanctuary and prison.

Michael was someone who was taken on fairly cautiously because of a history of violence. On a number of occasions he had a potentially hostile person in his flat when I called. The man was a burly alcoholic and his presence made doing any useful work impossible. Michael was small and lame and not much of an actual physical threat, unlike his friend who could act out Michael's resistant and aggressive feelings. I left after a short time, recognizing that work was not possible. I became very identified, in my response to this situation, with the plight of Michael. I felt I had deprived him of support and left him to the mercy of a brutal, dangerous man and that I had to rescue him. The scenario touched me in a difficult area personally and I had to control the urge simply to call the police.

Sexual issues and their relationship to the gender of the counsellor need to be thought about but the problem can never be totally eliminated and is always potentially present. On my first visit to Michael, after a long pause, about halfway through the hour, he asked whether or not we were going to masturbate together. Such a comment may reflect his despair: will this be a fruitful relationship or a frustrating fruitless and isolating one? It might also have indicated a possible eroticized transference to me.

Without the consistency of stable surroundings and because of being right in the middle of what can, in some cases, be a very bizarre and abnormal environment reflecting the client's emotional state, one can be prone to extremely powerful anxieties. Such anxieties in the counsellor will be related to the split-off but ever present aggressive, explosive, and uncontained sexual anxieties of the client. It could be that the inclusion of a third party in the relationship with Michael was a way of diffusing such anxieties.

A man called Arthur went through a period of trying to persuade me to go out walking with him. Although I found his place almost unbearable, I resisted his attempts because I gathered that a previous worker had run into all sorts of problems when they did leave the flat together. On one occasion he left me in his flat alone while he went out to do some small job and returned about ten minutes later. This was a very difficult experience for me during which I struggled to keep my attention on a part of myself, hardly daring to explore my surroundings because of strong feelings of dread. However subjective or personal my reaction was, it showed me clearly the tragic bind that a man like Arthur is in, that he dare not take in the dreadful state of his environment becaue of the awful feelings that would be evoked. Also that the counsellor has in such a case a need for the presence of the client to help him or her to manage the overpowering effect of the environment.

Once a relationship has been set up, the client is in a position to take some risks. He or she may expect hostility or retaliation of some sort but, if such anxieties can be looked at, the person may, for periods, come to feel accepted as they are and in the environment they are in. A woman named Sandra was physically able to go out but unable emotionally to leave the house for more than a few minutes at a time, and never (unless accompanied) to a distance beyond which she could no longer see her home. She presented herself as a victim, and often spoke of the demands and cruelty she was subjected to in the past and from relatives in the present. Whenever she was shown any kindness, however small, she would respond by offering everything that she had regardless of the reliability and trustworthiness of the person. We gradually started to make some connections between her extreme need for love and her complete vulnerability to the provider of anything remotely resembling it. She started to make some insightful connections about the dynamics of her home life and the role that she plays. She also started to express some sadness over her life being in such a 'mess'. By experiencing the counselling right in the middle of the 'mess' and in response to her particular situation, Sandra was able to have an experience of a different way of considering an age-old, stuck pattern. Because I made no particular demands on her and given that I remained relatively consistent and non-retaliatory, she, on occasion, came to recognize the tremendous pressure that she tried to put on me.

The environment, for an hour at least, will feel slightly different than usual. An elderly man called David was living in an old people's home where I would visit him once a fortnight. After some months he told me that having me come to visit him made all the difference as to how he felt and that it made him feel a lot better. In one meeting he complained a lot about his residence but towards the end said how much my visit had helped him and later that the place he was staying in wasn't so bad after all, that the people there were good to him and that he has a laugh sometimes, 'it could be a lot worse'. David was able to recognize both good and bad aspects of his environment and to see it in a somewhat more realistic light.

In some instances the presence of the counsellor and effect of the work can seem to have a disturbing effect. In the case of Peter, in one particularly painful session he expressed very directly his feelings of worthlessness, of having had a useless life, and his belief that he should never have been born. The following week he reported having had a bad week with sleepless nights. The previous evening he had become convinced that he had heard footsteps in his flat but a check revealed nothing. Eventually it was possible to refer to the difficult themes of the week before. He told me how, after I had left, he had started to hallucinate. He said how exploring his emotions too much can leave him in a bad way and he spoke of having no support. The end of the hour was experienced as a desertion and abandonment to hostile feelings. Technique and consciousness of time are therefore important factors in this. One client, at the very end of an hour that I stopped rather abruptly, told me how frustrating it was sometimes when a film that he had recorded and then watched on the television had finished before the denouement because the tape had run out.

A person who is very isolated can come to see the counsellor as, among other things, someone who keeps an eye on them. There have been cases when other services have been alerted because of a crisis. Again these situations must be carefully thought through to see that unnecessary, complicated involvement with other agencies is avoided. Alternatively the client could get the message that all the necessary help will appear if they just stay put. An example of this kind of confusion occurred with Gerald. He was bed-bound with limited walking ability because of an accident four years previously. Consequently he had suffered brain damage and was often very confused. He would speak about a time in his youth when he did the same job as I was doing. A number of times he explained that it was his job to keep an eye on the people he visited to see how they were getting along. I said that perhaps he felt that I was there to check to see how he was getting along. He responded by saying that perhaps I would soon be able to tell him that he was able to return to work, and that I would tell his doctor this.

WHAT THE HOME ENVIRONMENT CONVEYS

Hanna Segal described the way in which Edward's environment, then the nursing home, came to contain certain projections and how in consequence he sought to protect his analyst from them:

> love itself was often felt to be wholly bad, giving me his love could give me his illness. As a result I could be good and safe only if he withdrew both hatred and love. He often expressed this by saying he wished I did not come to the Nursing Home where the voices would change me. I was much safer outside. *The Nursing Home represented himself* and I could not be safe near to his madness.[7] (My italics.)

It could be said that for the disturbed person their environment (the things in it and their relation to each other) contains projected psychic contents, some of which are unacceptable. The sane person knows that he ends at his own skin. Beyond that is a transitional space which can be utilized for self-expression. This imaginative space is an acknowledged and often cherished extension of a person's inner world, both conscious and unconscious.

The things in a person's living environment are separated by space the quality of which is influenced by internal factors particular to the inhabitant. The disturbed person's experience of their living space can really only be inferred. However, a counsellor can often get a feeling for the client's experience by entering their physical world, together with some understanding of the person's internal resources.

The actual composition of a person's living space will obviously be determined also by economic and social factors. The range of environmental set-ups is very broad. In my experience, at one extreme was Arthur who was not prepared, although physically able, to do any cleaning at all. In consequence the Council's clean-up department would have to come in and clean the place up quite frequently. During my period of visiting him, for two months he acquired two puppies that he failed to house train, the result being that the sitting-room floor was thick with dog faeces. At the other end of the range was a man called Phillip who self-referred and was quite disabled. However, he kept his flat fastidiously tidy and pretty and even did some gardening. He in fact inhabited and used his space in an ordinary way.

Perhaps these two examples can be seen as illustrating at one end the psychotic or very disturbed relationship to the environment and at the other the normal or neurotic relationship. In the more disturbed case the sense is often conveyed that the inhabitant exists there but with no conscious relationship with the surrounding items, as if there is very little in the way of relationship or exchange between the individual and the environment.

Often a room will have no obvious focus or symmetry and be devoid of an orientating theme, any personal touches or ornamentation. This will relate to aspects of the client's damaged personality that are permanently projected into the environment and denied.

In a more normal space there is evidence of self-expression. Aspects of the personality, personal history, taste, etc., are expressed through the objects chosen and the relationships between them. In a lecture on schizophrenia Jung made a helpful comparison: 'whereas the neurotic dissociation never loses its systematic character, schizophrenia shows a picture of unsystematic randomness so to speak, in which the continuity of meaning so distinctive of the neurosis is often mutilated to the point of unintelligibility'.[8] In an environment that makes a strong impact upon the counsellor, the counsellor's attention can, as it were, be tugged and pulled away from the verbal material onto particularly striking aspects of the surroundings.

More usually, odd bits of information are noticed, revealed, or experienced and they then serve to broaden and deepen the counsellor's feeling for the client's world. This is perhaps similar to the usual setting when the client, in a developing relationship, reveals more of him- or herself in a verbal manner. For the counsellor things that were initially ideas and fragments start to link up, patterns emerge.

A man called Gerald was suffering from pathological mourning and was unable to refer to his deceased wife directly. It was evident that he used only a portion of his flat, sleeping in the sitting room and using the toilet and kitchenette, not the bedroom. There were many outlines on the walls of where ornaments and pictures had once hung. Gradually it emerged that his wife had died next to Gerald while they were in bed. Gerald had actually gone back to sleep before calling for help in the morning. In connection with the unused bedroom, he told me that he could not bear to go in there and would never sleep in there again. The unacceptable painful feelings seemed to be reflected in aspects of the environment. The outlines on the walls were like ghostly allusions to one-time feminine and homely touches. These features in the room were, for me, symbolic of his shadowy and barely perceptible references to his wife and her death. The room had somehow taken on the quality of a half-present, half-deceased presence.

In my experience it is rare that a person will raise the subject of the condition of their environment, so it is difficult to draw any firm conclusions about what the environment represents for the client. There is often a narrowing down of interest and awareness in the surroundings and a consequent kind of point-to-point existence. The man named Michael exhibited this feature to a considerable degree. On a number of visits it was barely possible to enter his flat because of some upended furniture right by the front door. Further obstructions made entry to his sitting room extremely difficult and, what with the piles of old electrical items, stacks of papers, and general rubbish, making it to an available seat was quite a delicate exercise. The layout of his room conveyed to me the feeling that my presence was rather tenuous and precarious. It seemed as though Michael was attempting to restrict his awareness to a very narrow area, as though the items in the room were felt to be bad or dangerous, the dead and lifeless appearance of the room reflecting this. Michael's habit of acquiring or buying items of damaged or useless second-hand electrical equipment could be viewed as a concretization of damaged or lifeless internal objects.

With Peter the significance of the very precise layout of his room did emerge. He self-referred because he felt unable to have visitors since his sister's death some years before. He had a full-time job of filing and cataloguing items. His room was laid out meticulously with everything in its proper place, never anything out of place. Peter constantly struggled to keep voices and hallucinations at bay which could, in times of stress and tiredness, easily swamp his fragile sense of reality. Things being confused or out of place represented a threat to his attempts to control his psychosis. His orderliness was a defence against delusions. He once said that the one thing he remembers ever being praised for in his life was his tidiness, so the room in some way was a testimony to the one quality that he felt was approved of.

With Peter from the outset the boundaries were not a problem. He was always there, the room was always the same, the seating was comfortable, face to face, and the room was warm and there were never any disturbances. All the difficulties were manifest through the transference and countertransference as in the usual set-up. After about twenty visits during a period of increased rapport, Peter started to show me important sentimental items from his past, including coloured drawings made during a period in therapy and some of his many photographs. Including these things indicated a readiness to let go of some defences and to take some risks with non-verbal material; the drawings were extremely powerful and evocative. Boundaries for Peter functioned in a similar way to the meticulous orderliness of his room: as a defence against overpowering and unpredictable anxieties. Consequently the contact was enriched and more spontaneous, the pictures perhaps representing a different type of boundary. Jung indicated how the apparently incomprehensible and unmanageable chaos of a patient's situation is visualized and objectified in a painting or drawing. This product can then be analysed and interpreted by the conscious mind:

> the effect of this method is evidently due to the fact that the originally chaotic or frightening impression is replaced by the picture which as it were . . . covers it up.[9]

Peter, in showing me these pictures, was revealing the deeper issue for him of containing and making sense of his psychotic anxieties.

The way in which static objects could come to illuminate an aspect of the client's inner world was evident with Arthur. After his place had been cleaned up, he seemed very much more buoyant. However, he soon expressed his dislike of cleaning and expressed anxieties about keeping the place clean. Over the next few weeks there was a gradual but inexorable progress towards the previous state. It was as though the tension set up by the differences between, on the one hand, his inner world and his feelings about himself and, on the other hand, a now clean outer world was too great and a more appropriate balance had to be struck. Around this time he spoke of his pet rabbit for the first time in detail. This very large rabbit, kept in a separate room and restricted to a container, sat in what must have been countless months' accumulation of its own droppings. After the clean-up the hutch remained the same. Arthur expressed some contradictory ideas about the rabbit, that it didn't mind the conditions it was in, that it was hygienic and did not smell, that he could not clean it out and that it would also be very easy to clean up. The rabbit, perhaps representing Arthur's vulnerability, could reflect the fact that for Arthur, despite changes in the outer world, his inner world and his feelings about himself remained the same.

THE THRESHOLD AND BEYOND

Complicated boundary issues arise from making home visits. Ideally the work should occur at the same time, in the same room, with the same furniture, etc. This steady state enables the counsellor to be attentive to the verbal material presented. In an environment that is changing it can be very hard to maintain boundaries and continuity. Movement from room to room, bringing items into the room, disturbances from the television or visitors, can all affect the boundaries. However, a gradual diminishing of the external and destructive factors, with associated increase in focus and consistency, will accompany a developing relationship. One of the clearest signs of this might be that someone who was prone to absence without notification becomes more mindful of the counsellor and phones in a message to cancel or plans a change of time in advance.

Ambivalence towards the counselling process can be seen by clients' attempting, over a period of time, to turn the contact into something different. In the case of David, it took a few months before he would lead me, more or less directly, to his own private room in the nursing home. Initially we would end up sitting for ten minutes or so in the common meeting area which made concentration very hard for me. Staff would then suggest that we went into his room or I would remind him of that option. Having something different from the rest of the group was difficult for him.

Much can be communicated on entry into the client's home. The length of time it takes to be let in can vary enormously with the same person and can reflect changing feelings towards the counsellor and the counselling. Over a period of time there may be a considerable irregularity at the doorstep and it can take some time before it settles down.

Sandra, whom I had been seeing for three months or so, had on a few occasions not answered the door, and it was unlikely that she had been out, given her reluctance to leave her home. She would not refer to this in the following session apart from, on occasions, saying that she had been out. One time, the following week, she said something about maybe having been in the garden. She then said that when I called in the future I should ring the doorbell once only. She was very concerned that I understood what she meant, though to me her reasons were unclear. She said that she did not want people in the other flats to think that the doorbell was ringing for them. I said I would comply if that is what she wanted but stressed that, given what had happened the week before, on occasions it could mean that we would not meet. At the time her request rather baffled me and only later did a number of possible explanations emerge. One, that she wished others not to know about our meetings and that they should be secret. Second, that her resolve not to see me on some occasions might be challenged too much by further rings on the bell which could be felt as persecutory. Perhaps Sandra gained a feeling of control. I experienced feelings of guilt associated with having lost an opportunity. Sometime later an opportunity arose to raise this question again with her in relation to her ambivalence towards many issues in her life. She explained that the procedure was appropriate as it stopped her daughter getting annoyed by Sandra letting in undesirable people. This made little sense in reality, given that her daughter was at work when I called. It illustrates the way in which her behaviour and the conditions that she set me were a means of dealing with her periodic negative feelings towards me.

Ambivalence can be seen when the client seems not to know 'where to put' the counsellor. Phillip (see p. 30) was ambivalent about the contact and finding a regular time was extremely difficult. Once we had, my ability to be flexible was never taken up when, for various reasons (usually hospital trips), he was unable to see me. In the initial weeks he was unwilling to provide a consistent place where we could talk. It could vary from week to week between his kitchen, bedroom, or sitting room, and we invariably had to finish early because he had to go out. This settled down for a period of about four months but fragmented again as the ending approached.

With Arthur it took me a long time to be able to start to make sense of his speech and ideas and to understand his anxieties. At the beginning there were many of what he referred to as misunderstandings which were a great source of concern to him. In a graphic and poignant way he attempted to communicate his distress concerning this to me. He started to move furniture around from week to week. Initially we sat more or less face to face. One week I arrived and he had placed a table between us and subsequently stuff was piled up on top of it, blocking my view of him. It also became harder to get into the room and the chair I used got covered up or had bits removed from it until I had to sit uncomfortably on the wooden arm. This all seemed to convey the feeling that there was an impenetrable barrier between us, that I wasn't seeing him and that I wasn't understanding how uncomfortable and precarious the whole situation was for him.

Absence with no notification is frequently encountered. It can be the result of anger about the previous session or of a recent announcement about a break or such like. It is something that can quite considerably 'put out' the counsellor, particularly if the process of getting there is troublesome, because of poor weather for instance. It can be extremely worrying and can encourage over-hasty responses, particularly in the case of a suicidal client. It encourages fantasies because it is an event that could have any number of causes. In the absence of information the counsellor's own response to the unopened door can be most helpful. On one occasion prior to a break Peter (see p. 28) did not come to the door. I was on time and waited for over five minutes and rang the bell a number of times. In the meantime I became more and more convinced that he had committed suicide or worse that he was actually in the process of attempting to take his life. It was out of office hours and I soon started to feel isolated, responsible, and helpless. He finally came to the door and spoke of his faulty doorbell! My feelings of being helpless and cut off gave me perhaps a taste of Peter's dilemma when his inner and outer life were most taxing for him.

The extreme threat that a holiday break represented to a client was evident in the case of Timothy whom I visited in hospital. Initially we would meet in a busy common room where disturbances were frequent. Timothy was then transferred to a much quieter and more private section and here we could meet with no disturbances. With the change of accommodation was a move away from a more acute ward where the patients were more disturbed. After I announced that I would be taking a long break over the Christmas period, Timothy resumed the meetings in the busy, noisy common-room area. He also, on a number of occasions, got up and left me alone with no explanation. His return to this place seemed to indicate how threatened he was with regression by the break, and leaving me alone for periods of time actually made me experience what it might be like for him to be deserted. These periods were not easy because of the often intense interest of the other patients. Also, as I sat with my back to the room I felt vulnerable to possible unpredictable behaviour. When Timothy was present, if anybody did approach and disturb us he would get rid of them. In such circumstances one can rely upon the client to protect the counsellor from certain aspects of the environment.

CONCLUSIONS

There is obviously a limitless number of ways in which the person uses their environment together with the objects in it, and it is often difficult to notice that certain events are attempts at communicating something to the counsellor. Because acted-out behaviour is by definition unconscious, it is often difficult to differentiate between behaviour that was part of the individual's normal manner and that which is aimed at the counsellor. So the value of the counsellor's hunches or insights developed from his or her experience of the client and their environment is often hard to determine.

The aim is to create a therapeutic potential within the client's customary physical space. Perhaps what can potentially happen is that the individual, for a time at least, comes to feel understood right where he or she is both physically and internally.

It is not always clear whether the information gained from observation of the environment and the way it is used is part of the therapeutic space or outside it. Often it would be far more comfortable to believe that some piece of complicated and destructive behaviour is entirely separated from the counselling.

In this chapter I have tried to show that counselling which is carried out in the client's usual surroundings, although full of particular difficulties and constraints, is a viable and valuable way of working. It is a response to a group in society for whom this approach is appropriate and necessary. When working with such individuals it is perhaps important for the counsellor to consider that he or she is faced with a situation that comprises the client *and* his or her environment. For a person who is unable to express emotions and fantasies directly, their environment contains and hence expresses aspects of themselves that are unconscious. The counsellor will, by being attentive also to the environment, come to 'see more' of the client.

A psychodynamic approach serves very well in the task of trying to contain and to make sense of the considerably extended field of interest presented to the counsellor when conducting counselling in the client's home environment.

NOTES

1 M. Klein, 'The psycho-analytic play technique' in Juliet Mitchell (ed.) *The Selected Melanie Klein* (Harmondsworth: Penguin, 1986), p. 38.
2 H. Segal, 'Some aspects of the analysis of a schizophrenic', in *Melanie Klein Today*, vol. 2 (London: Maresfield Library, 1988), p. 103.
3 Ibid., p. 104.
4 D. W. Winnicott, *Through Paediatrics to Psycho-Analysis* (London: Hogarth Press and the Institute of Psycho-Analysis, 1987), p. 281.
5 D. W. Winnicott, *The Maturational Processes and the Facilitating Environment* (London: Hogarth Press and the Institute of Psycho-Analysis, 1987), p. 229.
6 Ibid., p. 194.
7 H. Segal, op. cit., p. 102.
8 C. G. Jung, 'The psychology of dementia praecox', *The Collected Works of C. G. Jung*, vol. 3 (London: Routledge & Kegan Paul; Princeton, NJ: Princeton University Press, Bollingen Series XX, 1960), p. 179.
9 Ibid., p. 182.

Chapter 3

'I was sick and you visited me'

Facilitating mourning with hospital patients and their relatives

Julia Buckroyd

For a period of nine months I worked part-time in the acute neurosurgery unit of a large hospital as a trainee counsellor and lay chaplain under the supervision of the chaplain. One of my original anxieties in taking up this work had been whether there would be anyone to whom I might offer counselling. It was almost immediately obvious that there was a vast need. I was very soon being given more referrals than I could manage. It was flattering to feel wanted and needed. However, it was also anxiety-provoking. Who was I to think that I had anything to offer people who were often mortally ill, or to their shocked and grieving relatives? Who was I to intervene in people's lives and assume that I had something they could make use of?

In a more professional way the question was something like 'How do I understand my function as a counsellor?' I came to think that the work with most patients and relatives could usefully be described as 'facilitating acceptance of the medical reality'. This was not the case for every single patient, and some of the exceptions will be considered later, but it is accurate as a broad indication of my purposes and intentions. In counselling terms what that most often implied was facilitating mourning.

For many patients and their families the early days of admission to the hospital were days of extremely high anxiety while the procedures which would lead to a diagnosis were carried out.

The combination of anxiety with tremendous hope and longing was common. The mother of a 2-year-old girl, Juliet, was distraught when her child went into a coma. Brain scans revealed a tumour. Surgery was planned but the child was too unwell for it to be carried out. While she waited for her baby to get well enough for major brain surgery, the mother struggled with the appalling situation in which she found herself. Her reaction was to read voraciously all she could find on the subject and canvass opinion all over as to Juliet's chances. She would triumphantly present me with new facts and figures about successful interventions in similar cases, but she did not sleep 'at all', she told me, for days on end. This woman was close to uncontrollable anxiety so I simply let her talk as long as she wanted in the hope that thereby some of the anxiety might be relieved. She fantasized a day, a month, in the future when Juliet's operation would have been carried out and she would be well on the way to recovery. It was painful to hear the enormous longing.

This initial stage of anxiety before the diagnosis is known might usefully be called 'worry work'. If the possibility of an unfavourable diagnosis has been confronted in fantasy, then to confront it in reality is less of a shock, and mourning will be able to proceed more easily. For that reason I try to assess whether this work is actually going on at a conscious level and if not I try to encourage it. Some patients are well defended against their fears; Juliet's mother was finding hers almost overwhelming.

The first stage of the mourning process is usually one of shock and disbelief, when an unfavourable diagnosis has been made. In order to maintain emotional health it is absolutely necessary for the denial in this phase to be succeeded by acceptance. Of course this cannot take place at once. The question for me is how can I promote this acceptance? What I do is ask people to tell me what has happened, how they find themselves in the unit, and what it's all about. 'Telling the story' re-acquaints the teller with the details and makes the account less unreal, more credible. It helps to integrate events into the mourner's experience.

Mrs Jackson had cancer. A spinal tumour had been compressing her spinal cord, making walking difficult at first and then impossible. The tumour had been successfully removed but the damage to the cord was already too great. She was paraplegic and would remain so. I knew I would see her only once because she was due to be returned to her referring hospital. What could I do in one meeting? I asked her to tell me her story and out poured a painful story with a rotten ending. She was a huge fat lady and one of the hardest things for her was to face the difficulty and embarrassment of having to be hauled on to a bed pan. 'Surely it won't always have to be like that,' she seemed to be saying. There was nothing I could say or do to make the reality any less painful. To reassure someone in those circumstances seems to me to be no kindness since it merely delays the necessary acknowledgement of the reality. What I can do is convey human understanding and sympathy – compassion in the strict meaning of the word. For most people there are few, if any, others who are willing to listen to the story in all its horrible detail without offering false hope and reassurance. What sometimes seems to me to be a merely passive role I can see in more hopeful moments to be actively giving space and time and a benevolent human presence.

I have been confirmed in my estimate of the importance of 'telling the story' by the urgency with which people sometimes seek to engage in it. One lady, Mrs Kelsh, stopped me in the corridor to ask if I could get a chaplain to visit her husband. What she really wanted was to tell me there and then about the appalling thing that had happened. Her husband had been referred to the hospital after what was thought to be a slight stroke, then affecting his co-ordination and speech. A brain scan had revealed a large, inoperable malignant tumour. 'I didn't expect good news,' she said, 'but I didn't expect this.' Mrs Kelsh, however, was also a good example of how simply being able to express something of what she was feeling gave her a little space and freedom. When she first spoke to me she was feeling faint and claustrophobic and was pacing the corridor in an agitated fashion, tearful. After telling me her story she was able to return to her husband's bedside and also to deal with the practical issue of how she was going to get home that night.

Sometimes, however, I have played a rather different role in this stage of shock and denial. Often it seems harder for the relatives than for the patient to accept an unfavourable diagnosis.

Mr Morris's wife, Nancy, was dying of cancer. He could not accept that and told his wife, 'I can't live without you.' He had thus made it impossible for her to share her fear that she was indeed dying. My feeling was that if Mr Morris could let himself acknowledge the possibility of his wife's death, then the last months of her life could be lived and shared in intimacy, honesty, and mutual support. I tried, therefore, to get him to let some of his feelings become conscious, but to each initiative along the lines of 'You must sometimes be afraid of the future' he could only respond 'I must hope'. It was only when their holiday was cut short by acute pain in Nancy's back, followed very shortly by the loss of the use of her legs, that his passionate desire for it all to be different had to give way to reality. Even then he maintained the fiction. He told me after her death that it was only in the last four days that he had begun to admit that she would die. On the day she died he was still denying to the extent that one of his two sons had gone to work and could not be contacted in time to be with his mother when she died. I felt sad for Mr Morris, faced with a reality which was plainly intolerable, but I grieved more for Nancy who had died alone with her fears, protecting her husband to the very end.

When once reality begins to be accepted, those who mourn experience all manner of different feelings. I would now like to describe my experience of trying to help people work through these different stages. One of those I commonly encounter is the point at which sick people ask the outraged question 'Why me?' I do not think it is a question so much as a cry of anguish about the unfairness of life.

Oliver had had cancer for some years. Radiotherapy had not stopped the spread of cancer and a short return to work had been followed by readmission to hospital because of difficulties in walking. Plainly Oliver had a very good idea of what was going on, even though up to that point the word cancer had never been mentioned and he had not been informed of the diagnosis. At one point he exclaimed 'I wish I were dead!' Regrettably the opportunity to recognize his despair was not taken. Instead a psychiatrist was summoned who took it upon himself to say that Oliver must not be told the diagnosis because he would not be able to tolerate it. The arrogance of this intervention and its imperception made me angry. What clearer evidence could possibly be required that Oliver both could tolerate and was tolerating his condition? May a man not be allowed a little despair? Whose fears are being treated by this recommendation? Oliver's wife was prepared to go along with this advice and so for six months this couple had lived a lie. Finally, Oliver was admitted to the neuro-surgery unit for investigations of his bladder incontinence. I was asked to see him because of his extreme distress. He was sitting in the middle of the ward in his pyjamas with his head on his hands, weeping. We talked for an hour, pacing round the garden together. He told me perhaps eight or nine times that 'Cancer is a hard thing to beat'. When I asked him if he thought his wife knew what was wrong with him he said he was sure she didn't. 'All I want', he said in anguish, 'is to live a normal life with my Pauline. Why has this happened to me? I'm not nasty like some people. I'm always prepared to do someone a good turn. I don't deserve this.' Much of the passionate intensity of this meeting derived from this man's enforced silence and isolation for six months. His 'Why me?' was real enough and in my judgement neither needed nor admitted of an answer. He was somewhat calmer later, simply, I think, because of having been able to express the question.

A closely allied and often experienced emotion is anger. People don't like being ill or disabled and neither do their relatives. The religiously minded sometimes get angry with God; the vast majority, angry that life is like that, look around for a target on whom to displace their rage. Sometimes I am that target but I have more often been needed to listen to expressions of rage about other people, most often doctors.

Quentin, a boy of 9, had a benign tumour the size of an apple removed from the side of his head. His father chose me, as not being a member of the medical profession and therefore without power to hurt him or his child, to listen to his fury that despite his considerable efforts to have a diagnosis made of the boy's evident perceptual deficit, nothing had been found.

Much of the work is about letting go, and that often implies great sadness. Even a successful intervention followed by complete recovery – as, for example, quite often occurs with laminectomies to relieve disc pressure on the spinal column – involves the loss of the fantasy of youth, health, and physical inviolability. Of course there is often gratitude for the relief of pain, but particularly before the wound has healed there seems often to be some regret as well. It is expressed in phrases like 'Ah well, it had to be done.' My function is such cases is, I think, to acknowledge the feeling and to accept that there are losses as well as gains, even in a successful outcome. I can perhaps provide the forum in which such feelings can be permitted and recognized.

There are, of course, many greater losses and much more pervasive sadness and regret for relatives as well as patients. Sometimes it can be seen only obliquely. One is the loss of the possibility of employment.

Trevor, a machine tool operator, had an operation for a double aneurism followed by severe memory loss and a deficit in functioning generally. His gradual return to some sort of health culminated in his being given a place in a job rehabilitation centre. His sadness for what he had lost was perhaps visible in his lack of interest in what he saw as childish tasks. Again, there can be little for me to do but to accompany people in their sadness and regret, and to refrain from offering false hopes.

Finally, among these intermediate stages of the mourning process, I am the witness of much alternating hope and despair. It is easier to hope than to despair, but I think that unless the worst has been considered as a possibility then it is impossible to have real hope. The hope without despair is false and defensive like that of Mr Morris. The vast majority of referrals I am given are presented to me as people who are depressed. It is the commonest mood I encounter.

Wilma, a lady of 65, was depressed. She had suffered from rheumatoid arthritis since her mid-30s. The disease had required the replacement of hip, knee, and ankle joints and had left her hands grossly deformed. Over the past few years, however, the disease had been in remission until three weeks before her admission to the hospital when she had begun to lose the use of her arms. When I saw her she had virtually no use of them and could not blow her nose or put on her spectacles unaided. Wilma was in hospital for almost two months before an operation was carried out and during that time she often felt despairing. The idea that she could not 'do for myself' was intolerable to her, and she made a number of covert threats of suicide if nothing were done to improve her condition. The idea that her husband might have to attend to her personal needs was torture to her, although she reported that he consistently asserted 'We'll manage somehow'.

Again, she had no one to voice these feelings to, and indeed became rather alienated from the staff. Her total incapacity to accept her condition made her contemptuous of their attempts to show her how to use various aids to enable life to go on despite her disability. It was not easy for them to endure this rejection of their efforts and Wilma's unvarying pessimism. I, too, found it hard to visit her over and over again and to feel in myself the hopelessness of moving her through this stage. I felt that her mourning was not only for this particular loss but for the whole of her mature life which had been blighted by the disease. When I could distance myself sufficiently to see it, two months' intensive mourning for thirty years of illness did not seem excessive. Her normal mode of being was stoical: 'I never complain, never have', so it is highly likely that she had never permitted herself such overt grief before.

The final phase of mourning is acceptance and reconstruction. Wilma repaid my sometimes reluctant devotion by her emotional growth during the last three weeks of her stay in the unit. The operation was carried out and was technically a complete success. The question was: had she regained the use of her arms? The answer seemed to be: to a very modest extent. She could spoon food into her mouth and she could grasp a tissue. Contrary to my expectations this did not thrust her back into despair. Instead she began to show some emotional movement. During the two months before the operation I had frequently suggested that she was angry. She had always denied it. Now she could own it. 'Oh yes, I am a very angry woman,' she said. The tentative 'Why me?' voiced early on became a strident clamour: 'WHY ME?' Then Wilma began to say:

> At least everything that can be done has been done. If I hadn't had the operation I would always have regretted it. If my arms don't improve I suppose we'll manage somehow. There are lots of people worse off than me. At least I have my faculties.

Simultaneously Wilma began to take better care of herself and her appetite and sleeping began to improve. Her surrender of herself to the institution came to an end and she began to long for home. I did not often see so much of the mourning process as I did with Wilma, and it was profoundly satisfying to have accompanied her to its resolution.

Sometimes I think it is possible for me to do more to promote acceptance of the medical reality than simply wait for it to happen. My acceptance of the damaged person sometimes seems a catalyst in this situation. I have been most aware of this in relation to babies and small children. Many parents of sick and damaged babies feel a powerful urge to reject them. Occasionally this is expressed verbally: when Will's father heard that Will would be almost certainly permanently and severely brain-damaged, he left the ward saying 'Well, put him in an institution'. More often the mother who stays with the child in hospital will express that urge to reject by neglect: not making sure that the baby is warm; letting the baby cry too long; but most often the care will be adequate while the mother's body language in relation to the child expresses her struggle.

Robbie went through several phases of seeming close to neglecting Will. She herself was only 18. Will had been born by Caesarian at thirty-eight weeks after a very difficult pregnancy, much of which Robbie had spent ill at home or in hospital. When the baby was born his brain was found to be imperfectly formed and at three weeks he was brought to the unit for the implantation of a shunt because he was hydrocephalic. Robbie's own internal baby screamed for attention which she expressed in gestures such as not eating properly, and she found the physical demands of getting up in the night to feed Will more or less overwhelming. Will's head was big and Robbie did not support it when she held him; she patted him in his cot just a little too hard; she held him in a tense and restless way so that he was agitated. He was not initially an attractive baby, especially connected up to drips and with his enlarged head. I thought that Robbie might benefit from seeing that I was not repelled by Will and so I used to ask her if I could hold him. It was plain, however, that one way for Robbie to resolve her desire to be rid of Will but at the same time to have him cared for was to let other people do it for her. It was essential that I did not promote that strategy. Further, it seemed to me that Robbie's problems were almost certainly related to an image of herself as the bad and damaging mother. In order to strengthen the good mother image I used to sit and tell Will how lucky he was to have such a lovely Mummy, what a lot she had been through and how brave she had been for his sake. At some point he would start to moan and cry and then I would hand him back to Robbie saying 'This boy needs his Mummy. Mummy's best.' Whether as a result of this approach or not Robbie was gradually more able to view herself as the good mother and to relate much more intimately to Will. For his part he grew fat and contented.

Sometimes the plea from adults seems to be 'Can you stand the sight of my damaged body?' I deduce this from the number of times I have been shown scars and paralysed limbs or the many times that reference has been made to shaven heads and head wounds. To begin with I was appalled by the horror of it all. Nowadays I hardly ever feel that in relation to an individual, but I am sometimes overcome by waves of nausea and revulsion when I am not on the unit. Many patients like to hold my hand and seem to derive comfort from what I think is a message of acceptance. This, of course, is rather contrary to the usual practice of counsellors who tend to maintain a physical distance. My reasoning for behaving differently is that many patients seem to feel invaded and damaged by the medical procedures but are simultaneously cut off from their ordinary sources of physical comfort. To be hurt, isolated in a bed, and distanced from those who mean most is a horrible experience. An attempt to heal the emotional wounds may sometimes appropriately include touching and holding physically.

Although I found this model of 'facilitating acceptance of the medical reality' useful for conceptualizing the work I did with a large number of the patients I saw in the unit, I came to be aware that there was a significant minority who did not fall into this category. I should now like to discuss my interaction with these people.

There was a surprisingly numerous group of patients who had suffered bereavement close to the time or even during the time they were themselves in hospital. This complicated and intensified their own sense of loss.

Alan, in his 40s, was in the unit for a spinal operation. He was unmarried and lived with his father, his mother being dead. I was asked to see him because after a very short illness of only three weeks Alan's father had died in another hospital. Alan had been found weeping by the nurses and was described as being very depressed. After trying to indicate to me that he was not grieving unduly, he went on to describe a relationship of extraordinary ambivalence. He had accepted this appointment even though he had been planning to visit his father who, he knew, was dying in another hospital. 'It was no good,' he said. 'I couldn't have visited him anyway. The pain in my back getting there was too bad.' It seemed to me that two things were operating: a denial of feelings – 'I didn't talk to the old man much' – and this powerful ambivalence which together were making for painful grieving. Added to these were Alan's own pain and distress following his operation. It seemed that what I could do was, by accepting his feelings, indicate that I was not overwhelmed by them and so Alan need not fear that he would be either.

Another group of patients was simultaneously trying to deal with their own problems and with another crisis in the family, often terribly torn by the competing demands of home and hospital. All that seemed possible to do was to permit the anxiety to be expressed and to hope that containing it offered some relief. One woman had a toddler seriously ill and a new baby between whom to divide herself. Another had a very sick baby and a dying mother. In such cases it must surely be impossible to do more than help these women to survive the crisis. Many mothers of sick children had the additional anxiety of another child or children at home. Elaine's mother, for example, spent her life circling from home to school to hospital to school to home to hospital. What is needed there is support to carry on doing that as long as necessary. This particular woman understood that well, indeed better than I did. She wanted me to be with her to listen to how she organized her life but she did not want to consider Elaine's future as a possibly/probably brain-damaged child: 'I'm just living one day at a time,' she told me, firmly.

A much more difficult problem is posed by people with life problems. Flora, now 18, had been born with spina bifida. She was admitted as an emergency to the unit suffering from dizziness and disorientation. She was admitted during Wednesday night and by Friday tests had been carried out and the decision made to refer her. I arrived on Friday afternoon and was asked to see her because she was said to be very depressed. As she talked about herself it became evident that she had not begun to adjust to the reality of her disability. My first inclination, knowing that I could see her once more at most, was to refer her, especially since the organization ASBAH (Association for Spina Bifida and Hydrocephalus) exists to help in precisely these situations. All my suggestions about where she might get the help she needed were turned down, and I began to see that Flora's needs were so urgent that she could only focus on this present moment and on me. I felt quite afraid of getting sucked into the enormous void of her need and longing, but I also felt great concern. I was needed to be a nurturing mother who would care for Flora totally, love her without reserve, and be strong enough to bear her disability and dependence. So, she told me on little or no acquaintance how kind, helpful, understanding I was, easy to talk to, if only she had a friend like me. . . . I would like to think there was a whisper of truth in some of this, but even allowing for vanity it was clear that we were talking about transference. Flora had already fallen in love with me. No doubt this is what she does repeatedly and it seemed desirable to try to work with it. Of course there was not the faintest chance of resolving the issue, but it seemed even less satisfactory to do nothing. At the end of that first session, therefore, I made a tentative beginning by talking about her reluctance to let me go. Had I to do it again I would be less tentative and would say something like 'You don't want to let me go because you are afraid that I might not come back and then you will feel totally abandoned again.'

I returned the following day (Saturday) – a clear indication of my countertransference that I felt I needed to do so. Whether any of the work did any good is hard to say. It seems wholly unrealistic to think that problems as serious and long-standing as Flora's will yield to the very limited contact possible in the unit. The alternative, however, seems to be to do nothing, a course of action that in Flora's case would have neatly matched her own despair.

Flora seems to be a good example of another issue which relates to my functioning as a chaplain. I had introduced myself as the chaplain, and early on in our conversation Flora made reference to the fact that she was a Roman Catholic. She went on to say that the priest had told her that she must be less 'selfish'. There might have been a temptation at that point to assume that God-talk might have meant something to Flora. I thought it more likely that I was being tested and decided to ignore that aspect. I think that was a sound judgement in that later she referred to the church with some fury (as well she might). That was, however, an example of me not taking up the religious issue, even when it was raised.

There was also a group of patients whose afflictions had an unconscious purpose. The most mysterious of these was Gerald, a white man who had lived in Africa all his life. About five months before he appeared in the unit he had suddenly developed weakness in his feet and then his legs. After various unsuccessful investigations in Africa he had come to Britain and had spent twelve weeks in one hospital with similarly negative results, before being referred to the unit. He stayed in the unit for about three months before being discharged, against his will, until such time as his symptoms became more florid.

He was referred to me shortly after his arrival because the nurses found it impossible to create a relationship with him and were puzzled and concerned by that. He was one patient whom the doctors also found it hard to deal with, so that I had considerable pressure/enthusiasm concerning my contacts with him. For reasons I do not understand I was able to make some sort of a relationship with Gerald. The first time I saw him he told me that he had been made redundant a few months before his illness began. He also told me, with tears in his eyes, that his wife had been killed in a road accident two years before. Finally, he mentioned that he had set himself up in business there only three weeks before he felt the weakness in his legs. I was aware of the great difficulty there had been in diagnosing his walking problem, so it seemed remarkable that Gerald should be telling me these things at a first meeting when he appeared to find it hard to tell anyone else anything. I tentatively formulated the idea that his leg weakness had at least a psychogenic element.

The problem was that if there was a psychogenic element how could that be dealt with? The medical staff remained convinced throughout his stay that there was organic disease, probably some form of malignancy, and that the problem lay only in identifying it. It caused them, particularly the registrar, considerable frustration that they were unable to do so. My suggestions did not seem helpful to them, although Gerald himself seemed to have some inkling of a possible other line of exploration and tried, without success, to get the consultant to let him see a psychiatrist. My efforts, then, were directed towards trying to put him in touch with his feelings, so that they could be expressed more directly than his leg weakness perhaps implied. My initial strategy was to identify and reflect back feelings to him. That was easy enough to do because he, in fact, often displayed very powerful feelings: anger, helplessness, sadness, depression; it did not, however, seem very productive, since it seemed to produce either denial or resistance. In fact I learned that this was to be expected in so far as psychosomatic illness deflects the pain of experience into physical pain simply because feelings are feared to be overwhelming. This happens because the child feels that his feelings cannot be contained and dealt with and must therefore assume another more acceptable and safer form: namely physical illness. I therefore began to try and find out whether this might be true in Gerald's case and to talk about some of the experience in feeling terms. This had some greater measure of success in that Gerald seemed to be willing to engage in this sort of exploration, saying that he was willing to try anything. Meanwhile his physical condition after his admission to the unit grew worse. It seemed that he was dying before our eyes, but then, gradually, for reasons medically as obscure as those that caused his deterioration, he began to improve. After three months it seemed not impossible that he was at least maintaining a condition rather better than that in which he had come to the hospital.

It would be hard to see this as success. Gerald was by no means 'well' when he left. I think, however, that he and I had the closest thing to a relationship that he made during the three months in the unit, which may in itself have been an achievement, and my containing his feelings provided a fragment of the 'corrective emotional experience' he so desperately seemed to need and which may have caused his deterioration.

A further example may underline my sense of the difficulty of working with patients whose physical problems seem to have psychogenic elements. Irene, who was 53, made a good start working with me but then, I think, lost courage. She had a history of undiagnosable ailments, was very thin, cancer-phobic, and identified by the staff as a hypochondriac. She came to the hospital complaining of back pain which proved to be undiagnosable although it dated from a particular incident of lifting a patient during the course of her work as a medical auxiliary. There was, therefore, some query in my mind about the 'hypochondriac' label. Her reaction to a test by injection of fluid which detects spinal abnormalities was a very severe and prolonged migraine. Our conversation got as far as a discussion of the headache and seemed to lapse, but in another of those moments where silence, waiting, hanging on seemed appropriate, I stayed with her until her story resumed:

Irene: I'm afraid people will think I'm a fraud. I feel ill, but nobody can put their finger on it. That's the story of my life. I'm afraid I'm a nuisance. I'm afraid I'm keeping somebody else out of a bed.

JB: Is that about a sense that you are not valued, not important?

Irene: My husband, he doesn't value me. I'm a bit afraid of him. He gets irritable with me for being ill. Oh, he looks after me, but he does things wrong and he won't bring my mother to see me.

JB: Does that seem like retaliation?

Irene: Yes. And now he'll say that he knew there was nothing wrong with me.

Irene continued for an hour telling me about her fear and anxiety, and cried at the end of our time. I certainly felt that we had made a good beginning. Perhaps, however, it had been too good and therefore too frightening. The next time I went she would not engage with me, although she responded warmly to the idea of another visit. On that occasion I went to the ward to find that she had discharged herself the day before.

The frustration I felt in Irene's case is, perhaps, typical of these more complex cases. It is by no means always easy to know what is going on, or how to respond. Is doing what I can in the limitations of the circumstances better than doing nothing, or should I refrain from intervening? I think in fact that it is only possible to intervene when the patient is willing that I should and I also believe that for most people it must be creative to find that I am not as afraid of their psychic pain and fantasies as they are themselves. Perhaps my short-term and limited interventions can at least be a symbol of hope for people who quite often seem to have very little. Must it not be true that it is better to light one candle than to curse the darkness?

Chapter 4

Who is afraid?

Managing anxieties in a youth club

Trudy Chapman

This chapter is based on my experience as a full-time youth worker managing a youth club in London. It was an eventful time, which coincided with the period when I was doing my counselling training. I wondered how the theoretical material I was studying could help me to understand what went on in this setting, and in generating insight into what decisions and policies were needed to run the club successfully.

At the time of first writing the dissertation on which this chapter is based, I thought it would be useful to focus on what adolescents bring along to a youth club. I hoped that this would show what particularly concerned them and illuminate the areas where they particularly needed help. What stood out in this regard was the way the young people communicated their difficulties in managing anxieties associated with the adolescent stage of development. While there were differences for each young person in the way these anxieties were experienced, there was much they had in common. This was why there were often events in the club which involved large groups of young people, or the entire group. Although it would be possible for me to describe much more fully interactions with individuals which would point to their personal struggles, I have decided to concentrate here mostly on the anxieties which were shared, and which are common to people of this age in our culture.

THE YOUTH CLUB SETTING

The club is part of the youth service provision of the local education authority, and its purpose is the informal social education of 11- to 21-year-olds. The aim of the work can broadly be described as promoting personal development. The staffing of the club consisted of myself as full-time worker, plus a team of part-time youth workers employed on a sessional basis.

The club is located on a small council housing estate of terraced houses and serves a stable local community with very little ethnic diversity. Unemployment and poverty are not major problems, although the area is not at all a prosperous one. The club's users (whom I shall also refer to as members) rarely continue their education past 16. Many have been expelled from one of the local secondary schools, attend special units, or simply do not go to school at all.

Housed in its own purpose-built premises, the club has good facilities, a congenial layout and is well kept. It is far smaller than some other nearby youth service units which offer extensive programmes of activities. Usually between twenty and thirty-five young people attend each club session.

ADOLESCENCE: A STAGE OF DEVELOPMENT OR A SOCIAL PROBLEM?

While adolescence is a stage in growing up that each person has to go through, it is also seen as constituting a social problem which needs attention, and it seems that establishing youth clubs is one way that society has devised for doing just this. However, it can sometimes seem to youth workers that a youth club is somehow meant to resolve all the difficulties associated with adolescent behaviour.

Winnicott says about this tendency for society to want adolescence to be somehow solved as a social problem:

> We do sometimes need to be reminded that although adolescence is something we always have with us, each adolescent boy or girl grows up in the course of a few years into an adult. Irritation with the phenomena of adolescence can easily be invoked by careless reference to adolescence as a permanent problem, forgetting that each individual is in the process of becoming a responsible society-minded adult.[1]

So what is it about adolescence as a stage in the life cycle that means that it is seen as problematic, and what is this stage of development like for the individual girl or boy? What are the crucial aspects of this stage of development for an agency that will be dealing with adolescents' difficulties as its stock-in-trade?

Adolescence can be defined as 'the period of experiencing and resolving the turbulence which is set into action by the biological process of puberty'.[2] Puberty brings with it sexual maturity and growth to an adult body size. Adolescence can be seen as a crisis, since it is a process of transition which involves 'transient "madness" which is necessary and healthy although painful'.[3] Young people are entering a phase in which it will be important to search for their own sense of identity and, until they do so, they do not know what they are going to become. Adolescents are involved in a struggle to feel real and, in this stage which Winnicott calls 'the doldrums', cannot yet do so. The struggling, searching, and not knowing, while being a normal and important part of the transition process, carry anxiety and distress which make this period difficult at times, both for the young people and for those around them.

Throughout the teenage years the dependence on parents that was quite proper in a child has to be relinquished, and the attachment loosened. Reliance on external authority will need to be reduced and replaced by an inner authority which mediates the struggle between the need to express instinctual impulses and the necessity to control them. It is this immense change which gives rise to the teenager's need for experimentation, for trying things out.

I will be arguing that in a youth-club setting anxieties around aggression and destructiveness and around sexuality are particularly crucial. In the case of aggression we can see that a teenager is acquiring new strength and size and with it increased potential for violence and destruction. Adolescents at the beginning of this stage do not know how this new power can be managed, how it can be internally controlled so that it is not let loose on those around them.

> How shall each one deal with something that is really new: the power to destroy and even to kill, a power that did not complicate the feelings of hate that were experienced at the toddler age?[4]

In the same way concerns about how sexuality will be expressed or controlled are most important. Adolescents are in the dark about how their sexuality will develop, and concerns about what adult sexuality is all about and how they themselves will be as sexual adults are very much around. Just as physical growth brings with it new and dangerous possibilities for aggressiveness and its expression, so sexual maturity raises new possibilities for sexual expression that are equally frightening. Again this uncertainty arouses strong anxieties in the teenage years, and teenagers are commonly preoccupied about whether they are normal or abnormal, particularly with regard to sexuality.

In the next sections I will be demonstrating how adolescent anxieties are powerfully expressed in the work with young people. There is space here only to deal with anxieties around aggression, although anxieties around sexuality are just as important. I think it is the intensity of the anxieties associated with adolescence that is being communicated when teenagers behave in ways that irritate and frighten adults. It is this intensity that leads adult society to view adolescence as a problem.

ANXIETIES ABOUT AGGRESSION IN THE YOUTH CLUB

Being with a group of adolescents can put a youth worker very much in touch with the anxieties that have been mentioned. It can be a most harrowing experience, and normally self-confident adults can feel intimidated, undermined, confused, helpless, stupid, and guilty. After a difficult time with a group of teenagers, youth workers will often talk of feeling as if they are losing their senses. As youth work is usually more informal and less structured than a classroom teaching situation, I think that youth workers may be even more likely to experience the full force of adolescent anxieties than are teachers. In these interactions I think that the anxieties that belong to the young people are projected, and are picked up by the youth workers, who find these intense feelings very difficult to tolerate.

It seems to me that it is when the work is going badly, and particularly when things feel out of control, that these anxieties become most evident. Adolescence brings with it the need to confront and defy authority figures, and these experiences will help a young person to test out and explore their own resources and to gradually assimilate a sense of their own authority. But when the adolescents' challenge to the authority of an institution is not effectively met, the anxieties will be exacerbated and can become overwhelming.

Small-scale challenges and confrontations are going on all the time in a youth club, often over quite trivial issues. Usually these exchanges are managed in a good-humoured way, and all is well. There are other times when an entire group of young people involves itself in defiance and disruption in a more severe testing out and challenge to the institution. Alternatively the group makes use of one or two more disturbed individuals who commit violent or destructive acts on behalf of the whole group.

The material which follows demonstrates how behaviour in the club may be showing the young people's anxieties. In my first months at the club the sessions were almost invariably affected by incidents of stealing, vandalism, disruptiveness, threats of violence, or actual fights between club members. The kind of incidents which frequently occurred were: spitting on tables or chairs, craft materials thrown around or set alight, damage to sports equipment, sweets or drinks thrown at people, and deliberate knocking over of pot plants. At the end of a session a fire extinguisher was often set off or a window would be broken.

I think it is important to try to understand the meaning of this kind of behaviour, to try to see what is being communicated. At first sight such behaviour can seem quite incomprehensible, and youth workers often express their bewilderment. Why do the young people seem intent on destroying a club that is there for them to use? Why do they smash sports equipment used by no one except themselves?

However, if we look at what is happening from the point of view of what is being communicated about adolescent anxieties, then I think an answer can be found. In this context it seems that the behaviour points to and emphasizes a worry that angry and destructive feelings are getting out of control. At this time it was clear that the youth-club workers were unable to prevent severely destructive behaviour. As adolescents are not yet able to be sure of their own internal controls over expressing aggression, the failure of the institution to exercise control effectively leaves them anxious about the possibilities of aggressiveness being completely let loose with disastrous consequences.

In order to understand what was happening here, I think it is useful to digress for a moment to look at a youth club in terms of a holding situation, similar to that which a mother can give to a distressed child. Looking at the mother and child: is the child's distress met by the mother's awareness of the distress and by confidence that the feelings are not so overwhelming that they cannot be coped with? Or is the mother's response one of fear and uncertainty? If the child feels that the mother is able to cope with the distress, the child is reassured by the knowledge that its feelings are not unmanageable. But if the child meets a response which communicates uncertainty about whether the feelings can be tolerated, then its anxieties and distress are increased.

I think that much of what is written about holding and containment in counselling, psychotherapy, or case work can be applied to youth work. Isca Salzberger-Wittenberg says of casework,

> Failure to respond appropriately, whether with a baby, child or adult leads to a feeling that aggression, depression, or terror cannot be borne. . . . It continues to be felt as an omnipotently powerful force that cannot be circumscribed or bound. It comes to be experienced as endless and unspecified . . . a 'nameless dread'.[5]

Effective holding, on the other hand,

> makes it possible for the client to introject a kind of container/mother holding this aspect of himself. Anxiety is thus modulated and his internal world becomes enriched, more manageable and stable.[6]

The reason why this function is so vital is not just that things can become unmanageable when there is a failure, but that proper holding of adolescents in a youth club will aid their development by helping them to learn how to hold themselves; that is, to internalize their own control. Failure in this regard can mean that the client group has an experience which is unhelpful and even damaging, and it is then imperative that something is done to allow effective holding to be re-established.

However, the club at that time was not adequately responding to the challenge presented to it by its users. There was just no sense of confidence that the staff could manage the young people's difficult behaviour. On the contrary, the club was being damaged, both physically and as a club, because of the impossibility of properly organizing any kind of activity. A youth club should offer opportunities for its users to involve themselves in creative, sporting, or cultural activities, since these activities themselves provide opportunities to modulate and work through anxieties. When disruption makes these things impossible then the club is not really surviving.

I conclude that the adequacy of the holding being provided in the setting is reflected in the ability to put effective limits on how aggressive and destructive impulses may be expressed. Exactly where the limits are set can be a difficult decision since there needs to be a balance between control and flexibility that allows room for confrontation, growth, and self-discovery. When there are no clear limits, anxiety escalates as adolescent fantasies about death and murder become strengthened. The increased anxiety can reach an unmanageable level and will then have to be discharged through a further violent or destructive act. The situation can worsen, with more and more serious acts as the young people try to find out when they are going to be stopped.

This can become a desperate search for the boundary that is missing. I think this was exactly what was happening at this time in the club. The members' behaviour became worse and worse as they sought to find out where the boundary lay. Having failed to find an adequate holding situation in the youth club, and possibly at home as well, young people may search for it elsewhere, perhaps in confrontations with the police. Throughout this period some of the members did express openly their fears about getting out of control. Later, I heard that two of these young people had been charged with jointly assaulting nine policemen in the local shopping precinct.

In order to explore further the implications of anxieties about destructiveness and the ability of an institution to put some boundaries on destructive behaviour, I am going to consider in detail the circumstances and possible meanings of one piece of behaviour – breaking windows.

Broken windows had long been fairly common at the club, which has huge areas of glass. Other local youth clubs and secondary schools also at times run up massive bills for replacing smashed glass. In my first six months in the job the number of broken windows decreased substantially at a time when it seemed that the staff group were succeeding in efforts to stop uncontrolled destruction. At that time the vandalism and disruption were much less marked, and the young people seemed happier. What was interesting, though, was that there was a change over this period in the way that windows and then other pieces of glass were broken. At first windows were often smashed just after the end of a session. As the staff were turning off the lights an object would be thrown from outside, and glass fragments would fly everywhere. This pattern of breaking windows stopped after I called the police to arrest a boy who had smashed a window in particularly dangerous circumstances. This 16-year-old, Jim, was a focus for many of the most damaging acts that happened in the club.

Before this incident the members had been warned that the police would be asked to take action over broken windows, so when I next saw Jim I informed him that I was calling the police to arrest him. Instead of disappearing, he stayed in the club quietly playing table tennis. When the police arrived, he came when I called him, and went without protest. His arrest happened in the most calm and undramatic way possible. I wonder if there was not some relief that something was being done to call a halt to destructiveness that was becoming more extreme, and that an outside agency, the police, had been brought in to help in making a prohibition effective.

In fact, after that windows were never broken in the same way. Sometimes they were smashed accidentally or else over the weekend holes made by an air rifle appeared in the glass panels. Around the same time a pane of glass over the front of a video game machine was shattered several times, but it was clear that this was not deliberate. I think that the broken glass still communicated something, but the message was muted and less shrill than before.

Unfortunately, this early progress was not maintained, and, after some alarming incidents, I came to believe that the club was not providing a good experience for its users and decided to close it down for a few weeks. By this time the number of broken windows had risen again and I thought it necessary to take drastic action in order to remedy what I saw as a serious mismatch between the task of the club and its ability to enforce the boundaries appropriate to that task. While many factors were involved, what mattered most was my conviction that at that time the club was exacerbating its users' anxieties rather than assisting with them. Disarray among the staff was the ingredient that finally tipped the balance the wrong way, and the incident which finally decided me occurred when the young people refused to leave the building one night at the end of the session. While some staff quietly sat down and waited, another member of staff announced that she had called the police even though she knew that this was not my chosen course of action. The obvious confusion among the staff about what strategy we were adopting resulted in an escalation in what was already a tense situation.

After that it seemed to me that the staff team needed to demonstrate greater cohesiveness in order to establish proper boundary control for the members. I felt that part of the problem lay in my own failure to provide effective boundaries for the staff team, so that some staff commonly took inappropriate actions. Part of the reason for closing the club was to allow the staff to meet together in order to become a more cohesive team. I produced some guidelines outlining staff conduct which I regarded as unhelpful, unprofessional, or unethical. Included was an item saying that, except in an emergency, the police would not be called without my permission. The guidelines were discussed, agreed, and soon became accepted as a basic guide to which we all adhered. The consistency thus provided was seen as valuable.

However, I thought it was also necessary to take further action to ensure that the club's task did not excessively tax the staff team's capacities. The only choice that seemed workable was to alter the client group to match our abilities. It seemed to me that we were not able to work in a constructive way with the older adolescents at that time, and therefore I decided to exclude this age group temporarily.

With the younger age group, aged 11 to 15, we were able to establish limits effectively, although considerable hard work was involved. With hindsight I could later see that once I had set up and maintained appropriate limits for staff, we were able to do the same thing for the young people. Crucially we were able to gain control over an important physical boundary: the doors of the club. This mattered a great deal because we had agreed that it must become clear that the staff would decide who came into the building, and this we succeeded in doing. Consequently we were able to set up and maintain an important boundary – one between the inside and the outside. The older ones, however, began to cause an enormous amount of trouble outside the building. They banged constantly on doors and windows, shouted abuse through the letterbox, threw firecrackers, and intimidated the younger members. I was often threatened in the street, and had to park my car some distance away after it became a target. Again considering boundary issues to be crucial, I directed the other staff to pay attention to what went on inside, and not to the young people outside. We were able to run successful sessions in spite of what was happening outside, and slowly the trouble diminished and then ceased altogether. Although I had decided that I would, if necessary, call the police to deal with goings on in the street outside, I never needed to take this step.

What amazed me was that through these weeks of almost riotous behaviour in the street in front of the club, only one window was broken, and there was no other damage to the building. While older members I met outside often said to me that every window would be smashed, nothing like this ever happened. At a point when the older ones could be expected to be most aggrieved, and were displaying great anger, damage to the building ceased almost totally.

I think that this can be explained if we look for a connection between broken glass and the effectiveness of the holding function. When the club reopened, effective holding was established which was robust enough for the task. Boundaries were maintained and were seen to be reliable. Crucially, it was seen that the club was able to continue functioning as a youth club in the face of all that was being done outside to disrupt it. Thus the attacks by the young people outside did not damage the institution's ability to carry on.

Perhaps it is helpful to think of broken glass as a symbol for the fragility of the holding situation in operation. Glass has the property of being solidly there one moment, yet being easily in fragments the next. In addition, glass in windows defines the physical boundaries of a building, so that breaking a window means that a building is no longer intact. I have been arguing that effective boundaries and effective holding are needed to keep a youth club's functioning intact. When windows are being broken, can it be that this is a message about the soundness of these boundaries – that the boundaries are perceived as insubstantial and likely to shatter if pushed against, leaving the institution damaged? If so, then it could be said that the club had now been able to establish a holding function that was sturdy enough for its task. The aggression, destructiveness, and anger directed at the institution could demonstrably be withstood, so broken glass was no longer meaningful or appropriate as a symbol.

After that the conduct of the club's users was much improved and the kinds of problem described here were only occasionally in evidence, and even then in much less extreme form. A broken window became a rare event. Some of the older members later returned to the club, but most of them quickly grew up and no longer went to youth clubs. So quickly did some of them change around this time, that I have often wondered if these events at the club could have helped them to make a leap in their maturation.

RECOGNIZING AND ACKNOWLEDGING DIFFICULT FEELINGS

So far I have discussed only the aspect of holding that is related to being able to continue functioning in an undamaged way. The other vital aspect is to do with being in touch with the feelings that the client group is unconsciously trying to communicate through its behaviour. While it is often unpleasant, confusing, and sometimes frightening to be aware of the young people's feelings, I think it matters greatly that avoidance does not become entrenched as a way of defending against the painfulness of this awareness. Some kind of acknowledgement that a youth worker recognizes a young person's feelings is often, I think, a real help. Just a few words that communicate awareness of what is being experienced at an emotional level, or even a simple comment on what is happening, can have a profound impact.

One example was when a well-built 17-year-old, who was fond of weight-lifting, followed up a confrontation with me by removing his shirt and walking around me displaying his muscles and delivering punches to the walls. I said to him, 'I think you're trying to frighten me.' At this he grinned and said nothing, but he stopped what he was doing and was calm for the rest of the evening. This straightforward observation was sufficient to relieve the tension, as it acknowledged an awareness of what was happening and indicated a willingness to talk about it. Certainly very frightening feelings were around at the time, and I think it is immensely reassuring when something can actually be said about them.

Sometimes a more interpretative comment is needed and can have a useful impact. On occasions a few words could reduce a room of noisy riotous teenagers to complete silence with good effect, and changes in behaviour following an interpretation were sometimes marked. On one such occasion in my early days at the club I had been struck by the frequent references to excrement. At the time when the young people were very disturbed and vandalism and destructiveness were rife, they often spat on their hands and then rubbed the spit on to the walls and windows. They also frequently complained that the club was 'crappy'. It struck me that there was a connection, and that it was possible to view what the young people were then doing as 'dumping'. Rubbing spit onto the walls seemed to symbolize smearing the club with excrement.

One evening when I was sitting with a group of young people, the conversation again was about shitting and farting. This had gone on for some time when one of the older teenage boys told a little story:

> There was this turd right, in the bog. I pulled the chain lots of times but the turd just wouldn't go down. I pulled the chain again, and this time the turd started to go down. Rrrr down and down. [He makes a downward spiral movement with his hand.] Rrrrrr. Then suddenly zoooooom it went flying up in the air, right out of the toilet. [He makes a whistling noise, and with his hand indicates a curved path through the air.]

There was an uproarious burst of laughter from the group. As it died away I used the opportunity to give an interpretation that I had reached some time before.

> You come here and you bring all your shit. No wonder the club is crappy.

There was a stunned silence which lasted some time, and then a rather sad and reflective atmosphere descended on the group as one of the young people remarked that she really missed a youth worker who had recently left. Others agreed and began to tell me about outings they had been on with him over the years. The sudden emergence of these sad and wistful feelings was striking. It was, I think, a response by the group to a recognition of their destructiveness.

I had earlier noted a widely held belief that this worker had left due to ill health caused by enduring the members' terrible behaviour. It could well be that this belief fed the young people's omnipotence, while also arousing considerable guilt. The conversation in progress seemed to reflect a worry that their actions had deprived them of something that they recognized as good. They are now acknowledging that the club they have previously derided as 'crappy' has provided them with many positive experiences.

Over the next few weeks I made several more similar interpretations about the meaning of acts such as rubbing spit on the walls and throwing pieces of chocolate at the staff. There was little said in response, but it was very noticeable that these behaviours became infrequent and then ceased altogether.

Although my intervention referred to a dynamic that was going on in the club at the time, it did not directly address the material in the story told by the boy. The story received such an enthusiastic response, and was so bizarre, that I thought it must have some kind of significance. Not until much later was I able to come up with any possible explanation of its meaning. Now it seems to me that the story may well show that the young people at the time *were* making an effort to try to improve things at the club and to curtail their damaging conduct. I think that they really were at times trying to make the shit go down the toilet, but found that somehow it just wouldn't. Somehow it just flew back out. It seems that the aggressive, spoiling feelings which are represented by the excrement sometimes feel quite out of control, and cannot be prevented from coming out and causing destruction. In the same way, the turd in the boy's story is quite out of control and seems to have a will of its own, managing even to defy the law of gravity. The laughter that followed the tale is perhaps an indication of the delight and pleasure that at times accompanied the uncontrolled acting out of destructive impulses. The shift from uproarious laughter to sad, miserable feelings reflects, I think, the group's awareness that their uncontrolled acting out was damaging the club that had so often helped them.

It was fascinating for me to see that the strange and often disgusting talk and behaviour that went on made some kind of sense, and shed light on what was happening for the young people in a way that was profoundly helpful. This was also the case where anxieties about sexuality were concerned. I found that it was worthwhile noting what was being said about sex even when the content was crude and distasteful. A lot can be learned about the nature of adolescent anxieties through paying attention to such material.

LEARNING TO BE A COUNSELLOR

One incident which illustrates how my experience in this job had great relevance for my learning how to be a counsellor comes from a time when generally things at the club had greatly improved. Nevertheless there were still tensions. Sometimes large crowds of unknown teenagers gathered outside the club and demanded to be admitted. The staff felt that it was detrimental to have lots of newcomers, since the norms we had worked so hard to establish were then easily undermined. We had seen this happen several times, so had decided to adopt a membership policy severely restricting the entry of newcomers. While the club's regular users often supported this policy, it was naturally not appreciated by the groups who made their appearance at our door. The incident described here happened at a time when there had recently been many disputes over this very issue.

One evening some hours before the club was due to open, I noticed that a crowd of young people had begun to gather outside. As I left the building on an errand, I realized that about fifty teenagers, nearly all strangers, were standing around outside. The atmosphere was tense. A young man I had never seen before approached me and, while others looked on, informed me that he intended to smash up my car that evening. At the time I did not comment, and drove off on my errand.

However, when the time came for me to return to the club, I found that I was very frightened. I could not face the thought of walking through this crowd of teenagers up to the door. I would be on my own, since the other staff were not due to arrive for some time. As I struggled with this, I found that I was even considering giving up the job on the grounds that it was just too scary. I began to look at alternatives: waiting for the other staff, cancelling the session, asking the police to disperse the crowd outside, etc., rejecting each one by turn. I was still scared. However eventually I was able to ask myself the obvious question. Why was I so frightened?

Once I was able to ask this, things began to improve. I acknowledged that I did not really think anything dreadful was likely to happen to me. I did not consider that it was at all likely that I would be physically harmed, for example. Neither was I concerned about the threat to my car, since I often left it some distance away. So why did I feel so paralysed by fear? Obviously there *was* something intimidating about a large group of teenagers, who were evidently in a bad mood, and not well disposed towards me. They were probably annoyed that we did not admit all comers, as was usual at local youth clubs. However, the degree of fear I was experiencing seemed out of proportion.

At this point I could begin to see that the fear was perhaps in some way coming from the young people themselves. They gathered together, possibly to test out the boundary that we had set at the club when we decided on a restricted admission policy. But perhaps this situation became rather worrying for *them*. What was going to happen? What were they going to do all gathered together out there? How much power did they really have? How much control did they have over themselves? Once I began to think this way the fear receded, and I began to appreciate again how frightening it can be for adolescents to have such big bodies when they still often feel like children.

I now felt much calmer, and I walked back towards the club. As I approached, the crowd outside turned to face me, watching in complete and utter silence. As I reached the gate one of the boys called out, 'Evening Miss', and then the tension broke. The young people began chattering among themselves as I went inside the building. Although the crowd remained outside for most of the session, nothing whatever happened. A few of the newcomers were brought in by the regular members as allowed, but the others did not even attempt to gain entry. Most of the them just stood around and eventually drifted away. The staff remarked how strange it was that so many teenagers should choose to spend the whole of a wintry evening just standing in the cold.

In this situation I think that any kind of action would have been a mistake, and was certainly unnecessary. Asking the crowd outside to leave, involving the police, cancelling the session, or any other move could have precipitated something dramatic and confrontational, whereas all that turned out to be necessary to contain the situation was for me and the other staff to carry on as normal. But it was just this that had been so very hard for me to do.

Although this example may seem trite, I have used it because I think there is something about it which is quite typical of youth work. So often the feelings generated are so intense that they are almost unbearable. Fear and anxiety are chief among these feelings. At times decisive action needs to be taken to ensure that things don't get out of control, but at other times it is best that nothing is done and the youth worker's task is simply to tolerate what is happening and to manage their own feelings.

This is where I found that being able to think about the situation came in as the means for allowing me to carry on. Once I had got to the stage of being able to ask myself 'What's going on here?', I began to recover myself. Similarly in a counselling situation, the counsellor in the face of strong emotions being experienced in a session must try to ask themselves, 'What is happening here?', even if the answer they arrive at is that they just don't know. There are times too when a counsellor just has to put up with very difficult feelings, while making an effort to try to understand them. I think it was a valuable experience for me as a counsellor to discover for myself that this process could be so helpful when I was under pressure.

The importance of boundaries and of maintaining effective holding was another aspect of what I learnt here that applies to counselling. To quote what Patrick Casement says of psychotherapy with his 8-year-old client Joy:

> I eventually had to hold Joy's wrists to control her, whilst she shouted: 'Let go, let go!' . . . *I had to control her with my holding of her until she was ready to hold herself.* Several times we went through a similar sequence, with the same kind of shift from destructive behaviour to something positive. I believe that her difficult behaviour had been expressing an unconscious hope that she might eventually find the holding that she needed, from someone able to survive her rages. Only thus was she able to experience herself as controllable, at first by someone else then by herself.
>
> In the analytic encounter, in different ways, we are presented with similar needs for firmness. We meet these differently, without having to provide a physical holding; but we still have to meet this challenge if the patient is going to feel securely held in the analytic relationship.[7]

Although there were times when this job was harrowing and even nightmarish, I came to see that the good, enjoyable, rewarding times came when I had not dodged the vital work of attending to the boundaries. If I let something slip because I thought it didn't matter, or because I found it tiresome, the detrimental result was nearly always in evidence. Members of the staff team often pointed out to me how a lapse in this regard had led to something negative happening, and these comments by my colleagues often forced me to see the results of my errors. The idea that there was indeed a point to the sometimes boring or seemingly trivial work of holding the boundaries became crucially important to me. Usually the benefits of holding firm without being unduly inflexible could, with hindsight, be clearly appreciated. I came to see that the work of tending to the boundaries, as well as being useful in itself, also created a space in which much that was valuable and enjoyable could happen in the club. The young people's creativity, exuberance, and sense of humour as well as their doubts, fears, and worries could be safely and productively expressed once the right environment had been established.

The importance of containment was also emphasized by my reliance on my own supervisor, a psychotherapist at the local child guidance centre, to contain my own anxiety. It was clear to me that without this, and without the support of my counselling tutors, I would probably not have survived in the job, and I certainly would not have learnt nearly as much as I did. As well as this I discovered over time that my own capacity for tolerating anxiety improved, and not least because I could see from examples like the one just described that there was often a lot to be gained through being able to put up with it and carry on.

Much of what I've written here has been about my efforts to understand what was being communicated in the young people's conduct and conversation. I think that it was very worthwhile for me in my counselling and youth work to see that it often was possible to discover meanings that helped me to know how I should proceed. Counselling, after all, is so often about trying to bring a meaning to what a client says, or to put it another way, trying to understand unconscious communications. In this regard I noticed too that it made a difference when I thought about an incident, or when I related it to my supervisor, if I bore in mind small and seemingly insignificant details of what had been said and done. The value in finding that little things could add another dimension to the entire picture was considerable. As a counsellor too, I have often found that the funny little things I hardly even notice can repay examination.

I have said little here about the fun, energy, and excitement a youth worker experiences through their contact with adolescents. These things too belong to the adolescent stage of development, and they make the good times with a group of teenagers very rewarding. I think, though, that a youth worker's primary task is to help the young people with the anxieties that can make this time of life so very difficult.

NOTES

1 D. W. Winnicott, 'Struggling through the doldrums', in *Deprivation and Delinquency* (London: Tavistock, 1984), p. 145.
2 A. Hyatt Williams, 'Problems of adolescence', in S. Meyerson (ed.) *Adolescence and Breakdown* (London: Allen & Unwin, 1975), p. 12.
3 E. Rayner, *Human Development* (London: Allen & Unwin, 1986), pp. 141–2.
4 D. W. Winnicott, op. cit., p. 146.
5 I. Salzberger-Wittenberg, *Psychoanalytic Insight and Relationships* (London: Routledge & Kegan Paul, 1970), p. 144.
6 Ibid., pp. 143–4.
7 P. Casement, *Further Learning from the Patient* (London: Routledge, 1990), pp. 114–15.

Chapter 5

The world turned upside down

Responses to trauma in the family

Elizabeth Nabarro

INTRODUCTION

The concept of trauma is used to describe:

> psychological occurrences . . . which happen unexpectedly and without the individual's own will being in any way implicated, which disrupt the individual's integrity and sense of continuity of being.[1]

The immediate response to traumatic events is a mixture of confusion and shock. The victim is unable to comprehend what has happened to him. Because of the difficulty in assimilating the event, memories of it remain disconnected from the continuum of the experience. Research carried out on the effects of major disasters on adult survivors shows that victims commonly exhibit symptoms such as emotional numbing, hyper-alertness, poor concentration, and intrusive flashbacks.

Children may also present some of these symptoms. However, their responses to unexpected traumatic events differ from those of adults for several important reasons:[2]

1 The trauma occurs at a time when the individual is developing, and it is thus likely to become an integral part of a distortion of the whole personality instead of remaining external to it.
2 In some cases children are exposed to repeated and distressing experiences, e.g. sexual abuse, which build up throughout childhood and have an adverse effect on all phases of development. Because of their immaturity, and because they find such experiences incomprehensible, they are often unable to communicate their distress except through a variety of symptoms.
3 Because of their helplessness and emotional dependence, children are more likely to be traumatized by unexpected events which affect their personal attachments, e.g. loss of a parent, than by environmental disasters such as earthquakes or transport accidents.

For the developing child, then, trauma is something which makes the bottom fall out of his world.

In the general course of events, the mother and, later on, the rest of the family give the growing child protection from trauma by exposing him gradually to a variety of experiences while shielding him from anxiety and distress. In a thousand ways, parents protect their children from traumatization and home becomes a safe place in which development can take place.

The *Shorter Oxford Dictionary* defines 'home' as 'the place of one's dwelling and nurturing . . . where one finds rest, refuge and satisfaction'.[3] For nomadic peoples, 'home' meant the centre of the world, the place from which the world could be *founded.* Without a home, one was not only shelterless, but also lost in non-being, in unreality. Without a home, everything was fragmentation.[4]

In the same way I would argue that trauma *within* the family, e.g. incest, parental madness, or sexual confusion, undermines the bedrock of reality on which the child's world is founded. It turns the world upside down. Life becomes perverse and unpredictable. Things begin to fall apart. In the face of this threat of annihilation, primitive defences are organized to prevent the child from being overwhelmed by anxiety. The form these defences take will vary according to the particular developmental phase in which the child finds himself when he experiences the trauma. Their severity will depend on the extent to which the child can be provided once more with a maximally adaptive and supportive environment.

Although the case studies referred to concern young adults, I have taken the fundamental Freudian view that people do not outgrow early childhood experiences, and that early acute anxieties are repressed to the unconscious, only to emerge at a later date when the defences against them begin to fail.

THE EMOTIONAL DEVELOPMENT OF THE CHILD AND THE EMERGENCE OF THE SELF

From the outset I should say that the framework I find most useful in looking at emotional growth in infancy and childhood is based on Winnicott's work.

For Winnicott, dependence is the prerequisite for development. Given 'good-enough' mothering, the infant passes gradually from absolute dependence at birth to relative dependence and on to independence. These are not discrete stages but form part of a continuum. Some individuals will achieve greater independence than others, but this can never be absolute, and at times of stress or illness they may slip back to a more dependent mode.

Winnicott postulates three basic processes in emotional development: integration, personalization, and, ultimately, realization.[5] At birth, the infant is in an unintegrated state – he is 'an armful of anatomy and physiology with a potential for development into a human personality'.[6] But in order to realize this potential he needs someone to gather all these pieces together.

Winnicott sees this as the mother's essential role: to provide adequate 'holding' for the baby. This means keeping the baby safe from unpredictable events which would be experienced as traumatic, and also understanding and attending to his physiological needs. Under these conditions the baby will experience moments of wholeness, will be able to return to the unintegrated state when resting, but will also be able to re-integrate. Because of the mother's ego-supportive function she is able to keep the child in her mind as a whole person so the thread of continuity is not lost.

If the holding environment is faulty, the result is disintegration. The baby experiences extreme distress – a sense of falling to pieces. Disintegration, by definition, presupposes some degree of integration.

It differs, however, from the concept of dissociation. Winnicott sees this as a primitive phenomenon occurring when a part of the infant is blocked off, is never integrated into the self. This split-off part remains dissociated – a sort of psychological cocoon which is never given the chance to develop. The result is that integration can only be partial and the resulting self is incomplete.

Integration is closely related to personalization. Winnicott talks of the infant's need for 'adaptive handling' which implies that 'the person who is looking after the child is able to manage the baby and the baby's body as if the two form a unit'.[7]

Gradually the baby comes to experience himself as a whole person – to feel that his self inhabits his body, and this contributes to his capacity to feel 'real' in relating to the actual world of objects and phenomena. This 'realization' (ability to relate to objects) is made possible by the mother who introduces 'the world in small doses'[8] to the infant, thus giving him an experience of omnipotence and shielding him from too brusque a confrontation with reality.

Under these conditions of good-enough maternal care, the infant begins to build up a continuity of being, and in a facilitating environment he will keep on developing and moving towards independence.

TRAUMA AND ITS RELATION TO THE FAMILY

What happens to the child for whom the environment has not been good enough? If mental health is the result of reliable care that enables a continuity of personal emotional growth, the central question must be – what is it that interrupts the going-on-being of the individual?

According to Winnicott:

> Trauma implies that the baby has experienced a break in life's continuity, so that primitive defences now become organized to defend against a repetition of 'unthinkable anxiety' or a return of the acute confusional state that belongs to disintegration of nascent ego structure. . . . Madness . . . means a *break-up* of whatever may exist at the time of *a personal continuity of existence.* After[wards] . . . a baby has to start

again permanently deprived of the root which could provide continuity with the personal beginning.[9]

Trauma results in a hitch in the individual's emotional development. The next question must be – 'what symptomatology will the child use to restore the continuity of his life if the environment fails him?'[10]

Symptoms and defences

We must remember that the meaning and effects of trauma will vary according to the stage of emotional development of the child at the time.

When something goes wrong in the very early stages of emotional development, there is a disturbance in the basic structuring of the self and in the ability to relate to external objects. In other words, splitting of the ego occurs and the individual will feel cut off from reality and unable to become involved in any real relationships. At its most extreme, the result is autism or latent schizophrenia. At a less extreme level 'a schizoid element may be hidden in a personality that is otherwise sane'.[11] Such individuals may appear normal and mature, but may break down, withdraw, and show psychotic elements under stress.

Another form of splitting can be seen in the creation of a false self. The implication here is that, because of faulty holding, the infant is forced prematurely to develop a caretaking role (false self) to protect the true self which is weak and frightened. Because it is hidden, the true self does not have a chance to grow, 'life is lived through the compliant false self, and the result, clinically, is a sense of unreality'.[12] Outwardly such individuals may function well, holding responsible jobs and raising families but they lack spontaneity and initiative and inwardly they are beset by feelings of futility.

But the true self can remain concealed and intact, waiting until conditions make it possible to emerge in later years. In counselling this may occur if the client feels secure enough to abandon his false self and allow the counsellor to 'hold' him during the period of confusion which follows while the true self is developing.

Individuals who have had good-enough care in infancy do not suffer this fundamental difficulty in making interpersonal relationships and entering fully into life. Faced with the stresses and strains of life, they develop defences, the chief one being regression. However, the important point is that, in doing so, they lose none of their early integration. The continuity of their lives is not broken. For them, trauma impinges on an intact personality.

The role of the family in protecting the child from trauma

As we have seen, Winnicott distinguishes between those who have had a good-enough start in infancy and those who have not. I would like to draw attention to a further important distinction – between those who have a secure base to sustain them during childhood and adolescence and those who do not.[13]

Bowlby argues for the importance of a secure base, stating that:

> human beings of all ages are happiest and able to deploy their talents to best advantage when they are confident that, standing behind them, there are one or more trusted persons who will come to their aid should difficulties arise. The person trusted, also known as an attachment figure . . . can be considered as providing his (or her) companion with a secure base from which to operate.[14]

This can be compared with Winnicott's 'good-enough maternal care', but Bowlby stresses the importance of experiences during all the years of childhood and adolescence, not just those of early infancy. He argues that the keystone for early development is the continuity of *potential* support and that this can be maintained best by the family, especially the parents, who provide the child with a secure base and encourage him to explore from it. The child who experiences this will grow up confident in his own ability to cope with the outside world, and also able to trust others and enter into mutually rewarding relationships with them.

Children suffer many anxieties in the course of their development. These may arise from difficulties with peers, academic problems, illnesses, and external traumata such as witnessing an accident or being involved in some disaster. The result is often some form of disturbed behaviour, generally known as regression.

In the face of threat, the child's immediate reaction will be to get back to a secure base – his home. He may feel the world is falling apart, but if he has an intact family (this may mean just one parent in whom he has basic trust) he can begin to rebuild his sense of integrity and trust in the world. Winnicott repeatedly states that in most cases it is the parents who do the therapeutic work,[15] often instinctively and sometimes with professional help.

They may allow the child to become more dependent, may give him time off school or extra 'spoiling'. In all kinds of ways they may act as a protective shield, keeping the demands of the world at bay, holding the child together until he is ready to resume his developmental tasks. In short, they offer a haven, a safe space to rest and recuperate.

Trauma may occur *within* the family, e.g. death of a parent or sibling, and, while it can cause intense distress, in many cases the family will survive it and remain intact. They may be able to share their grief, to reorganize, and to keep on providing a secure base for the child.

My concern, however, is for those children for whom trauma, occurring within the family, destroys basic trust and erodes the foundations on which the self is built. This may result from actual loss of a parent through suicide or desertion, or from symbolic loss when the trusted figure turns out to be untrustworthy, as in sexual abuse, or unable to provide reliable basic care as in mental illness. This reawakens primitive anxieties but, unlike for the child with an intact family, there is no safe space to retreat to. The situation is frequently complicated by feelings of shame and secrecy which increase the child's feelings of isolation. The following case studies will illustrate this further.

PSYCHIATRIC ILLNESS IN A PARENT

Psychosis

Let me begin with the example of a girl who grew up with a schizophrenic mother.

Renata is 22 years old – attractive and articulate, with a confident friendly manner. Her father is German, and she was brought up in Berlin, but her mother was Vietnamese. She has little memory of her early life, but knows that her parents' marriage was always difficult, and they had several separations during this time.

When she was 5 years old, her parents separated for good. She saw her father rarely after this, so the family unit consisted of mother and daughter. Her mother was a rather isolated, obsessive woman and her only friends were other expatriate Vietnamese. Her German was not very good, but she did not teach her daughter Vietnamese, so there was some poverty of communication between them, as indeed there must have been between husband and wife. In these early days Renata remembers thinking that her mother was 'different' from other mothers, but attributed this to her being Vietnamese.

However, when she was 8, her mother had a schizophrenic breakdown and spent a month in hospital. Renata stayed with a teacher from her school. It was at this stage that she realized her mother was not just different, but mentally ill. In future she would have to look after, not only herself, but her mother too. She had no father to turn to and her mother's family were in Hanoi. But Renata had made friends at school, and their parents were good to her. She managed to build up a sort of extended network for herself. This worked fairly well, except that she felt she could never *completely* depend on her friends. She could *ask* for help – and it seems she was good at this – but she could never *expect* it as her right (as she felt she could have if she had had an intact family). If her friends or their parents let her down, she would just smile and say: 'Never mind!' She could never risk being angry with them.

Her mother had four or five hospital admissions over the next ten years. Renata would stay at the flat alone during these periods, would pay the bills, collect her mother's disability pension, look after herself, etc. Prior to admission, her mother was often in a very florid state, but when she came home she was drugged and lethargic – 'like a vegetable'. In between, she was chaotic and unpredictable and Renata felt she had to get away from her to preserve her own sanity. At 18, she went to university in another town, to read English and drama. She went home rarely and her mother became more and more withdrawn.

After university, Renata came to London to work in the theatre. When she returned home briefly in the summer, she found her mother was in hospital, but she was discharged into Renata's care. They spent two weeks together, and for the first time there was a closeness and they talked a lot. When she left to return to England, her mother hugged her goodbye.

A month later her mother hanged herself.

Renata returned to Berlin, organized the cremation, and disposed of her mother's things. She felt she had coped well – though it had never occurred to her that she wouldn't cope.

About six weeks after her return to England, she began to feel tearful and depressed. She was afraid she was going to have a breakdown.

Winnicott's axiom is: 'Fear of breakdown is the fear of a breakdown that has already been experienced'.[16]

He maintains that the original breakdown occurred in the individual's very early childhood and resulted in the defences now displayed as an illness by the client. In this case the defence is the false self, and the fear is that this is crumbling.

This case history is sketchy and incomplete, particularly about early childhood, of which Renata retains few memories. With a psychotic mother and a disturbed marital relationship the early environment may well have been erratic, compelling the baby to comply with it and to develop a 'caretaker' self in order to survive. It seems Renata's real memories date from the moment she found out that her mother was ill. At this moment she realized that she was alone and that she had no family to support her. She had no safe place to retreat to and nowhere she could regress and be looked after for even a limited period to ease the strain.

It was not until her mother died that the crisis came. She was exhausted from looking after herself for so long, and this, coupled with the ambivalence (relief and guilt) which she felt at her mother's death, made her vulnerable to all those feelings of dependence, anger, sadness, and hate which she had repressed for so long. She needed truly to mourn her mother and to mourn her own childhood self, which had never had a chance to develop.

It was the false self which brought her to counselling, and it continued to fulfil a protective function. For instance, when I first saw Renata in mid-February, I could offer her counselling only until the Easter break (mid-March). She accepted this. However, in the second session, she told me she had looked at the calendar and realized this would mean only four sessions.

She explained that this would be too big a risk – she felt too much would be stirred up and she would not be able to cope. We arranged to continue for another term. She also asked if I could warn her when we were getting towards the end of the session, so she would not be left 'up in the air' (fear of falling?) and could get herself back together before going back to the outside world.

We can speculate that Renata's lot would have been easier if she had had an intact family – father and siblings – who could have helped bear the strain of the mother's psychosis. For this girl, the mother's illness meant the fragmentation of her entire world, which she then had to hold together by her own efforts.

Depression

The following brief outline illustrates the protective role of the family in the face of the mother's depression.

This family comprises Mr and Mrs A and three children: a boy and two girls. Mr A runs a well-established family business, Mrs A is a part-time art teacher at a sixth form college, and all three children are now at secondary school and doing well. When the children were younger, Mrs A was easily exhausted if she had to deal with them alone, and she had several bouts of severe depression, which blocked her capacity to respond to them. However, the father is a stable and realistic man who loves his wife. They have a large extended family and money is not a problem. With his support, the mother has been able to face the situation without feeling too threatened. She has had good professional help and domestic help, and has been well, apart from some anxiety, for the past five years. They have a permanent 'nanny' who has been with them since the first child was born, and who has now taken on the role of housekeeper. The children always spend part of the school holidays with grandparents and cousins, and all three are lively and outgoing.

The family is fortunate in having good resources, and also in being able to use them to their full extent. In this way, the mother has been able to spend as much time as she could manage with the children, but there has always been a well-functioning safety net – in the form of father, nanny, grandparents – who could deal with the children's demands without being exhausted (as mother would have been on her own). So these children have not been forced into premature caretaking of themselves or their mother, and they have been able to develop at their own pace. As far as possible they have been protected from any trauma which could have been caused by their mother's illness.

Children react differently to maternal depression,[17] and this may be related to their stage of development at the time of depression. If this occurs at the stage of absolute dependence, the child, finding his mother unresponsive, will feel abandoned and filled with terror. In the absence of reliable maternal care, he will organize a false self as a defence, and this may fit in with the mother's feeling of internal deadness. At a slightly later stage the child with a depressed mother may feel the necessity to alleviate the mother's heavy mood with an exaggerated show of aliveness. This is another example of the way in which the defensive false self reacts by compliance, by doing what is expected of him. This puts an enormous strain on the child who feels he must deal with his mother's moods before he can get started on his own developmental tasks.

Other aspects of psychiatric illness

In the case described above, the children were shielded from trauma by a stable father, an intact family, and an auxiliary caretaker (nanny). In some families, however, there may not be a healthy parent to keep things together, or the healthy parent may abandon the family to save his own sanity.

The case of Renata illustrates how psychotic illness in a parent can cast a 'shadow' on the emotional development of the child. The child is obliged to develop prematurely in order to cope with the world and his parent's problems. Many children, from a young age, become adept at gauging their parent's mood and monitoring their behaviour accordingly, but where there are rapid mood swings this can be traumatic, causing the child to be hyper-vigilant and robbing him of all spontaneity.

There may be a chaotic element in the parent's illness, so that communication is erratic and full of double meanings. Winnicott[18] suggests that this organized chaos is a defence against underlying disintegration and describes a mother who:

> always muddled everything up with distractions and unpredictable and therefore traumatic actions. When talking to her child, she employed puns and nonsense rhymes, jingles and half-truths, science fiction and facts all dressed up as imagination. The havoc she wrought was almost complete.

One can imagine the fragmentation and confusion this must cause in the child.

SEXUAL CONFUSION IN THE FAMILY

The following case is about confusion as an organized defence against inner chaos precipitated by trauma in the family.

Catherine, aged 17, came for counselling because she was having trouble concentrating at school. The previous year, she had been anorexic and had been in hospital for six weeks because of this. She had changed schools, but was afraid she would soon be asked to leave if her work did not improve. She was still very thin, but assured me she was now eating properly.

Her story is as follows:

When she was 11 years old, she discovered that her father was a transvestite. But he was a transvestite only on Saturday nights, and she had been able to cope with this by isolating it as a 'Saturday night phenomenon'. Although Saturday nights were very tense, the rest of the week they were a 'normal happy family' and she described him as 'a lovely dad'.

A little over a year ago, her mother had told her that her father was going to have sex-change treatment. The implications of this – in terms of disruption to the family and home life – were devastating for her. She became obsessive about food, explaining that as long as she could occupy her mind counting calories, she could effectively suppress her anxiety about the situation at home.

Winnicott draws attention to the fact that in obsessive thinking:

> every attempt is made to annul one idea by another, but nothing succeeds. Behind the whole process is a confusion, and no amount of tidying that the patient can do alters this confusion, because it is something very simple: namely the fact that in some specific setting of which the patient is unaware, hate is more powerful than love.[19]

It took Catherine some time to get in touch with her own anger and hate.

When I first saw her she was complaining of confusion. She described her family (mother, father, sister (24), and herself) in idealized terms as a close and loving family. (Later she was able to describe them more realistically.) She had coped with the transvestism by 'splitting it off', but, faced with the sex change, her world fell to pieces. The threat of losing her secure base (parents would separate, house would be sold) disorientated her completely.

A 'mad' feeling came over her when she thought about it – sometimes she would laugh hysterically – but on a deeper level she felt the whole world was mad. If a man could become a woman – if the person who talked to you as a father yesterday could today dress as a woman and talk of nothing but the colour of his/her nail polish – if you loved him when he was 'him' and you hated him when he was 'her' – if the hormone tablets he was taking actually made him look younger (smoother skin, etc.), though you knew that internally they were taking their toll and would shorten his life span – then everything was turned upside down.

Added to this was a schizoid feeling of isolation 'as if I'm in a glass cage'. Because she had told none of her friends, she remained apart from them, guarding her secret, not able to invite them home or talk about it. Because of the fear of stigmatization she had told none of her teachers, so she had no sympathy or excuse for her lapses in attention. Because her mother was finding it difficult to cope, Catherine had become protective towards her, trying to deny her own distress, which, however, was evident in her somatic symptoms. Because she (unconsciously) feared her aggressive impulses towards her father, she became excessively concerned about him. It was all topsy-turvy.

Gradually, she is becoming less confused and is able to see things more clearly. Sometimes I get the impression that the immediate crisis about the sex-change has been resolved and that she now realizes that no amount of worrying is going to stop it taking place. In fact, at times she just wishes it could be over and done with so she can get on with the rest of her life. But no sooner does she think this than she becomes confused again, and I think this is because 'getting on with her life' will include coming to grips with her own sexuality.

At the moment she feels both anger and hatred towards her father. The anger is both thwarted and fuelled by the fact that he appears pathetic and lonely and accuses the family of deserting him. Catherine feels this is a travesty. She is the one who feels betrayed and abandoned. The hatred is more threatening for her and she tries to deal with it by splitting the object – she loves her dad but she hates 'her'. She says: 'When he changes into her I do not ever want to see him again, but I won't desert my dad.' Notice the constant muddling up of 'him' and 'her' in the same sentence, and the conflicting statements that although she doesn't ever want to see 'her' again, she won't be able to desert 'him'.

This kind of crazy, circular, confused thinking gives her a 'splitting(!) headache' which I think is a sign that some progress has been made compared with her earlier psychosomatic symptoms (anorexia) in which there was a denial of mind-content. Winnicott suggests that, in an anorexic, this may represent 'a shift from the dissociated state, since headache could be accepted as associated with a confusion of ideas and responsibilities'.[20]

If this girl survives, it will be because her relationship with her mother has remained intact throughout, and because she is secure in the knowledge that her mother loves her and believes in her. From this point of view, although their family life has been shattered, her primary attachment figure (mother) has not faltered or let her down.

SEXUAL ABUSE

> 'I can't explain *myself*, I'm afraid, sir,'
> said Alice, 'because I'm not myself, you see.'
> 'I don't see,' said the Caterpillar.
>
> Lewis Carroll, *Alice's Adventures in Wonderland*

Of all the forms of childhood trauma, sexual abuse within the family (incest) is probably the most damaging in terms of long-term psychological consequences for the victim. Recent research[21] has shown that suicidal acts, depression, substance abuse, and hysterical symptoms are major clinical problems among incest survivors, and Steele[22] estimates that at least half of the difficult patients known as 'borderlines' have been sexually abused.

Each culture has its own version of the incest taboo, and there are numerous examples in fairy tales and myths of the misery and misfortunes which beset incest victims: Oedipus gouges out his eyes and his mother, Jocasta, hangs herself; Hippolytus is trampled by his chariot horses when he flees from his seductive stepmother Phaedra. In more primitive societies, incest participants are believed to become witches, and to bring on natural disasters, such as earthquakes and fires.[23]

However, despite the universality of the incest taboo, it remains a serious and persistent problem, which society has repeatedly tried to deny. To admit its pervasiveness and prevalence would be to challenge fundamental assumptions in our society about men and women, children and sex. Thus adults have been unwilling to listen to children, and much abuse has been overlooked or denied.

But perhaps the most striking factor is the silence of the survivors. If this really happens to children, why don't they tell someone – their non-abusing parent, a teacher, or a friend? And why should adult survivors hide from exposure and try to avoid the past? I think this is where the two questions overlap and we get some indication of the pathogenic nature of the consequences.

When sexual abuse occurs within the family the perpetrator is usually a trusted adult, e.g. father. The degree of ambiguity surrounding the interaction is high. The experience is frequently defined as loving by the abuser. Sometimes the child is made to feel she is responsible for the abuse. It is nearly always a secret and accompanied by threats of reprisal should the child tell anyone about it. This produces a profound internal confusion for the child who, wanting to behave correctly in order not to lose the attachment figure she loves, now finds she has been betrayed.

Even if a sympathetic and supportive person is available, feelings of shame and guilt will often stop the child from talking about the abuse. She feels isolated and helpless, and has no choice but to repress the trauma which then appears in disguised form as symptoms – neuroses, psychoses, psychosomatic disorders, and delinquency.

Some survivors cope with it by dissociation. They may have no memory of the abuse, although the content may be preserved in fantasy. In the most extreme cases, this may result in multiple-personality disorder.[24]

This brings me to another point. Incest is rarely limited to a specific event. It usually goes on for a period, and is more like a 'relationship' or a 'situation' than an isolated incident. The cumulative effect reinforces the child's sense of helplessness, worthlessness, and self-blame. The longer the child is abused, the greater the psychological damage.

The trauma may arise from being trapped in a pathogenic environment rather than from one overwhelming event. Frequently there is a high degree of ambiguity surrounding the trauma (i.e. the child's relationship to the abuser) and the child is put in a double bind. This is a situation in which the victim is weaker than the binder, she is subject to incompatible emotional demands, and she cannot leave the relationship.[25]

It can be seen that these conditions often apply to children who have been sexually abused within the family. In addition, there may be collusion or denial from the non-abusive parent or other adults who fail to protect the child. Most of these elements can be identified in the following case history.

Minna is an 18-year-old West Indian girl. Shortly after her birth, her father came to work in England, leaving Minna and her mother in Trinidad. When she was 4 years old, her mother went to New York leaving Minna with her paternal grandparents who had a large and still young family. After initial difficulties, Minna settled down and came to regard them as her real family. She had no further contact with her real mother.

However, when she was 11 her father wrote, asking her to come to London. Although she protested, her grandparents said she must do as her father wanted. She spent the next four years living alone with him in a small flat in South London. She kept house and tried to please him. He was physically intimate with her, fondling her and wanting her to sleep in his bed, telling her this was 'the West Indian way', and that if she loved him she would do what he wanted. She felt confused and unwilling, but had no family to turn to, and most of the girls at her school were white, so she couldn't ask them about 'West Indian ways'. She loved her father, and feared she would lose him (as she had lost her mother and her grandparents) if she wasn't ready to comply with his expectations. So, for a while, she went along with this and just tried not to think about it.

However, one day, when he was being sexually intimate with her, she 'saw the look in his eyes' and she knew this had nothing to do with the kind of love a father should have for his daughter. This was the moment of real trauma for her. She felt hatred and anger towards him, and yet she had no means of escape. She was also terrified to arouse his anger as he quickly became violent.

She began to employ dissociation as a coping mechanism, learning to dissociate from her body during sexual contact. Although this may at first seem to be an adaptive mechanism, the individual may find that to repress the experience effectively, she has to cut off a whole range of experiences and emotions. This ultimately leads to an impoverishment of the personality, which may manifest itself in depression.

For this girl, her father's betrayal broke up the last possibility of having any kind of 'home' or safe place. Eventually she ran away and lived in a hostel for a year before getting her own flat. But her present difficulties owe much to the fact that the experience of getting close to someone and beginning to trust him have been disastrous for her, so she now reacts by retreating from any real emotional contact. Individuals from intact families who have been abused as children report similiar experiences. In two autobiographical novels,[26,27] the writers tell of persistent abuse at the hands of their fathers, and of the anger they felt towards their mothers, who, though living in the same house, remained seemingly oblivious to the situation, and did nothing to protect them.

Every child who has been abused carries with her a dreadful and burdensome secret. She can never again think of herself as 'normal'. In order to conceal a turbulent, confused interior, she may present a confident, coping false self. This may be so effective in terms of the outside world that she fears losing sight of her 'true self'. She may try to explain that she is not her real self – like Alice, but, like the caterpillar, the rest of the world doesn't want to see. This may exacerbate her feelings of madness and isolation.

SEPARATION AND LOSS

It is generally accepted now that disruptions in maternal care in early childhood may result in faulty emotional development and proneness to psychiatric illness.

Winnicott[28] stresses the essential role of the mother in facilitating the integration of the ego in infancy. Lack of maternal ego-support at this stage leads to 'unthinkable anxiety'. For Winnicott, this is the origin of the vulnerability to psychotic disorder, which can show itself at any stage in the individual's life.

He describes the way in which the baby is increasingly able to tolerate separation from the mother as follows: the baby comes to bear the mother's absence for X minutes, but then feels he has lost her unless she comes back. If she is away X + Y minutes she must restore her image and ease the baby's distress by special attention. But if she is away X + Y + Z minutes, the baby is traumatized, and he sees her as a stranger because his ego has begun to disintegrate.[29] Acute anxiety of this kind leads to the schizoid state.

In a similar vein, Bowlby draws attention to the sequence of behaviour shown by young children when separated from their mothers. First comes the phase of protest, which is linked with the child's anxiety and hope that his mother will come back. After several days his hopes begin to fade (phase of despair). He becomes disorganized and yearns for his mother. Eventually, however, he gives up, and seems to forget her. If she returns at this stage, he may even seem not to recognize her. Bowlby calls this the phase of detachment, and states that 'having undergone disorganization in the phase of despair, behaviour in this stage becomes reorganized on the basis of the person's permanent absence'.[30]

Bowlby maintains that these responses to loss occur irrespective of age and are part of the basic mourning process. However, he suggests that in young children the process may be accelerated. Detachment may develop prematurely, masking unresolved anger and yearning for the lost person. If these persist, they may become split-off or repressed, leaving the individual vulnerable to later disturbance.

Separation from mother

Kathleen (aged 21) spent the early years of her life with her single mother in London. When she was 4, her mother took her to Ireland, and left her there with her aunt and uncle. It seems she went through the sequence of behaviour described above, protest, despair, and detachment. She remembers that for the first week she refused to change her dress or let her aunt look after her, because she was sure her mother would come back to get her (protest). She then became withdrawn and shy (despair) but then appeared to settle down, and came to regard them as her real family (detachment).

Her mother emigrated to Canada, married there, and lost touch with her family in Ireland. When she was 18 Kathleen went to Canada to find her, but when they met she felt nothing: 'It was just like seeing a family friend.' Since then their only contact has been occasional (late) birthday cards.

Kathleen came to counselling because of sexual difficulties with her boyfriend Jack. She felt these had been caused by her experiences with her two older male cousins who had sexually abused her when she was 12 years old.

Over a period of eighteen months we dealt with many problems, particularly those to do with her cousins, but we never managed to get very far in discussing her mother. She and Jack decided to see a sex therapist together. This appeared to be a genuine commitment to their relationship.

After the initial interview with the sex therapist, however, she became panic-stricken. It seemed that she was terrified that if the sexual problems were resolved, both Jack and I would think she was 'normal' and would cease to be concerned about her, i.e. abandon her. We would also never get to the bottom of her most primitive anxieties. In a chaotic session in which she was full of hate and ambivalence I asked her what she really wanted and she burst into tears and said 'my mother'.

A week later, just before the holidays, she rang me to say she had just taken an overdose. When I arrived at her flat she was sitting, cross-legged, in a trance – rocking backwards and forwards. When I tried to take her to the hospital, she suddenly dived under the bed saying,

> I can't go till I've found her – the little girl – I've lost her and she keeps calling me, but I can't find her. I can find her when I go to sleep and that's why I took the pills. I just wanted to go to sleep so I could find her again.

In this psychotic episode Kathleen was re-experiencing the overwhelming terror and disintegration she felt when her mother left her. It showed a desperate need to communicate to those of us who know her that we had missed something – that behind the false self, a young adult who was planning to get married, there was a little girl who needed to be rescued or she would be lost for ever. It was also meant to be a specific communication to me (her mother in the transference) – both a cry for help and one of anger and yearning.

I think this shows how the experience of losing one's mother in early life can have a profound and devastating effect on emotional development.

Death of a father

Up till now, I have spoken only of mothers. But in some families, father may be the primary attachment figure, or may fulfil some other important function, as can be seen in the following example.

This second case concerns a dance student from Martinique. She came for counselling complaining of a general feeling of confusion and anxiety. She spoke hardly any English, French being her native language, and she felt extremely isolated. She was beginning to feel 'invisible' and to lose her sense of identity.

This was her story:

She was the youngest of six girls. As a baby she suffered from bad eczema, and her first memory was of acute loneliness – of lying in her pram, crying, but nobody could pick her up and cuddle her becaue of her skin condition. She described her mother as very domineering, a born-again Christian who had little time or affection for her youngest child. She doesn't remember ever being able to say she liked or disliked anything until she was 14, when an older sister said to her – apropos of a dress: 'But Martine, you must *say* what you like and don't like – it's *your* dress you know.' It seems that, although this girl had received adequate physical care (hers was a wealthy family with servants), there had been no maternal ego-support or 'mirroring', so she had not had the chance to integrate herself into a unit – to develop a self.

However, there had been some compensation from her father. He was an elderly and benign man, rather henpecked by his domineering wife, but he loved his little daughter. She felt safe with him and used to seek him out and climb on to his knee. In this way she felt she had begun to exist. While she was in England, she spoke to him every Sunday night on the telephone and she had a photo of him in her room at the hostel. She had no photo of her mother.

This girl had little ongoing experience of feeling real, alive, and complete, but she had fragments of experience – her relationship with her father and her dancing – and these just about kept her going. She had to work extremely hard at feeling real, and she knew this was necessary, but it was exhausting. She had a 'caretaker' self which kept up the contact with her father, and made sure she continued with her dancing, and which had brought her to counselling so she could at least communicate with someone and feel she mattered. She needed to be *seen* and recognized in order to feel she was a person. Perhaps this is why she chose to be a dancer, but in this school there were regular technique classes but few performances and she had begun to feel she was fading away. This filled her with acute anxiety. She was like Tinker Bell – in order to exist she needed someone to believe in her existence. Her relationship to me (the counsellor) was a bit like that of the Unicorn in *Through the Looking Glass*.

> 'Well, now that we *have* seen each other,'
> said the Unicorn, 'if you'll believe in me,
> I'll believe in you. Is that a bargain?'
>
> Lewis Carroll, *Through the Looking Glass*

In this way, with her father's phone calls, the counselling sessions, and the dancing, she could *just about hang on* but it felt precarious.

In the middle of the third term, her father died. When she came to tell me, I was struck by the fact that her reaction was not one of grief or sadness, but of overwhelming panic. It was as if she really thought she might disintegrate and disappear without her father to affirm her existence. She went back to Martinique for the funeral, and didn't return to the school so I do not know what became of her.

This girl had not had a 'good-enough' mother, and had never properly achieved integration but her relationship with her father had helped her survive. Without his support, she felt, the world and her 'self' would become fragmented.

SUMMARY

In this chapter I have tried to show some of the long-term sequelae of childhood trauma on emotional development.

Trauma occurring at critical stages of development will have profound effects on an individual's psychological make-up. Defences against anxiety will be organized which may subsequently hinder further development or lead to bizarre and inappropriate behaviour.

I have relied most heavily on Winnicott's theory of emotional development as a general framework. However, I have also incorporated ideas from other sources where this seemed appropriate, e.g. Bowlby's concept of the secure base.

I have concentrated particularly on the effects of those traumata which may arise within the family, and which, by their very nature, threaten to disrupt the family unit. I have argued that an intact family (a safe base, or even just one reliable attachment figure) offers security and protection for the growing child, and this does much to alleviate the effects of traumatic events.

My concern, however, is for those children for whom trauma destroys basic trust and erodes the foundations of their world. The proximity and intimacy of the family relationships within which the trauma occurs may be distorted (as in parental psychiatric illness) or perverted (as in sexual abuse). In these situations the effects are more complex and profound than if the trauma were external to the family.

I have used case material to illustrate these points. There are many types of trauma, and, equally, many variations in response. I have managed to describe only a few of these, but they are linked by a common denominator – they all involve some kind of loss, whether actual (death of a parent) or symbolic (parental sex change). I hope they give some idea of the feelings of confusion, rootlessness, and abandonment experienced by these individuals.

I am reminded of John Berger's description of home as 'the return to where distance did not yet count'.[31] For those whose fundamental trust in life has been shattered by trauma within the family, there is no way home. The centre of the world has been dismantled, and they move in a lost, disorientated one of fragments. The role of the counsellor is to help them reassemble these fragments and once again make sense of their world.

NOTES

I have used the terms 'incest' and 'child sexual abuse' interchangeably. Strictly speaking, incest refers to sexual relations between blood relatives (irrespective of age), while child sexual abuse refers to sexual relations between (any) adult and (any) child. As this paper deals with traumatic events within the family, both terms have been used to mean 'the sexual abuse of a child within the family by a family member'.

In the same section, I have used the terms 'victim' and 'survivor' interchangeably. There is no contradiction here, except in emotive terms, so both words have been used to avoid monotony.

I have been erratic in my use of he/she, him/her when referring to 'the child'. Most of the time I have referred to 'him' since a lot of the material refers back to the mother–infant couple, so this reduces confusion. In the section on sexual abuse, however, I have referred to the child as 'her' because I have taken the father/daughter relationship as the prototype. Of course there are many variations on incestuous relationships – boys may be victims and mothers may be perpetrators – so this is purely for convenience.

1 C. Rycroft, *Anxiety and Neurosis* (Harmondsworth: Penguin, 1968), p. 22.
2 Ibid., p. 26.
3 C. T. Onions (ed.), *The Shorter Oxford Dictionary*, p. 914.
4 J. Berger, *And Our Faces, My Heart, Brief as Photos* (London: Writers & Readers, 1984).
5 M. Davis and D. Wallbridge, *Boundary and Space* (Harmondsworth: Penguin, 1983).
6 Ibid., p. 47.
7 Ibid., p. 53.
8 D. W. Winnicott, 'The world in small doses', in *The Child, the Family and the Outside World* (Harmondsworth: Penguin, 1964), p. 69.
9 D. W. Winnicott, 'The location of cultural experience', in *Playing and Reality* (London: Tavistock, 1971), p. 97.

10 A. Phillips, *Winnicott* (London: Fontana, 1988), p. 103.
11 D. W. Winnicott, 'Ego integration in child development', in *The Maturational Processes and the Facilitating Environment* (London: Hogarth Press, 1965), p. 58.
12 D. W. Winnicott, *Psycho-Analytic Explorations* (London: Karnac, 1989), p. 43.
13 J. Bowlby, *The Making and Breaking of Affectional Bonds* (London: Tavistock, 1979).
14 Ibid., p. 103.
15 D. W. Winnicott, 'Dependence in various settings', in 1965, op. cit.
16 D. W. Winnicott, 'Fear of breakdown', in 1989, op. cit., p. 90.
17 D. W. Winnicott, 'The effects of psychotic parents on the emotional development of the child', in *The Family and Individual Development* (London: Tavistock, 1965).
18 Ibid., pp. 74–5.
19 D. W. Winnicott, 'Psycho-analysis and the sense of guilt', in *The Maturational Processes and the Facilitating Environment*, 1965, p. 20.
20 D. W. Winnicott, 'Psycho-somatic disorder', in 1989, op. cit., p. 107.
21 D. Jehu, *Beyond Sexual Abuse: Therapy with Women Who Were Childhood Victims* (New York: Wiley, 1988).
22 B. Steele, 'Notes on the lasting effects of early child abuse throughout the life cycle', in R. E. Helfer and C. H. Kempe (eds), *Child Abuse and Neglect*, (Cambridge, MA: Ballinger, 1976), pp. 283–91.
23 J. M. Goodwin, 'Obstacles in policymaking about incest', in G. E. Wyatt and G. J. Powell (eds), *Lasting Effects of Child Sexual Abuse* (Beverly Hills, CA: Sage, 1988).
24 J. Snedgar, 'The impossible life of a woman split in 10', *The Independent* (London), 20 March 1990.
25 G. Bateson *et al.*, 'Towards a theory of schizophrenia', *Behavioural Science* I (1956): 251–64.
26 J. Spring, *Cry Hard and Swim* (London: Virago, 1987).
27 S. Fraser, *My Father's House* (London: Virago, 1989).
28 D. W. Winnicott, 'The theory of the parent–infant relationship', in 1965, op. cit.
29 D. W. Winnicott, 'The location of cultural experience', in 1971, op. cit.
30 J. Bowlby, op. cit., p. 49.
31 J. Berger, op. cit., p. 92.

BIBLIOGRAPHY

Bateson, G. *et al.* (1956) 'Towards a theory of schizophrenia', *Behavioural Science* I: 251–64.

Berger, J. (1984) *And Our Faces, My Heart, Brief as Photos*, London: Writers & Readers.

Bowlby, J. (1979) *The Making and Breaking of Affectional Bonds*, London: Tavistock.

Carroll, L. (1872) *Alice's Adventures in Wonderland*, London: Macmillan.

—— (1872) *Through the Looking-Glass*, London: Macmillan.

Chasseguet-Smirgel, J. (1986) *Creativity and Perversion*, London: Free Association Books.

Davis, M. and Wallbridge, D. (1983) *Boundary and Space*, Harmondsworth: Penguin.

Dawes, D. and Boston, M. (1977) *The Child Psychotherapist*, London: Wildwood House.

Fielding, J. and Newman, A. (1987) *Winnicott Studies*, London: The Squiggle Foundation.
Fraser, S. (1989) *My Father's House*, London: Virago.
Freud, A. (1948) *The Ego and the Mechanisms of Defence*, London: Hogarth Press.
Freud, S. and Breuer, J. (1895) *Studies on Hysteria*, Harmondsworth: Pelican Freud Library 3, 1974.
—— (1977) *On Sexuality*, Harmondsworth: Pelican Freud Library 7.
Guntrip, H. (1896) *Schizoid Phenomena, Object Relations and the Self*, London: Hogarth Press.
Jehu, D. (1988) *Beyond Sexual Abuse: Therapy with Women Who Were Childhood Victims*, New York: Wiley.
Khan, M. M. R. (1974) *The Privacy of the Self*, London: Hogarth Press.
—— (1983) *Hidden Selves*, London: Hogarth Press.
Klein, M. (1957) *Envy and Gratitude*, London: Virago, 1988.
Laing, R. D. (1960) *The Divided Self*, London: Tavistock.
Masson, J. M. (1984) *Assault on the Truth: Freud's Suppression of the Seduction Theory*, New York: Farrar, Straus & Giroux.
Meyerson, S. (1975) *Adolescence and Breakdown*, London: Allen & Unwin.
Miller, A. (1985) *Thou Shalt not be Aware*, London: Pluto Press.
Mitchell, J. (1974) *Psychoanalysis and Feminism*, Harmondsworth: Penguin.
Noonan, E. (1983) *Counselling Young People*, London: Methuen.
Phillips, A. (1988) *Winnicott*, London: Fontana.
Pincus, L. and Dare, C. (1978) *Secrets in the Family*, London: Faber.
Rycroft, C. (1968) *Anxiety and Neurosis*, Harmondsworth: Penguin.
—— (1968) *A Critical Dictionary of Psychoanalysis*, Harmondsworth: Penguin.
—— (1985) *Psychoanalysis and Beyond*, London: Hogarth Press.
Segal, H. (1988) *Introduction to the Work of Melanie Klein*, London: Karnac.
Spring, J. (1987) *Cry Hard and Swim*, London: Virago.
Stephens, W. N. (1962) *The Oedipus Complex: Cross-cultural Evidence*, Glencoe, IL: Free Press.
Symington, N. (1986) *The Analytic Experience*, London: Free Association Books.
Tustin, F. (1986) *Autistic Barriers in Neurotic Patients*, London: Karnac.
Winnicott, D. W. (1958) *Through Paediatrics to Psycho-Analysis*, London: Hogarth Press, 1987.
—— (1964) *The Child, the Family and the Outside World*, Harmondsworth: Penguin.
—— (1965) *The Family and Individual Development*, London: Tavistock.
—— (1965) *The Maturational Processes and the Facilitating Environment*, London: Hogarth Press.
—— (1971) *Playing and Reality*, London: Tavistock.
—— (1986) *Home is Where We Start From*, Harmondsworth: Penguin.
—— (1989) *Psycho-Analytic Explorations*, London: Karnac.
Wyatt, G. E. and Powell, G. J. (1988) *Lasting Effects of Child Sexual Abuse*, Beverly Hills, CA: Sage.

Chapter 6

Culture shock

Personal and organizational responses to an expatriate life-style

Sally Holder

INTRODUCTION

This chapter is about some of the emotional reactions that arise among those who find themselves in a country and culture with which they are unfamiliar. These reactions are usually termed 'culture shock', a term which in general has a negative connotation, associated with feelings of unfamiliarity and alienation. The material is based on the experiences of employees working for an organization with branches worldwide and has been collected by one of the staff members responsible for the welfare of employees and their families overseas. This chapter will also consider the organization's part in helping to allay or exacerbate anxiety in those it sends overseas.

The term 'culture shock' was first used in 1960 by the anthropologist Oberg who described it thus:

> Culture Shock is precipitated by the anxiety that results from losing all our familiar signs and symbols of social intercourse. These signs or cues include the 1,001 ways in which we orient ourselves to the situations of daily life: when to shake hands, and what to say when we meet people, when and how to give tips, how to give orders to servants, when to accept, and when to refuse invitations. Now these cues which may be words, gestures, facial expressions, customs or norms are acquired by all of us in the course of growing up, and are as much a part of our culture as the language we speak, or the beliefs we accept.[1]

The loss of such cues, as happens in a move to a different culture or country, may cause no more than brief embarrassment while people respond awkwardly or get things wrong, but it can result in feelings of total alienation if people feel that adaptation to the new regime requires them to betray their earlier attachments. Peter Marris explains that we tend to feel immediately threatened if our basic assumptions and emotional attachments are challenged or taken away from us.[2]

The threat is intensely real, for it is these assumptions which provide the basis of regularity on which depends our ability to predict our own behaviour and that of others, and to feel comfortable and in control. Take them away, and we can feel cast adrift in a world where A is no longer followed by B, but by X, causing feelings very much akin to those arising after bereavement. Thus it appears that people's reaction to loss of any kind, whether it be through death or a change of environment, is very similar. These similarities will be considered in detail later.

Culture shock may be experienced by anyone who comes in contact with a culture different from his own: tourist, refugee, student, immigrant, diplomat, or business person. The category considered in this paper is the latter: the business person who, working for the same organization, will spend the majority of his[3] working life overseas, on postings of roughly three to four years' duration. Because he is not travelling alone, but as the representative of an organization, the interaction between him and the organization, and the organization's reactions to the responsibility of deploying and caring for staff and their families around the world will also be given some consideration.

WHY PEOPLE JOIN THE ORGANIZATION

Individuals seem to be motivated to pursue this type of career for a variety of reasons, conscious and unconscious.

For some it yields an opportunity to pack variety into their life, without the usual stresses that would be inherent in such a life-style. Thus, employees are assured of a working lifetime of travel, but with the support of a large, international organization behind them able to provide a high standard of living, but also to extricate, help out, guide, and support should the going get rough. So some can be seen to be looking for adventure the safe way, working for an operation which 'cares' and provides a rule and regulation for almost every conceivable occurrence. Those looking for adventure and variety are unlikely to suffer from severe culture shock as the very aim of their life is to be rootless: so, for them, the pattern of continuous moves will prove more stimulating than disorientating, provided the organization keeps its part of the deal and gives continuing support. The expectation that the organization will do so, and thus meet their unconscious dependency needs, leads many employees to demand that accommodation be found for them, estate agents and accountants be recommended, and the everyday difficulties of life be smoothed away. This would seem to indicate a strong wish, in Kleinian terms, to put the responsibility of being a good parent on to the organization.

In Melanie Klein's description of the paranoid-schizoid position, she maintains that the feelings of tremendous warmth and affection felt by the helpless baby towards its mother when its needs are being met go side by side with feelings of intense frustration and hatred towards the same mother when those needs are left unmet.[4]

The fantasy that the mother is knowingly depriving the baby and keeping her love and milk to herself causes the baby to turn destructively against her and what she provides. In addition, the baby's envy of the tremendous power she has (thereby highlighting its own helplessness) can lead to its spoiling in fantasy that good which the mother has to offer. The baby's destructive impulses towards the mother lead it to expect retaliation on her part, and so the baby, at this stage of development, feels intensely persecuted.

Similarly, at an organizational level, the more staff have to endure the feelings of helplessness arising from untimely postings made by all-powerful management to unpleasant spots, the more their anxiety causes them to revert to the ways of interacting described by Klein.

Some join the organization in the belief that, by working overseas, they will be creating a better life for themselves and their families: this may be in terms of weather, availability of servants to help in the house, the standard of housing itself, and also by offering the possibility of a boarding-school education for children. Underlying this search for a better life is often the perception that Britain is no longer a country with which these employees wish to align themselves: the violence, dirt, education system, and ailing National Health Service have become unacceptable, and so something better is looked for abroad.

On an unconscious level, the life-style seems to attract some with a need to deal with anxiety by splitting – thus they have never to come to terms with the good and bad in Britain, which is too close to coming to terms with the good and bad in themselves. So the real Britain becomes split into good and bad parts. Employees prefer to associate themselves only with the good parts as represented in the organization by its promotion of what management calls 'the best that Britain has to offer' in its particular field. That this narrow field cannot be a true representation of what the whole of Britain is actually about today gives a distinctly archaic feel to many overseas offices, more reminiscent of the 1950s when the belief that Britain was 'top dog' was prevalent. Pictures of the monarchy adorn the walls of many offices and a life-style revolving to some extent around non-working wives and a diary of formal social entertaining seems to belong to a bygone age.

This split ensures that the dirty, messed-up part of the mother country which is no longer able to provide care (National Health Service) or to nurture (education) is kept well apart from the idealized one as represented by the Queen. The desire of employees to work overseas represents their flight from the bad object, which is experienced as persecuting and tainted by dirt, to the good, which is experienced as creative, protecting, and benevolent.

Those who join the organization in search of a better life in another country can find the effects of continuous moving very stressful, for, having found the right spot, their impulse is to put down roots there and not to move on. For them, the adverse effects of culture shock arise when they are posted on from somewhere they have felt at home and where they have begun to put down roots. Sue, as the wife of an employee, had spent four years in Italy and loved it there. When the time came for them to move, she desperately wanted to stay on and urged her husband to resign and get another job in Italy. Although her husband had also enjoyed Italy, he was very committed to his career and knew that to stay on would mean professional suicide. They were moved on to India where Sue became deeply depressed in the knowledge that the life-style they had would mean she would never be able to settle down anywhere.

For some, the opportunity of spending time overseas may offer an escape from home and the family, and the patterns established there, in order to achieve some sort of separate identity. If that succeeds, all is well – if not, then breakdown may occur.

Mary was the youngest in a family of three girls, with two academic older sisters with whom her father always adversely compared her. For her, going overseas represented a way of proving her individuality and her capacity to cope alone both to herself and to her father. However, before leaving she was careful to ensure that she had a 'substitute family' waiting for her and went to live with two older women employees. She broke down when she discovered, on arrival, that these two women brought their own work home every night, just as her sisters had done, and were not prepared to look after her.

Feelings of culture shock and alienation arise for many when their conscious and unconscious needs are not met. For the most part, staff choose to work overseas because by so doing they are able to fulfil some of their more conscious needs such as working in countries in which they have a particular interest or whose language they already speak. However, the organization is often required to accept and react to the unconscious dependency needs of staff from whom they have taken away all other avenues for getting those needs fulfilled. The degree of culture shock experienced by employees will depend partly on how well the organization is able to respond to these unconscious needs.

WHERE PEOPLE GO

Any move may bring in its wake a conflict of interests involving members of the family – not only those going, but those staying as well – brothers, sisters, cousins may all find that their roles in the family must change as a result of someone leaving. So, as a defence against the anxiety of having to decide when and where they go overseas, employees agree to hand over to the parent organization such far-reaching decisions, absolving themselves of any responsibility, and casting themselves firmly in the dependent role in this parent/child relationship. Although there is a notional choice as to where they go (staff are asked to state their preferences annually), in most cases the actual choice is negligible: employees, on signing their contract, make a commitment to 'total mobility' and thus agree to go where they are sent, when they are sent, even at the most inconvenient times for the well-being of the family unit (possibly just before the birth of a baby or during the last year of a child's A-level course).

In effect, as a defence against the anxiety of having to make decisions about when to leave and where to go, the individual hands over to the organization responsibility not only for his career structure, but also for much of his life: home, furniture, children's schooling, etc. From an organizational viewpoint this ensures that all overseas vacancies will be filled speedily – the hell-holes, as well as the corners of paradise. But equally the role of the stern organizational parent who will brook no argument also suits many staff members who collude with the inflexibility of the organization in order to alleviate their own anxiety and guilt at leaving behind their own family responsibilities.

One example of this was seen in a couple with a severely handicapped child whom they managed to place, at an early age, in a boarding school in Britain. Their commitment to the organization's ideal of 'total mobility' helped to allay their feeling of guilt about something which a part of them wanted – that someone else take long-term care of their child so that they might lead a more normal life.

The unconscious expectation on signing the 'mobility' clause is that the parent organization will be a consistently good and understanding one, ensuring that regular promotion is forthcoming, and that every inconvenience arising from working overseas will be compensated for. When it is not, the anger can be intense, compounded by the fear that to complain and express this anger may only result in the all-powerful parent taking away the trouble-maker's privileges and blighting his career prospects.

Bill was encouraged to 'train up' a new manager for his department in London so that in nine months' time he could be promoted to a new job. However, within six months, instead of the expected promotion, he was transferred abroad at the same level to fill an emergency vacancy which had arisen. The organization, in its guilt at having thus misled him, reacted defensively to his anger, reminding him of his commitment to mobility and assuring him that he could have been sent to many worse places! The perception of the injustice done to him enraged him, but he also felt quite helpless in the face of parental power. So, instead of directing his anger at the department which had sent him abroad (but which also had a responsibility for his future career and was therefore too dangerous to alienate), he vented it on other departments which made small administrative errors. His suspicion that to complain to anyone with any clout would serve only to convince them of his inability to cope with stress caused the displacement of his anger away from its proper source and on to an unconnected area.

The conflict between what the organization requires and what is best for an individual can sometimes be insoluble. Management needs to have a staff it can send to fill vacancies as and when they arise. The virtual impossibility of the task of successfully deploying staff, at varying stages of their career and with differing family needs, around the world makes it collude with the all-powerful role projected on to it by staff. However, because the organization receives no feedback from staff as to how it is doing on the personal front, it is able to assume that it behaves as a continuously good and nurturing parent. At the same time, it has no wish to receive any negative feedback because it has an underlying awareness that it cannot always be good, and that it does sometimes move people to fill empty slots rather than with any thought to their ultimate well-being or career. So in order to allay its own anxiety at sometimes having to be 'bad', management organizes itself into a position where it receives no feedback. It also denies its own 'badness', claiming that staff who have signed a 'total mobility' agreement can have no grounds for complaint no matter what treatment they receive. Given this impasse, management becomes isolated and out of touch with the implications of the life-style for staff. It is unable to improve its performance because it cannot acknowledge (and then improve on) its own deficiencies.

MOVING ON

On average, jobs last three to four years, although the reasons for this length of employment seem not to be known by those operating the system; perhaps such a term represents a compromise between staying somewhere long enough to become effective in the job (the personnel department quotes an efficiency curve peaking at one year) but not so long as to put down roots and make moving on more difficult. The necessity of not putting down roots and making real and close relationships with local people, as opposed to business relationships, may rest partly on the necessity in management's eyes of retaining the organization's Britishness and separateness from the local community. Management must also feel less guilty at uprooting someone after a short spell in a country than when they have become firmly embedded in the locality. The use of the expression 'we must get him out' for staff working in even the more pleasant countries seems to indicate a belief that to stay anywhere too long represents disaster.

The organization purports to be looking to recruit good administrators, whose success will be at least partly judged on their ability to withstand regular uprooting and replanting in another spot without this having too adverse an effect on their performance. The belief that anyone can do any job anywhere in the world as well as anyone else, and the reference to employees by the name of their job rather than by their given name, denies the significance of the individual and prevents management from having to confront feelings of guilt at moving people on at times which can be severely and destructively disruptive for them personally.

In moving people around in this way, the organization assumes that psychic health does not depend on environmental ties and close personal relationships, and that individuals are able to live happily while continually moving on from one country to the next. For some this is possible: the roots are provided by their partner, and the umbilical link with the organization's headquarters is sufficiently strong to provide the support that cannot be got abroad. Colleagues worldwide are referred to as a kind of substitute global family with whom it is possible to re-establish contact from time to time as postings coincide. However, for those whose dependency needs are not so easily fulfilled, the effects of culture shock begin to be felt, and the attractions of worldwide travel begin to be inadequate compensation for the disadvantages of a hobo existence spent away from family and old friends, and from important transitional objects (baby's first shoes and the horseshoe off the wedding cake) for which there is no room in the suitcase.

THE ELEMENTS OF CULTURE SHOCK

Going to work overseas represents change and the loss of what is familiar. Peter Marris sees types of change as falling into three distinct categories: first, the change which 'is consistent with our purposes and the way we are used to interpret life' – that is, when change is merely substitution or improvement.

Second, 'change as growth comes from imposing new purposes on circumstances whose meaning has not been disrupted.' Such changes do not threaten the integrity of what has already been learnt, and the person is confident enough to explore new experiences because the basis of their understanding seems secure.

Third, however, Marris cites the changes which follow from the disintegration of a meaningful environment – although out of such change a new sense of purpose may eventually emerge.[5] Although all three types of change may be experienced on going overseas, the 'shock' felt at coming into contact with a new environment falls into the third category: the environment no longer makes sense, and cannot be relied upon to behave in a consistent way, and for some, this is a profoundly disconcerting experience which causes tremendous anxiety.

It must be said, however, that not everyone experiences culture shock. Some enjoy the experience of the unfamiliar, and are able to incorporate any changes encountered into the first two of Marris's categories. Much will depend on an individual's early experiences of loss as to how they cope with loss later in life: those with a secure family base are likely to cope better than those who lost, say, a parent through death or divorce early in life.

Kate, married to a company employee, had given up her job as an office administrator to accompany her husband overseas. Although he had some experience with Voluntary Service Overseas, she had not lived abroad before, but was excited at the prospect and looking forward to it. Her father had died when she was 7, leaving herself, her sister, aged 9, and her mother. Her mother, as Kate remembers, reacted to the loss by becoming very distant and constantly 'too busy'. She was eventually unable to cope, and Kate and her sister were taken to their aunt's to be looked after. There was a cousin there, just older than Kate, whom she adored; however, when they arrived, it was her older sister who joined forces with the cousin, leaving Kate lonely and isolated, with no one to turn to. When she went overseas, the tremendous anxiety of these earlier experiences of loss were stirred up again for her, and, although she did not break down, she became extremely depressed and withdrawn for the first few months. It was not until she was able to befriend another newcomer that she began to feel better.

Some may find certain cultures more alienating than others, depending on their own personality and how that is accepted by the local population. Kevin had a strong line in raucous laughter and enjoyed racy jokes and innuendoes. His ebullience was received well in Italy where the locals thought he behaved wonderfully – so unlike his restrained and 'typically British' colleagues.

However, a move to India brought a totally different reaction from the Indians he met, who found him coarse and aggressive. He found Italy a wonderful experience, and began to experience culture shock only when he arrived in India, and felt that he did not understand the currency of social communication and interaction any more. In Marris's terms, Kevin's experience in Italy would fall into the second category of change as growth where the integrity of what was already known was not threatened. The experiences in India fall into the third category: the culture was so alien to his nature that it no longer made sense, and he was unable to link any thread of meaning between his past and present environments.

For the purposes of this chapter, I have concentrated on those who do experience some distress on finding themselves in an alien environment, and who fall into Marris's third category. Their anxiety is based on loss. This loss embraces almost everything with which they have become familiar, including a familiar physical setting and a predictable environment. One woman, unfamiliar with Canadian weather patterns, found she had to stay overnight in the office when a sunny morning had led her to dress for spring. She was completely unprepared for the 'white out' which happened later in the day and found her own unpreparedness quite out of character and disturbing.

Another type of loss experienced by expatriates is the loss of familiarity with a country's etiquette. Conflict may subsequently arise, not simply in learning the new country's etiquette, but in deciding whether this etiquette conflicts with personal values. Very often it becomes necessary to adopt new moral standards or modes of behaviour for the sake of survival. Whereas a Londoner may prefer to wait for the next tube train rather than push a way on to the present one, he may have to adopt vastly different tactics in Tokyo, where, unless he pushes along with the rest, he will never get to his destination. On a slightly more serious note, in a country where the main currency is bribery and black-market dealing, the decision not to bribe can mean that certain goods or services become unobtainable. Ideas of fairness and 'first come, first served' can be totally undermined in a country where what matters is money and power. Even if expatriates decide that they cannot fall in with such behaviour, the issue becomes more blurred further down the line: if the household plumbing is not working as it should and the water is running down the walls of one of the rooms, is it possible to wait the three weeks the plumber specifies, or is this a case where it is acceptable to give him a sizeable 'tip'?

Decisions on how to approach such dilemmas seem to hark back to the crisis of adolescence where the issue is to decide on one's personal moral stance in life and to find one's own conscience. Reactions to both the crisis of adolescence and the crisis of culture shock are similar in that in both the individual swings between acts which assert independence (exploring, eating unfamiliar food) and acts of complete dependence accompanied by feelings of inability to cope without parental/organizational support.

The loss of familiarity with a country's etiquette means that anyone who is to settle must be able to tolerate not knowing the right thing to do in social situations. This in itself can be particularly difficult for educated and articulate employees who would never normally find themselves at such a loss. The areas of difficulty, which re-emerge in every new country with a different emphasis, range from knowing how to eat (which hand is unclean), what social chat is acceptable (in India the first question asked at any social gathering is how much you earn), to how late to arrive as a guest (in Brazil to arrive late shows your level of success in life). Families moving regularly to new countries have to live with these uncertainties all the time. As soon as they get to know the currency in one country they are moved on to yet another where they have to start again from scratch, and so their anxiety level barely diminishes.

For some, the fear that they will inadvertently commit an unpardonable social *faux pas* develops into a contempt for the local population into whom is projected the gauche, inadequate, and unacceptable part of themselves. Brenda was on her fourth servant since her arrival: she had had to dismiss them all as they were, according to her, lazy, sullen, and rude. She did not know why she was so unlucky – all her friends seemed to have better luck. She would appear to have been projecting on to her servants the dirty and lazy side of herself which wished not to clean or cook and then harshly punishing that part of herself as personified by the servants.

The feeling of being 'different' is ever-present if you are readily visible because of your colour/accent/height, so the loss of anonymity can become an important factor. One man described it as feeling like the Queen must feel: every time he set foot outside the house, he would attract attention. It wasn't malicious, in fact just the opposite, people were fascinated by him, but this type of behaviour became very wearing after a time.

Many expatriates lose their anonymity in that they enjoy a far better life-style than the majority of those around them, even those with whom they are dealing on a business basis. This is particularly so in developing countries, and can lead to increased isolation as locals are too embarrassed to invite expatriate employees to their own less salubrious homes. The fear of being different and the guilt of perceiving oneself as someone to be envied by locals can lead to the use of splitting and projective mechanisms whereby fellow nationals are seen as being totally good and the locals totally bad.

Lee had got out of Vietnam by marrying a British man. Her family remained there, unable to leave. When her husband was sent to Indonesia, a country not so far removed from Vietnam in climate and spirit, she became withdrawn and was convinced that the locals were cheating and robbing her. She had locks and bars put on her house, and for most of the day remained at home virtually a prisoner while her husband was at work. When she did go out, it was to go shopping at the local market. She took a motorized rickshaw like the locals, not a taxi as the other expatriates might have done, and her colouring and command of the language were such that both she and her husband commented that no one guessed that she wasn't Indonesian. It would seem that her guilt at getting out of Vietnam and leaving the rest of her family there was a major factor in her behaviour. She undoubtedly identified the native Indonesians with her native Vietnamese and feared their hatred and envy of her for having escaped to something better. On one level she wanted to be as like them as possible, using their transport and speaking their language so that they would not envy her, but on the other hand this envy was inescapable – she had got out of Vietnam – and her guilt about this made her fear that terrible reprisals against her would come from the locals.

The sudden loss of a familiar role in life takes a good deal of adjusting to. Parents with expatriate life-styles often choose to send their children to boarding schools so that their education will have continuity. The loss of the child creates a gap in the lives of both parents, but is a particular problem for a non-employed partner for whom the raising of children has provided a focus for many years. The guilt at being uncontactable by phone and up to three weeks away by letter can lead to much anguish in relation both to children and to ageing parents left at home. By sending children back to boarding school in Britain parents are re-enacting their own experiences with the 'parent' organization, from which they, too, are separated.

Along with the loss of those they are responsible for, employees and partners also have to come to terms with the loss of those who provided them with support: those they shared happy or sad occasions with, often people going back a long way who provided comfort and stability. This applies not only to family and friends, but also to trusted doctors or dentists – even hairdressers. Younger employees often report spending much of the early months in a new country planning and catering for visits from those at home to compensate for this loss. Older employees comment on their diminishing circle of friends as, over the years, the ties become increasingly tenuous and include, eventually, only the closest relatives.

There is no doubt that the very real loss of safety in some countries contributes to feelings of culture shock. Staff can work in countries with unstable governments where coups, curfews, and the sound of gunfire are everyday occurrences. In other countries, Britain itself is a target for political reasons. Physical danger is something which has to be lived with. Purse snatching at knife-point, house break-ins, and rape are daily facts of life in some countries, and the ineffectiveness of the police force as a means of protection can make for feelings of complete and unsupported isolation. So atrocities can be committed without reprisals or any apparent concern from the host community. The fact that in some countries the alien is automatically found guilty only increases the hopelessness of ever seeing justice done, and crimes may go unreported – sometimes because of the police lack of interest and sometimes because the system of punishment appears to be excessive to British eyes. One woman felt unable to report the theft of her purse as, in the country she was in, those found guilty of stealing would have a hand cut off. Living in a country where the system for upholding law and order is so vastly different from the British one can lead to some conflict within the individual as he tries to decide how many (if any) of his true feelings it is safe to expose to host nationals and to come to terms with how he feels about having to suppress part of himself.

REACTIONS TO LOSS: THE STAGES OF MOURNING

The familiar mourning response to loss as described by Lily Pincus[6] can be observed in the behaviour of many going overseas, and most acutely in those with the least motivation: the incentive of promotion or a particular interest in a country can help to alleviate the extent of the loss. An individual's reactions to loss will differ according to how he has been able to come to terms with past experiences of loss, but, as Marris points out, 'Loss generates a conflict which must be worked out, so as to restore a vital sense of continuity of experience'.[7] That conflict is how to take on board all the new demands made of a person, while still remaining true to the past. Losses must be grieved for, as Marris says:

> If we accept that life can only be defined in the particular experiences of each individual, we cannot at the same time treat that experience as

> indifferent – uprooting people from their homes, disrupting their relationships with patently facile exhortations to adaptability. Such change implies loss, and these losses must be grieved for, unless life is meaningless anyway.[8]

The first acts of mourning attenuate leave-taking. They continue the relationship with the dead person, enabling the bereaved to give that person as central a place in their lives as they had previously. Overseas, this phase is often marked by furious letter-writing home and a need to arrange holiday visits to the new country. The phase is also marked by regression, a phase which is acknowledged in real death by the conventions of mourning, when status is given to grief and the bereaved are protected from demands for action which they are unable and unready to make.

Overseas, however, this need to regress is seldom acknowledged, or, if it is, for a period insufficiently long to allow for real working-through. Laura reported that her first few weeks in Bangkok were fine – she was a newcomer, and as such was introduced all round and generally made much of. The problem arose when she was no longer given such treatment, but neither had she been there long enough to make her own friends or find her own way. For a few weeks she felt alone, estranged, and lost, without the protection of her colleagues to support her through her loss.

Feelings of apathy and withdrawal may arise as the lost objects of affection remain unrecovered, and all that is worth living for becomes the next visit home or the children's holiday visit. This stage is characterized by withdrawal and an inability to make use of whatever facilities may be available. As with the bereaved, whose greatest wish is often to be with people but who yet cannot accept invitations to enjoy themselves for fear of betraying the dead person, so those in the grip of loss overseas are unable to go out and enjoy themselves for fear of being untrue to all that they have left behind. One woman who missed her children dreadfully was unable to integrate at all into the country her husband had been sent to: she refused invitations from all her colleagues on the grounds that she had to do her housework and her cooking (she had made sure to sack her servant for not being up to the mark very early on in her stay).

One of the most familiar reactions to loss or change is the loss of inventiveness and spontaneity in an individual. The active and enquiring part of his nature ceases to function effectively as a result of tremendous anxiety, and he becomes obsessed with minor details as the only thing over which he has any control. In his helplessness, he demands the support of headquarters at home to sort out minor problems, while the larger policy issues remain unconsidered. In enlisting such support, the individual is ensuring that he is not alone, abandoned in a strange land, but that he has contact with the past which he understood and could cope with.

The lack of space and time to mourn what has been lost or the idea that it is wrong to mourn can, in extreme cases, lead to breakdown. James, on being told he had to leave for Mexico in six weeks' time, immediately propelled himself into a frantic round of clothes-buying and leave-taking. The reaction of all his friends left him no space for mourning: he was left in no doubt that he was largely envied by them and that he was very lucky to have been given such an opportunity. On arrival in Mexico, he was immediately plunged into meeting new colleagues and learning the new job. He was living with an 'old hand' who coped with his own feelings by working all hours and leaving himself no time to think unhappy thoughts. James certainly felt unable to confide in him and talk about his feelings of homesickness. He also felt a failure, in that he had been given this wonderful opportunity which everyone envied him but which he was not enjoying at all. Eventually his anxiety reached such a pitch that he was no longer able to function and was brought home.

Finally, as with real mourning, most, having gone through some of the above phases, are able to develop a new structure of response which helps them adapt to the new country while holding on to the essence of what was important for them in the old. So in enjoying what the new country has to offer, the old remains unbetrayed. Marris describes this:

> Confidence in the original commitment is restored by extracting its essential meaning and grafting it upon the present. This process involves repeated reassurances of the strength and inviolability of the original commitment, as much as a search for the terms on which reattachment would still make life worth living. Until this ambivalent testing of past and future has retrieved the thread of continuity, it is itself the only really meaningful activity in which the bereaved can be engaged.[9]

The responses described above occur most strongly, but by no means exclusively, in those going overseas for the first time. Those on successive postings appear to learn how to cope with the upheaval so as to make it less disruptive to their lives and to recognize familiar emotions for what they are – a reaction to loss – and to feel less overwhelmed by them. Many also opt for social or business contact in preference to true friendship because they have learnt that the loss of a true friend causes pain and they are unwilling to face such pain on a regular basis.

FAMILIAR COPING MECHANISMS

Marris talks about 'the impulse to conservatism – to ignore or avoid events which do not match our understanding'.[10] So some deal with the tremendous anxiety of being in an alien culture by denying that they are overseas, and that things are any different from how they were at home. These people's existence is limited to the British expatriate community which knows which shops stock the Weetabix and the Mars bars. Their social life revolves exclusively around fellow members of the community, and almost their only contact with the local population is via the servant they employ. Anything local (food, culture, remedies for minor ailments) is scorned. Envy of those already there and perceived as coping can prevent newcomers from asking for help and assistance from them – explained always as 'not wanting to bother people'!

It is certain that support from others in the early stages of a stay is vital in helping adaptation. People often report coping better in the so-called 'harder' countries where the difficulties of living and the differences between locals and expatriates create more of what Marris would call a 'tribal'[11] or Dunkirk spirit. The boundaries around the tribe

> prevent people from having to confront confusion as an aspect of their own uncertain identity, unmediated by any given sense of where they belong. . . . The more nakedly people are exposed to the anxieties of change, the more uncompromisingly they will try to erect protective barriers about their precarious sense of self.[12]

Thus all internal conflict is projected on to society and the environment and not felt within the individual. In 'easier' countries the necessity to do this is not so marked – the environment is not so threateningly different from what is known that it becomes necessary to erect such barriers and retreat into the tribe.

In Nigeria the environment is so alien that one company has formed a compound – separate dwelling places within a guarded perimeter fence. On the surface, the reasons are that such a compound is easier to defend against robbers and that it makes good economic sense to buy a plot of land when rental prices are escalating. Unconsciously, however, there would seem to be a desire to form a 'tribe', and to align oneself with and cling to the known and trustworthy in an alien, dangerous, and unpredictable environment.

Denial may also take the form of 'going native' in an effort to allay feelings of difference between oneself and the local community – and the guilt at having so much more, in material terms, than the local population. The denial may involve taking substandard accommodation, choosing not to employ servants, and eating the local food bought at the cheapest (not always cleanest) unwesternized markets.

For those constantly on the move, identification with the parent organization can become a very important factor. Marris says: 'If people cannot protect their personal sense of identity they will begin to demand that the social framework itself should provide the structure of meaning they cannot find in their own experience.'[13]

So the organization becomes the only safe place – and one's colleagues the only people who will understand the life-style and remain stable when all else behaves like an ongoing game of musical chairs. The truth of Marris's comment is shown particularly clearly in the behaviour of those who have retired from the organization but who, none the less, still expect it to provide them with advice, care, and protection as well as a pension.

It is sometimes easier for individuals if identification with the 'tribe' is total rather than partial. In Syria in 1986 prior to the severance of diplomatic relations, many staff had good relationships with locals and had never felt under any threat. Thus the severing of diplomatic relations, although possibly making political sense, seemed incomprehensible on a personal level. Employees on their return spoke of their confusion at being used as political pawns, and they emphasized their good relations with locals. Here, if their identification with Britain and the British government had been more total, they might have found the decision to recall them easier to accept.

It has already been shown that splitting and projection are ways of coping with the acute anxiety aroused by being in an alien environment. People project their own internal feelings of anxiety and confusion on to the new environment or society in which they find themselves so that they might keep inside themselves an idealized picture of Britain, seen as being all good in comparison with the new country which is seen as being all bad (the water will give you typhoid, the food will give you food poisoning, the servants are dirty, and the locals will cheat you if they can).

The hostility shown towards the host culture goes along with a re-identification with the home culture of which the bad aspects have been forgotten and the good aspects excessively idealized. The difficulty that some have on their return home is to come to terms with the reality of present-day Britain (good and bad), which they previously had to deny.

CONCLUSION

It has been argued that the extent to which individuals experience culture shock on going overseas will depend on a variety of factors, including their level of motivation, the extent to which their conscious and unconscious needs are met, the degree of support from local people and friends, what practice they have had in coping with culture shock before, and what preparation their early experiences of loss have given them to cope with subsequent loss encountered later in life. Inevitably the distance between the culture of origin and the new culture will also play its part. But exposure to any new culture is stressful and will continue to be so until the losses associated with the past life have been mourned and sense made of the new life in terms of the previous one. During the period of adaptation (the length of which will vary from person to person), while an individual is unable to interpret events or predict from experience, the urge to move forward will be frustrated by the guilt of betraying the past by so doing. Only when the past can be incorporated into the new system of thinking can the person move forward without guilt.

For many, exposure to a new culture will eventually result in personal growth and the adoption of new values, attitudes, and behaviour patterns. For some, however, the anxiety caused by such exposure will be overwhelming, causing them never to emerge from the defensive position adopted to cope with anxiety, and sometimes leading to breakdown.

For those working in jobs where they are continually uprooted, the tremendous anxiety caused by the moves and subsequent losses can produce regression to a state of dependency, whereby the organization is endowed with all the power and the individual with virtually none. The perception of many, that they are 'stuck' in the organization, unable to leave because they have no specialist skills, emphasizes this dependent feeling.

The organization, for its part, confronted with the impossible task of carrying the projections of so many while still needing to achieve its own task of filling vacant posts, can, when the going gets tough, respond only by becoming heavy-handed and invoking the 'total mobility' clause, to remind staff of their commitment.

I have concentrated largely on the negative effects of culture shock which, when experienced, can override the positive and exciting aspects of living overseas. A few never experience culture shock at all, but find a new environment stimulating and exciting. Most do manage sooner or later to overcome the negative effects and are then able to gain a great deal from the life-style they have chosen: they do mourn what they have lost by going overseas and subsequently manage to extract a meaning from the past which may then be applied to the present. Without this continuity of meaning, the present can make no sense, and, until this has been achieved, the anxiety of culture shock will inevitably be felt.

NOTES

1 K. Oberg, 'Cultural Shock: adjustment to new cultural environments', *Practical Anthropology* 7 (1960): 176.
2 P. Marris, *Loss and Change* (London: Routledge & Kegan Paul, 1974).
3 For the sake of clarity, I have throughout referred to the employee overseas as 'he', although the observations apply equally to both men and women working overseas.
4 J. Mitchell (ed.), *The Selected Melanie Klein* (London: Penguin, 1986), p. 176.
5 P. Marris, op. cit., p. 20.
6 L. Pincus, *Death and the Family* (London: Faber, 1976), p. 112.
7 P. Marris, op. cit., p. 92.
8 Ibid., p. 91.
9 Ibid., p. 21.
10 Ibid., p. 92.
11 Ibid., p. 59.

12 Ibid., p. 82.
13 Ibid., p. 90.

BIBLIOGRAPHY

Bion, W. (1961) *Experience in Groups*, London: Tavistock.
Dally, P. (1985) 'Psychiatric illness in expatriates', *Journal of the Royal College of Physicians of London* 19 (2).
de Board, R. (1970) *The Psychoanalysis of Organisations*, London: Tavistock.
Furnham, A. and Bochner, S. (1986) *Culture Shock*, London: Methuen.
Julius, C. (1986) 'How to cope with culture shock', *The Times*, 23 January.
Marris, P. (1974) *Loss and Change*, London: Routledge & Kegan Paul.
Menzies, I. (1970) *The Functioning of Social Systems as a Defence against Anxiety*, London: Tavistock.
Mitchell, J. (ed.) (1986) *The Selected Melanie Klein*, Harmondsworth: Penguin.
Pincus, L. (1976) *Death and the Family*, London: Faber.

Chapter 7

Exam failure in the accountancy profession

Julia Bridgment

INTRODUCTION

Every year approximately 7000 graduates enter three-year training contracts with chartered accountancy practices, with the wish to become members of the Institute of Chartered Accountants in England and Wales. This figure represents about 10 per cent of the graduates seeking employment in the United Kingdom. Of these approximately 70 per cent will eventually become members of the Institute, the majority taking longer than three years to do so. To be eligible to apply for membership the student has to have completed a prescribed amount and type of work experience and, during the same period of time, has had to pass a series of examinations, these being Conversion (for the large majority who have not taken an accountancy degree) and Professional Examinations 1 and 2 (known as PE1 and PE2). The examinations are devised so that all of the subjects must be passed at the same sitting, although a marginal failure in one paper means that only that paper need be retaken. (This is known as a referral.) The student cannot move on to the next stage until the previous examination is passed, and there are time limits within which the examinations must be passed. Individually neither the examinations nor the work requirements are onerous; the difficulty lies in passing examinations while in full-time employment. Coping with these dual pressures means a period of considerable hardship for all students, however bright, and whether eventually successful or not.

I wish to address the reasons why large numbers of graduates continue to enter the profession every year despite pass rates which vary around 50 per cent for PE1 and 45 per cent for PE2. In this chapter I wish to explore, too, the needs, motivation, and defences used by students and the firms and the collusion between them, by drawing on information gathered through interviews with qualified accountants, together with my own experiences in my role as Student Examination Manager where I act as a personal tutor for the trainees on behalf of the institution. It should be noted that, because of the nature of my work, it is difficult to gain experience of the students' internal worlds, as I have a role in management which precludes such access.

In looking at the process I will consider three stages: recruitment, initial training, and examination failure.

Looking at the situation from my point of view as a personal tutor for the students in training, I am puzzled as to why a training system has been devised which has such a high failure rate and why so many graduates are willing to pay this price.

Looking at the situation from the firm's point of view, the primary objective of the firm is to operate a profitable accountancy practice. In order to achieve this they have traditionally required an adequate supply of cheap labour to carry out the more mundane tasks and fewer, more specialized members of staff to supervise and deal with complicated or specialist areas. Recruiting graduates meets both these requirements as they can be trained to carry out the more complex tasks, yet while being trained are unqualified and as such are on lower salaries. In compensation for their salary level and mundane work the firm must train them at considerable cost to itself.

In order to explore this question I used the idea of unconscious processes operating at an individual and at an institutional level. I propose that these interact with each other in a symbiotic way to meet their mutual needs and in this way perpetuate the system. The firm employs the student in order that they can staff their assignments; in order to attract the student to the firm to carry out work that can be tedious they have to offer the student training. A relationship built on this understanding must be subject to tensions, which I believe get played out by the students in their problems of balancing work and study while they prepare for their examinations.

Within both institutions and individuals there are unconscious processes in operation, often relating to very primitive phantasies. As Menzies Lyth[1] explores in her study on social systems, primitive anxieties are dealt with by using primitive defences, both by individuals and by institutions. Individuals cope with difficult experiences in a certain way and these coping mechanisms can become institutionalized and taken on as rules and regulations.

RECRUITMENT

Graduates moving into their first job will be making a transition from education to work. This may be felt to be the final transition from child to adult and therefore in some cases be difficult to manage.

They may encounter particular problems dependent upon past history and how they coped with previous changes, e.g. from primary to secondary school or even their experience of weaning. Phillipson, in a paper on career guidance, states:

> Readiness for career choice and for work life is clearly an important achievement in a long process of growth. This kind of readiness includes

> an ability to envisage and a confidence in being able to realise in an adult context, some pattern of interests, abilities and skills that have developed within the dependent experience of childhood and in the transitional experience of adolescence.[2]

Among the various problems encountered when making a career choice are having to cope with making the final steps away from parents and having to grow up. New graduates worry about their loss of freedom and that they might lose their own identity. They also fear they could make the wrong career choice and be stuck with their decision for life.

For each of these problems accountancy recruitment has an answer; those doing the recruiting are not dishonest, but they do ensure the recruitment message plays to what the students want to hear.

The aspect of leaving higher education is hidden by the training contract offered. Originally trainee accountants were called articled clerks and served a period of articles. Now trainees have to serve a three-year training contract, the three years equating to the usual number of years at university, and they are usually referred to as students. Overall, the emphasis is placed on training, and the work required by the firm is played down. Many graduates join practices in large cohorts as with university. Although they have to wear suits for their interviews, and the kind of work they will do is explained to them, it is as if the realities are only skin-deep. The message conveyed to them is that life is not changing, that they will continue to study and will have their hands held as before; the firm colludes with the idea that the students do not have to grow up.

One further factor which highlights the similarity with university is the structure of the firms. The pyramid structure, with large numbers of students at the bottom, exists not only as far as responsibility is concerned but also in terms of age. The majority of staff with whom the trainee will be working are in their early twenties. As part of the recruitment drive the older partners, while they might be tough interviewers, will also appear approachable and friendly in order to encourage the student to join their firm as opposed to any other. The fact that the trainees will be working with line managers near their own age helps allay fears of having nothing to offer and gives them people with whom they can identify. The gap between childhood and adult life has narrowed, and the student anticipates it will be easier to cope with the changes.

There is the suggestion that, as there are plenty of jobs for all, there is no competition, and so students do not have to experience the related feeling of rivalry.

Their fears of making the wrong choice or of being tied down are also allayed by the Institute which, together with the firms, offers a 'first-class business training'. The student intends that after three years they will reassess the position and work out what they really want to do. In the meantime they have chosen a very respectable and grown-up way to put off the decision. After training they believe they will be fully equipped and will have gained that extra something that will enable them to be expert and adult.

Some students join by default and this viewpoint is often expressed by trainees and was mentioned by the accountants interviewed. One said: 'I crossed off the careers I couldn't do and then chose accountancy because I thought it would give me the ability later on to choose what I really wanted to do.' Another said he could not stand the sight of blood and was not clever enough to be a solicitor, so accountancy was the only thing left for him.

Students also choose due to peer pressure. Quoting one interviewee: 'There is not so much a peer pressure but a peer comfort of knowing that some of one's friends are going into this.'

Finally, students become accountants for the 'money and the security' – as one interviewee put it, 'I have never seen a destitute accountant' – meaning that, even if they do have to grow up and look after themselves, they will not be taking any risks in doing so.

If the students don't put much thought into making a positive career choice, neither do the firms. They seem to agree to collude in not looking closely at the 'rightness' of choice, as if it weren't important for either in the long term. The recruitment process is not onerous for the student who has prepared well by reading and visiting the careers service and who has a sound academic background. This is because firms have their own needs in recruiting students. They recruit large numbers and are well aware a percentage will drop out each year. Therefore they choose to invest resources in attracting, rather the selecting, the students. One interviewee said 'large firms are desperate for people'. This is in order to carry out their basic auditing function and to maintain their position in the hierarchy of firms.

ON COMMENCEMENT OF TRAINING

Once students join the firm they soon find out that their expectations are not going to be met. Firms offer to *give* the students a training, and so generate unconscious expectations that they will be able to be dependent upon the firm. In fact, when the students join they quickly realize that the firm actually requires hard work, and they have to cope with the shock and stress of this realization. It can lead them to react by becoming even more dependent by refusing to try and do the necessary work. Conversely, as one interviewee said, 'From day one I knew I was starting a three-year prison sentence, there was no point getting upset about it, nothing could be done, I just knew I didn't want to make the sentence any longer by failing any exams.'

The training normally commences with a period of intensive theory which often takes place at premises external to the firm. The nature of the teaching process and the course the trainees attend are more reminiscent of school than university, and trainees tend to cope by relating to the situation as if it were one in the past and reverting to patterns of behaviour used at school. In particular, they can become very dependent, asking for help with money or the provision of stationery, things I am sure they coped with quite well at university. 'In this, as in so many cases, fear of possible failure in the new life can retard the process of relinquishing the old.'[3] In many ways this might be the only way firms and students manage to cope with the stresses of training, as the students come to see the disparity between the reality and the phantasy of training. This realization causes them to reflect upon their career choice and a number leave in the first few days.

I will invariably see a number of students in their first two months with the firm because they are having problems adjusting to working life and coping with the fact they are expected to be adults. The problems of adjustment are real in that it is difficult to move from university, where there is a lot more time to fit in studying with a personal life. One of the accountants interviewed said how much he resented the loss of his social life during his training and the isolation from his friends. Presenting problems normally revolve around difficulties with the material which, in turn, are often a result of problems in balancing work, study, and social life.

June was one such student: She came to tell me that she was not coping with one of the subjects and to ask for help. I knew from her marks that, although she was not strong, neither was she particularly weak.

It turned out that June had decided to train as an accountant at the end of her summer vacation when she realized that she wished to secure employment. Because she had not taken part in the recruitment milk-round she was not aware of what was involved in the training. Her problem was that she felt she was not coping, but because of her particular role she was somewhat isolated from other students and had not spoken to anyone else about these problems. She therefore felt that she should be able to cope or should not be finding the transition to work so difficult. As I spent time with her and accepted her problems of balancing work, study, and social life as real, she calmed down and visibly started to relax. Her very real problem of isolation had fed into her phantasy that she should be able to cope.

Another example of how students cope with the transition was seen in a student, Simon, whom I was able to monitor closely as the course was held at a residential centre.

Simon asked to see me on the third day of the course. I knew he had been experiencing problems because his tutor had already mentioned him to me. The tutor said that not only was Simon having problems with the material, but that he appeared unwilling to try to work things out for himself. We had both been surprised the previous evening when, despite the necessity for him to study, Simon had been one of the first to the bar.

Simon told me that he had chosen accountancy as a career because he had wanted a respectable job and that accountancy had been easy to get into. However, he was having problems with the studying and found the subject really difficult. I asked him if he was prepared to put the necessary work into mastering the topics. Simon talked about the subjects and the course for a while and then said no. I asked if he wanted to leave and Simon said that he really did wish to go but was worried about the future. I then asked if he had discussed the matter with his parents and he said he was very anxious about doing so because they had been so pleased he had chosen accountancy; if it were not for them he would leave immediately. Once he had spoken to his parents and found them supportive, he decided that he could spend some time doing what he wanted to do which was to travel and enjoy his youth a little longer. He was not yet ready to grow up.

In the case of Simon I was able to recognize that his leaving would benefit him and also benefit the firm. A similar student was not so fortunate in that neither his parents nor his office manager were supportive, his parents in that they wanted their son to be an accountant and his manager in that he was unable to recognize his own failure in recruiting this student. The manager's defence was to take omnipotent control of the situation: he agreed with the student to forget the problems of the course and to make a new start. On the surface the student's problems had been resolved. However, he left the firm three months later by which time his manager was very pleased to see him go. The manager, again omnipotently, maintained that he had taken the right course of action as, by keeping the student working for three months, he was able to recoup the costs of recruitment and training.

While Simon was helped to deal with shock of his expectation not being met by the fact that those around him were prepared to listen, the second student did not get much support and so reacted in a markedly different manner.

It is a puzzle to me why every year a number of students are recruited to enter a profession that deals predominantly with numbers when they are not happy doing so. It is as if the students hope the problem will go away.

Claire came to see me having been with the firm two months. She was finding accounting a very difficult subject to master and had done very badly in her first examination. Her main grievance was that she had asked about the need for a mathematical background at the interview, and had been told that, although she would need to work hard, she should be able to cope, and that in compensation the written subjects should come more easily to her.

Unfortunately, Claire could not get to grips with the maths however hard she worked. Yet she would not countenance the thought of giving up, becoming very angry with me when I suggested it. As the exam drew nearer she slowly started to admit that her chances of passing were slim and, when she did fail, seemed to cope well. However, before reaching that point she had gone through periods of feeling very bitter towards the firm, in particular towards me for pointing out the reality to her and towards the manager whom she felt had misled her during recruitment.

Firms now realize that this problem of students with poor mathematical ability is one they don't wish to have and build safeguards into their selection criteria. Before we introduced such measures one student joined us having already failed an aptitude test set by another firm and having been told, as a result, that he did not have the necessary numerical ability. He left us after four days by which time he realized the advice was well founded. There must have been a number of dynamics involved (for example, the student's feelings about authority and control), but his reluctance to look at the reality of the situation was remarkable, and he was not prepared to do so until it could no longer be denied.

A clue to the need for a massive denial of one's ability to master mathematics could be found in work on symbol formation. 'Numbers are symbols, and symbols are associated consciously or unconsciously, with feelings.'[4] Mathematical functions can be equated on an unconscious level with relationships within the family. It is 'this ability to use maths symbolically to puzzle over family relationships, and to explain them, that distinguishes those who achieve in the subject from those who do not'.[5] If the difficulty arises for these symbolic reasons there may well be denial, because acknowledgements would be too near admission that we are influenced by family dynamics. Students might prefer Jung's view that 'The truth is that mathematics presupposes a definite mental aptitude which by no means everybody possesses and which cannot be acquired.'[6] This allows mathematics to be a magical ability and gives the student the freedom to believe problems will magically be put right on commencement of training. The student has the blind faith that things will work out and if they do not it is not their fault as this magical ability was not bestowed on them.

FAILING EXAMINATIONS

The firm and students both invest a considerable amount in the examinations. The student spends much time studying, expending mental and emotional effort, and making many sacrifices. The firm invests money, in paying both course fees and salaries for the students on courses. As one interviewee put it, 'there are a lot of personal statements encapsulated in the failure of the individual which are failures about the firm and its management process'.

High pass rates are important because they are a reflection of the firm and its status. Candidates coming for interview always ask what pass rates are in the belief that if they join a firm with good statistics they will also pass. Because firms are in competition for the candidates, statistics are 'massaged' to produce the best possible picture. The adage 'lies, damn lies and statistics' here comes into its own. The examination pass rate is part of a firm's sense of self. A good pass rate means a good feeling; a bad one and the whole firm shares in the sense of failure. Pass rates are displayed on notice-boards and lists of successful candidates are published in in-house magazines and the national press. Competition between firms for the highest pass rates is unnecessarily strong, suggesting that feelings about how practices are perceived by their rivals and their own self-image are interdependent.

It is as if the Institute and the firms are concerned solely with the pass rates per se. Two interviewees mentioned that the people who passed the examinations were not necessarily those who would make the best accountants, and I would suggest that this is because accountants are driven by quantitative rather than qualitative measures, and this will be evidenced in the way in which future members are examined.

During the interviews I carried out I discovered that failure was seen as important for the profession in order to maintain the worth of the qualification. In fact, the high possibility of failure was given as the reason the qualification was worth anything at all. One person said: 'If we didn't have failure we would have to prove the training was of value in itself. There is an exclusiveness to people who pass.'

The Institute had gone on record as saying it never alters the pass mark, but it will alter the marking guide. It states that it does not operate a quota system in passing a set number of students, yet the pass rates remain relatively consistent. An alternative viewpoint put forward by an interviewee is that the Institute does wish to maintain a standard despite having no absolute measure for that standard. 'If the Institute found they had a 100 per cent pass rate it would say "I cannot believe that 6000 people this time have got themselves totally together, all had adequate time for study and are all mega motivated. It has to be something wrong with our examination process" and they are probably right.' Perhaps the profession needs to have a 'fair' means by which to deal with the rivalrous feeling of its members.

The fact that the division between passing and failure is relatively clear-cut could represent the profession's need to split good from bad. Klein described one phase of the infant's development as being the paranoid-schizoid position: that is, that good objects which generate feelings of love and gratitude will be kept widely apart from bad objects which are felt to be frustrating and which there is a wish to destroy.

In later life, situations that involve anxiety can result in a return to these primitive ways of functioning. Primitive defences include splitting, projection, and denial. In examining the aspects of splitting the difference between passing and failing PE2 is substantial. Until the trainee is successful they are very much tied to the firm; on passing they are a free agent and this new status is recognized by increased respect and salary. Those newly qualified are told that the world is their oyster and, as they are wooed by recruitment agencies and praised by their firms, they believe that it is. They become the idealized object.

It is unlikely that anyone within the firm would be unpleasant to a student who had failed. However, this is where the rules and regulations take over in order to allow the profession and firms to deal with failure in the way that, at an unconscious level, they might wish. If the failures do represent all the negative factors that need splitting off it is not surprising that they are treated so harshly by expulsion from the firm. Every accountant has taken the examination, and all had the possibility of failure, whether they recognized it or not: every accountant is probably very relieved to get rid of that part by locating it in someone else.

The rules and regulations surrounding failure vary from firm to firm. One firm might, for its own reasons, initially operate a particularly harsh policy so the Institute will step in and incorporate the policy into the training contract, in order that firms no longer have to take the blame upon themselves but can use the Institute as scapegoat.

The institutional rules mean that we, as individuals, can appear supportive and helpful to the students who fail and who must leave. We allow the firm to carry all our bad feelings; no one has to take personal responsibility for them.

One interesting aspect of the splitting is the attitude towards people who have obtained a referral in the examination. These students can be seen as very near passing, but, having not yet done so, they can still be regarded as failures. These students are ripe for the projections of those around them who, regardless of the feelings the students have about the ambiguity of the situation, will wish to see the situation in either a positive or a negative light and so congratulate or commiserate with the student accordingly. However, neither the firm nor the Institute will treat them as passing until they have actually done so.

One further consequence of failure in the profession which must be considered is the economic importance of failure to the larger practices where much of the work undertaken is auditing. This work requires large numbers of junior staff who report to one manager and partner. This pyramid structure requires a large number of trainees to leave before they reach the manager and partner level. In addition, once students have qualified, their salary level is increased, and firms can make more profit from those with a similar level of experience who have not passed their examinations.

REASONS FOR FAILURE

Looking at individuals, the main reason most of the interviewees gave when asked why trainees fail was the lack of motivation which results in the student not doing sufficient work. Malleson[7] recognizes two sorts of study difficulty: primary, where the work itself is a problem, and secondary, where the student is unhappy for some other reason which gets in the way of studying. From my own experience I am aware that both these reasons can account for a trainee's difficulties, but an overriding factor in examination success seems to be their desire to pass the examinations and to obtain the final qualification, regardless of what they then do with it. They are able to cope with the short-term pain of studying for the longer-term reward of letters after their name. Here the reality principle overrides the pleasure principle. Jaques suggests that:

> The capacity to work depends upon the coherence of the unconscious and upon the integration and strength of the ego and its capacity, in the face of anxiety and uncertainty, to sustain its function to maintain the reality principle.[8]

In many cases I deal with, the problem of not studying is a reflection of the trainees' ambivalence with regard to their accountancy training. Often, unfortunately, the student cannot see this, or admit it to themselves, until they have failed an examination. The students cannot allow themselves to tell their parents their feelings directly and therefore use examination failure as a means of communicating their lack of enthusiasm for accountancy. I wish to give an example of a student who left just before sitting an examination, for reasons that are fairly typical.

William joined the firm with the intention of returning to his home town to work for his parents once qualified. William phoned me three weeks before he was due to sit an examination to say that he wished to leave.

I met with him the next day, as did other managers, and it appeared that it was very important to William to have our approval of his plans. He said that he had spoken to his parents, and his mother had not been interested. She wanted him to be a qualified accountant. However, his father had been supportive and wanted him to return to the family business. William talked with great enthusiasm about the new job he had found and said he wanted to have some fun. He knew accountancy was not for him, and said that he had chosen it because he hadn't wanted to return home after university, yet had needed security and, at the time, accountancy had seemed to meet both his requirements.

During that meeting and others that followed, it emerged that all William really wanted to do was to have some fun away from his family. He wanted to enjoy his youth, and needed to break away from his parents. His family and their business were very important to him, yet they also represented being bored and trapped, just like accountancy. He was going to a new job where he perceived there would be fun and excitement, and where 'everyone is very young'.

This came to a head at a time when William was under a lot of pressure and he could no longer cope with meeting both his own needs and his perception of his parents' wishes for him. However, his conflicting feelings had been evident throughout his period with the firm as his mock examinations had often been poor or not done until chased by me as a parental authority figure.

This case illustrates the conflict students have in their reluctance to grow up, the problems of dealing with parental wishes, and how these feelings get projected on to the management. In William's case I very much felt that I had to be the approving mother and give my blessing before he could happily leave. By contrast, other students have dropped out because they do not wish to separate from their parents and several have left to work in the family business.

Another reason for failure is much more subtle and that is the anxiety about success – what passing will mean to an individual about to take an examination. I have been told of the depression students may feel after qualification, as if they have suddenly broken free and are finding it lonely and frightening to be on their own. A fear of this final separation from parents, as represented by the training firm, must influence students as they prepare for and take their final examinations, especially if there are phantasies that growing up might damage the family in some way.

REACTION TO FAILURE

Failure leads to the use of primitive defences by all parties involved. One defence is a form of denial by looking only on the bright side. The Institute always issues a press release at the same time as they publish the pass list and this tends to be very positive. For example, when a pass rate was exceptionally low the release concentrated on the fact that more students than ever had passed, not mentioning the fact that more than ever had taken the exam; the manipulation of figures meant the true situation could be denied.

Another form of defence against recognizing failure is to find scapegoats. This is where the external tuition firms are particularly useful, and could be one of the reasons that the English Institute uses external firms. Following a poor pass rate a 'witch hunt' will ensue and much analysis will be carried out by the firms. The tuition firms will also carry out their own analysis in order to defend against attacks from firms. Having carried out many such analyses myself, I am well aware there are normally no simple answers. However, it is usually possible to identify something – for example, a subject that was examined but was not taught or the fact that the students had poor academic backgrounds – and at that point the investigation can stop. Having a central function dealing with examinations, I normally receive a few angry phone calls demanding explanations after the publication of poor sets of examination results. These attacks are powerful and I will also have my defence prepared, as do the recruitment department and anyone else who might be a target! Ultimately it is the students who have failed who receive the angry projections.

The students too have their defences. I may see them when they are still dealing with the shock of failing, and they wish to deny their failure, or project the reasons on to a small element of the examination process.

James could not believe that he had failed and came to see me to ask if it was possible for his paper to be re-marked. I explained the procedure, but added that there was virtually no chance of his result changing. At this James became very despondent and said there must have been a mistake. It was as if the failure was so painful that there was no way in which he could cope with taking the responsibility on himself. I am sure this feeling was made worse for him because he had invested much in the accountancy career, and his father was a successful accountant.

My feeling that his reaction was a defence stemmed from the fact that I was not surprised he had failed. He had the necessary ability but had not studied as much as was needed, and so his marks for his mock examinations were below average and the tuition firm predicted failure. In addition both myself and a tutor had spoken to him while he was on the pre-exam course to warn him that he was underestimating what needed to be done. Through addressing these facts I was able to help James come to terms with the reality of the situation, and we were able to identify how his avoidance of looking at the reality of his situation (the poor mock results) had contributed to his failure. He had always been strong academically and could not believe he would not pull through in the end, his past experiences colouring his view of the present.

Other students do not even need to find an explanation for their failure. They virtually deny the fact they have failed and make statements such as 'I've never failed an exam before, I don't know why this happened. I won't fail next time.' I find such students particularly difficult to deal with, not least because I tend to pick up the anger they cannot express, but mainly because I am aware that if they do not get in touch with the reality of their failure and the reasons behind doing so they are more than likely to repeat the failure when re-taking.

Not all students react by using the mechanisms of denial and projection to help them cope with their failure. Their reactions will depend upon their individual characters and the make-up of their inner world. Students who have a poor self-image can react particularly badly to failure, taking responsibility for the whole system on to themselves.

Sarah had failed PE2, which was the first examination she had failed during her accountancy training. She was upset and very cross with herself, and was not going to let anything or anyone get in the way of her blaming herself. Sarah had been conscientious in her preparation for the exam, and my feeling was that she had been unlucky because she was of above average ability and had just failed to make it (as evidenced by her marks) at a sitting when the pass rate had been particularly low. In addition the hall in which she sat the exams had suffered building work; a number of other students put that fact forward as a contributory factor to their own failure. Sarah showed her anger with herself by booking herself onto an excessive number of evening and weekend revision courses, and in wishing to approach her re-take as if it were her first attempt. She was denigrating herself by treating all the work she had done prior to her first attempt as worthless.

CONCLUSION

In looking at the obstacles graduates have to overcome in order to gain admission to the Institute of Chartered Accountants various themes emerge which reflect the conscious and unconscious issues. The main themes are the transition from child to adult and the concept of splitting, particularly as a reaction to failure. These themes appear to be related in that if the student does not achieve the adult status gained on qualification they retreat or are forced back into a more primitive way of coping.

In addressing the issues of recruitment, it is clear that the firms wish to encourage large numbers to join, and one of the ways they will attract more students is by appealing to the part of them that wishes to avoid growing up. The manner in which this is done, by subtly playing into the students' phantasies, ensures that the firm does not have to take any responsibility for misleading the students, and the students are left struggling with the feelings by themselves. To counteract this, the students are supported by a fairly rigid authoritarian environment, where the rules offer containment as well as restriction. In addition, the students are with many other young people who are dealing with or who have dealt with the same problems. This means that unless the student is unusually isolated they will probably be able to cope and will survive to help the next intake.

The process of passing or failing the examinations is seen to be clear-cut, the student is either a success or a failure, there is a complete split between passing and failing with no middle ground. This perhaps reflects the processes which go on within the profession, which is generally black and white, values being either debits or credits. The good is not to be contaminated by the bad. Splitting occurs in the way individuals react to failure, the way in which firms treat those who pass or fail examinations, the manner by which the Institute admits new members, and the way the market reacts in its remuneration and recruitment of newly qualified accountants.

Finally, in considering why the high failure rate is tolerated by the institutions and the students, my feeling is that it is not merely tolerated but required by those involved in the process. Failure is a necessary corollary to success, and for the qualification to retain its value it has to be obtained at the expense of those who have failed. The interviewees said the qualification is worth nothing in itself; its only virtue is because it is so difficult to obtain. For qualified accountants to retain their value, both economically and as far as their self-esteem is concerned, there must be failures.

The members from the Institute and the firms who develop and maintain the policies and practices for the examination system are those who have passed and qualified. The whole system is devised around success; the failures are not considered because they are kept outside the profession and will have no input into the manner of evaluation. The individuals who fail ultimately have to cope with the failure by themselves.

When reviewing the overall process it appears that the firm and the student enter into a relationship that is mutually beneficial in that the firm needs labour and the student needs to buy time. There is a lack of commitment on both sides and so if the relationship fails, as it will if the student fails, it is not to be grieved. The relationship becomes ritualized and institutionalized to guard against a strong relationship being developed. The relationship is built on the basis that it has as much chance of ending as it has of continuing and so is designed to defend against stress and anxiety. The manner in which this is done succeeds to the point that very little is actually felt. The relationship is sado-masochistic yet the ritualization prevents both parties having to face this fact, and prevents the pain having to be acknowledged. The ones who really suffer, however, are the students who truly want to be accountants from the outset and are shown no compassion if they fail.

For my own part, I also try not to be in touch with the feelings that are generated by the system and usually tend not to be bothered by results. Fortunately, it is not possible to cut myself off from the students once I get to know them, as then I am confronted by the reality of the individual, not the rules and regulations. When a student does not behave as expected, for example does little work during the year, is predicted to fail and is told so, but is then devastated by that failure, it brings home to me the personal cost. Those who fail are no longer protected by the system.

NOTES

1 I. Menzies Lyth, *The Functioning of Social Systems as a Defence Against Anxiety* (London: Tavistock, 1970).
2 H. Phillipson, 'Career guidance work and its relation to theory and practice in education', unpublished paper.
3 C. M. Parkes, 'Psycho-social transitions: a field for study', *Journal of Social Science & Medicine*, 1971, p. 101.
4 E. Blyth, 'Mirrors on girls and maths', 1985, also this volume, p. 156.
5 Ibid., p. 149.
6 C. G. Jung, *The Development of Personality*, *CW* 17 (London: Routledge & Kegan Paul, 1954), p. 152.

7 N. Malleson, 'The influence of emotional factors on achievement in university education', in *Students in Need* (Guildford: University of Surrey, 1978), 1963.
8 E. Jaques, 'Disturbances in the capacity to work', *International Journal of Psycho-Analysis* 41: 357–67.

BIBLIOGRAPHY

Blyth, E. (1985) 'Mirrors on girls and maths', *Bulletin of the British Association of Psychotherapists* 1: 79–83 (reprinted in this volume).

Hopwood, A. (1974) *Accounting and Human Behaviour*, London: Haymarket.

Jaques, E. (1960) 'Disturbances in the capacity to work', *International Journal of Psycho-Analysis* 41: 357–67.

Jung, C. G. (1954) *The Development of Personality, The Collected Works*, Vol. 17, London: Routledge & Kegan Paul.

Klein, M. (1957) *Envy and Gratitude*, London: Virago, 1988.

Malleson, N. (1963) 'The influence of emotional factors on achievement in university education', in Society for Research into Higher Education (ed.) *Students in Need: Essays in Memory of Nicholas Malleson*, Guildford: University of Surrey, 1978.

Menzies-Lyth, I. E. P. (1970) *The Functioning of Social Systems as a Defence Against Anxiety*, London: Tavistock.

Noonan, E. (1983) *Counselling Young People*, London: Methuen.

Parkes, C. M. (1971) 'Psycho-social transitions: a field for study', *Journal of Social Science and Medicine* 5: 101–15.

Phillipson, H. 'Career guidance work and its relation to theory and practice in education', unpublished paper, The Tavistock Centre, London.

Salzberger-Wittenberg, I. *et al.* (1983) *The Emotional Experience of Learning and Teaching*, London: Routledge & Kegan Paul.

Chapter 8

Being and becoming

A study of gifted young musicians

Anne Bell

INTRODUCTION

How is it that a 16- or 17-year-old boy or girl is able to interpret a highly complex piece of music? What internal qualities and strength are being drawn upon and what difficulties have had to be overcome?

These questions and others flashed through my mind recently as I was at an informal concert given at the music school where I have been a member of the academic staff for eight years. During that time I have been to many concerts, both formal and informal, so the experience was not a new one, and yet the impression of awe and wonder is one that seizes me afresh each time. How is it that a child whom I know to be quite 'ordinary' – and I use the term in a non-derogatory way – in other spheres of life can be so transformed? What energies is he/she harnessing?

Rosemary Shuter-Dyson in her article 'Musical giftedness'[1] cites numerous studies that have been undertaken (both in Great Britain and in the United States) to try to assess musical talent and its relationship to other abilities, such as long- and short-term memory, visual and auditory perception, perceptual speed. She also examines a series of articles written by Kemp in 1981 and 1982 for the journal *Psychology of Music*, in which he found that certain personality characteristics 'could be interpreted as facilitating the process of developing the motor, perceptive and cognitive skills necessary for performance'.

However, relatively little research has been done into the internal psychological world of very musical children. Hence I decided that it would be interesting to conduct a series of in-depth conversations with five music students, in order to explore their feelings about specific aspects of their life and, from these, to see if any patterns could be discerned. It seems to me that, in his striving to express himself creatively through his musical talent, the young musician is attempting to develop and integrate aspects of his personality in a way that is perhaps more *conscious* than that of his non-musical peers.[2] Thus, of the many 'opposites' which form part of life, some have emerged as being of particular relevance to the five students with whom I talked: for example, the need to internalize and reflect upon the music on the one hand and the possession of a real desire to communicate it on the other; a sensitivity to the feelings and ideas of other players on one hand and a confidence in one's own intuitions and opinions on the other; the courage to take risks and make oneself vulnerable versus a certain capacity to 'show off'; the inner freedom to give free rein to one's imagination and feelings when interpreting the music while yet mastering the necessary technique and retaining emotional control over it; the ability to let things 'flow' and 'happen' while at the same time striving towards a greater degree of perfection; the possession of a generosity of spirit towards fellow-musicians coupled with a degree of self-seeking and competitiveness.

I have not specifically sought out details on early mothering experiences or on the influence of the environment on the nurturing of exceptional talent. Above all, I realize that the impact of a musical gift cannot be seen *in vacuo* and that these students are also, as I mentioned earlier, 'ordinary' adolescents, coping with all the 'normal' tasks of adolescence. Their struggles, joys, and discoveries obviously take place within the context of the whole of their life, of which music is but a part, albeit a very significant one.

I have written in depth about three of the five students. However, individual difference apart, much of what these three said was reinforced by the other two, and I have used material from all five in my concluding section on the role of chamber music and the development of their personality.

I chose the five pupils, who are between 16 and 19 years old, carefully and for several reasons. First, I had taught (and in one case am still teaching) all of them at some stage within the last three years. Thus, because of the very small classes – between three and five pupils at a time – we had been able to get to know each other reasonably well. I deliberately say 'we' here because an important factor in the conversations I proposed to have with them was that they already felt at ease with me.

Second, all the students shine out as excellent among a group of extremely talented musicians, and all of them are dedicated to making careers as performers.

Third, between them they represent a variety of instruments, and, last, they are all articulate. However, that does not necessarily mean that they always found it easy to describe what they wanted to say.

When we met together for the first time I explained the reason for my dissertation – most of them already knew that I was doing the student counselling course – and I stressed two things in particular: first, that whatever they said to me would be in confidence in that I would not bring in to one person's session by way of comparison or confirmation what had been said by another; furthermore, that I would not discuss any of the details with anybody else in the school and that ultimately when I wrote up the dissertation their names and identifying details would of course be changed. I felt that it was important to stress these safeguards because of the gossipy and often very unconfidential atmosphere in which they live.

Second, what we would be doing together was in the nature of an exploration rather than an 'interrogation'. Thus, although I had drawn up a list of questions, these were intended more as a guide to certain areas on which it could be fruitful to reflect, rather than as a 'questionnaire'.

Of course, because ours was not a counselling relationship I felt that this imposed limitations on how far I could 'dig' into their internal world or make transference links with past experiences. However, I often felt both amazed and humble at the openness with which the students explored their feelings and by the way in which they felt able to reveal very intimate details, some of which they had never spoken of before. Each student, at some stage during our sessions, voiced a wonder, coupled with excitement, at what they were finding out about themselves.

THE STUDENTS

Patrick

Patrick is 16½, a violist and an accomplished pianist, and has chosen to go to university first before embarking on a musical career. He comes from a family where music has always been important: both his parents are musicians and his older sister also participates in the music-making around which their social life revolves. For Patrick it was his grandmother who introduced him to the piano at about the age of 2½, and he started formal lessons at 6. He asked to play the viola at 8, chiefly because he liked the violist who played chamber music with the family.

However, although this very early parental and environmental encouragement of his talent was obviously of great importance, he insists that in other ways he led a perfectly 'normal' life, going to a local primary school and mixing easily with other children.

> Throughout my childhood I have wanted to do all the usual things – be a train driver, airline pilot, etc., but music has been the one *constant* factor.

And, although music has now become the focus of his life, he stresses that it is by no means exclusive:

> I enjoy – in fact, often *prefer* – talking about things other than music. I still have a very good friend from primary school who is totally non-musical, and we simply share other interests.

Later on in our conversation the importance of being open to other influences came up again. I had asked him what helped to inspire him in his musical expression and, very animatedly, he said:

> *Everything*! From a sunset to a plastic chair! I think that you should be

> constantly aware of everything around you – immerse yourself not just in your music but in *life*, so that it gets inside you and then inspires you.

He then paused thoughtfully for a moment before adding:

> However, you do need some sort of a screening faculty, a critical faculty so as not just to be a sponge. You must be able to make something your own.

This needs an ego which is strong enough not to be overwhelmed by external influences on the one hand nor merely to act as a passive receptacle on the other. Winnicott's development of the idea of 'transitional objects' as the first symbols on the path to other forms of creative living and the whole field of play, culture and religion, demanded as a *sine qua non* that the infant already possess a secure enough feeling of 'continuity-of-being'.[3] Only when the infant feels sure enough in relation to both his internal and his external objects will he be able to enjoy and *use* his experiences with objects in the intermediate area between the 'me' and the 'not-me'. Those infants who, undisturbed by the anxieties of having to react constantly to an unpredictable or even hostile environment, are able to enjoy a rich phantasy life as well as a gradual experience of reality, will be all the better equipped in later life to receive new external stimuli, to 'play' with ideas and feelings and from that to create something which is uniquely personal.

Unlike many, Patrick found the transition, at 13½, from home to this school relatively easy. He said that his parents had:

> Nurtured but not pushed me. They didn't force me to sit and practise, but they did make me aware of the importance of regular practice. They encouraged me gently!

Thus, although he admitted that he probably does not practise as much as he should, he *is* able to discipline himself when necessary, and the lack of supervision of music practice at school did not 'throw' him unduly. Of the five students, Patrick is probably the one who has achieved the greatest amount of harmony so far between the demands of id, ego, and superego. When I asked him what personal characteristics he felt he possessed which contributed to his musical creativity, he named two in particular: the ability to feel emotions inside and the ability to stand back.

> You can't afford to be reserved while performing (unless of course it is specifically called for in a particular piece), but must give your all. You must be able to lose track of yourself, although being moved yourself is only helpful if you have got enough technique to cope with it. You need to keep hold of the central thread of the music; you can only afford to let yourself 'go' if you have a firm centre in yourself to which to return.

He felt that what he lacked was a sufficient degree of patience with himself when things were not going right and tenacity in the sense of being able to 'stay with' the difficulties.

> I need to learn more how to hold on to problems – to allow myself to play a passage wrong for a while, for example.

And when I asked him if he thought he was a perfectionist, he saw a contradiction in the term:

> Yes, I do strive for, work towards, perfection. But there is no such thing as perfection. If I achieved it, all possibility of development would end. It would be the antithesis of growth!

Patrick is the only one of the five students who composes as well as plays, and it was in this sphere that he said he felt the most solitary and vulnerable to the opinion of others.

> Composing is being truly creative, whereas I would say that performing is more re-creative. Composing is exhilarating because I feel I have total freedom, but I am also throwing open my personality, my *self*, in a way which is terrifying! The most nerve-wracking moments are waiting for a piece of mine to be performed. . . .

He then paused and said with a smile:

> But I often get a pleasant surprise when I hear it played and I find things in it that I never even knew were there!

It was in this way that he thought that a performer could re-create and enhance the richness of a piece without in any way distorting it. One of the most difficult tasks of a composer, although he felt that it also applied as a performer, was coping with the frustration of creative blocks.

> There are various things that I can 'do' – such as listen to some other music, talk with friends, go out or lie on my bed, but the most important thing of all is to wait and trust that something will turn up. To let time go by and try not to notice it – that is, *not* to try to control things.

This sounds very similar to what can happen in therapy, when the therapeutic relationship feels blocked for one reason or another; then both therapist and client need to have the courage and sufficient trust in the process to stop using the conscious ego as an ingenious battering ram and allow new material to surface unbidden from the unconscious. It is not easy to continue to hold on while at the same time letting go. The phrase 'waiting on God' describes a similar state of being, called for in those who practise meditation in their search for God and the further dimensions of the spirit.

Outwardly, Patrick gives the impression of being quietly self-confident, expressing himself with measured ease, yet, when we came to discuss anxiety in performing, he took me by surprise by the change of his manner as he spoke feelingly of the nightmares he sometimes had before a performance:

> I have had memory blanks in the past and the thought that they could happen again is very frightening, because when I am performing I am not just playing for myself – I feel that I have the responsibility to make the performance interesting for the audience. Ideally, I want to feel excited, rather than anxious, before a concert, because too much anxiety leads to over-cautious playing and too little anxiety often leads to a 'flat' performance. And for me, that is even worse than a 'bad' performance!

This echoes the work of Yerkes and Dodson who examined to what point anxiety could rise and still act as a spur to achievement, before becoming too great and thence causing the performance of the sufferer to diminish. In constructing a graph they found there to be an optimal level of anxiety in relation to effectiveness of output, which of course varies from person to person and from task to task.

We then moved on to the subject of competitiveness, which for Patrick has a particular resonance at the moment since he is succeeding in a national music competition in which he is – and has been – competing against close friends. However, it is also something which he has lived with and has thought about for a long time, and while his subjective feelings were obviously very much engaged, he was able to explore then in a thoughtfully 'objective' way.

> In a broad sense, a spirit of competitiveness can be helpful, even inspiring. Hearing someone play beautifully can spur you on to greater achievements, and this is an ongoing process. Competitions in particular are slightly different: I feel I need a certain amount of inner arrogance – to cultivate it if necessary – to give me the confidence in my ability to win. However, this has got to be a realistic self-confidence, and of course the trouble is that it often manifests itself as outward arrogance.

So here again it is a question of balance – or balancing one's inner needs with the expectations of the external world and also of integrating within *oneself* the capacity to show off fearlessly while maintaining a realistic humility. When I pressed him a little on how he was feeling at present he sighed rather wryly and admitted to being wary of being over-competitive, especially against a friend. He then went on to make the distinction between competition and rivalry:

> For me, competitiveness which entails 'doing down' someone else is unhealthy; then it turns into a form of rivalry in which the common goal – the pursuit of excellence – is forgotten. That is where the danger lies; in some competitions, especially when there is television or press exposure, with a lot at stake, you can feel 'put down' if you don't win, and be left

> with a terrible sense of being a failure. It is hard to keep a sense of proportion about your own abilities: to accept that someone else's success doesn't necessarily mean your own failure.

I think I could fruitfully have explored the extent and nature of Patrick's aggressive drives a little further, but time was at a premium for both of us and so we turned instead to how he felt about chamber music – as apart from orchestral or solo work. At this point his face lit up:

> I *love* it. Whether here, with musicians of a high standard, or at home with my family and friends who are talented amateurs, what matters is that we are playing for love of the music. I find the collective enthusiasm very exciting.

However, it cannot always work perfectly, I suggested.

> No, it doesn't. In a quartet, for example, the need to retain your personality and yet blend in with the others is a very complex achievement – and *marvellous* when it happens! You need to be willing to try out other people's ideas, but not have to compromise. I can't *exactly* describe how, but I know that it is possible to achieve a unified 'feel' in a quartet by an atmosphere of give and take.

Patrick went on to give specific examples of how he felt compromise to be a damaging, negative resolution to a conflict in the context of a chamber group. For him it always entailed a compromise 'down' to the lowest common denominator, which *ipso facto* had no real 'life' of its own. Thus he is using the term differently from Winnicott, who believes that, in health, the true self must also be capable of having a compliant aspect – that is, an ability to comply in order not to be totally exposed when exposure could be a threat. In this case, Winnicott perceives the ability to compromise – the development of a social manner – as a *positive* achievement. However, he does go on to say that when an issue becomes critical, compromise is then no longer deemed possible and the 'true self' overrides the false (compliant) self. This is particularly true in adolescence when a young person often feels as if he is fighting for his life, so to speak, and to give in and be compliant would mean the mutilation of his self. I would like to discuss this further, in relation to the life of a chamber group, later on.

Patrick became very animated during this part of our discussion, stressing his need to be true to himself, while at the same time being only a part of the whole which was greater than him. He even went on to say that:

> I feel that the whole political scene would be better off if it functioned more like a string quartet, reaching harmonious solutions not through sterile compromise but through an enriching experience of working together.

One might be tempted to dismiss this with a smile as a typically 'idealistic' adolescent fantasy, and yet Patrick is basing his judgement on real experiments in feeling, evaluating, and integrating opposing points of view. And it is only through many thousands of personal achievements that global achievements become possible.

Tina

Tina is a slim girl of 17, with a reserved quality about her. Both her parents are musicians and the fact that Tina is the middle of three children, having a brother two years younger and a sister five years older than herself, has had a significant influence on her. She started playing the violin at the age of 3, by the Suzuki method, and she says that her mother was a perfect 'Suzuki mother' – that is, attending the classes and encouraging at home. Between 3 and 10 violin playing was a part of her life, but not a specially important one. She was diffident about telling me that she was the one in the group most often chosen to play solos and she also remembers the edge of competitiveness she felt emanating from the parents of the other children in the group. At her primary school she felt she was no different from her peers, but this changed at her secondary school where she was singled out as 'odd' because she didn't have a favourite pop group, preferring classical music.

However, of greater importance to Tina was an event when she was 11, after which:

> I consciously set about changing my behaviour. I had overheard a friend of the family talking about me and my sister and saying that Joanna was an introvert whereas of course I was an extravert.

Tina took this as a terrible slur, because she perceived her sister as being both more beautiful and more 'interesting' than her. What is more, Joanna and Jeremy, Tina's brother, were also very clever and destined for university careers, whereas Tina felt that she just 'did music'. Hence, at 11, she set about cultivating a 'withdrawn' personality, which was how she interpreted the word introvert.

At roughly the same period she also started to modify her behaviour in another context, namely *vis-à-vis* her mother.

> I began to feel ashamed of the previous arguments I had had with her and so I just stopped arguing and blotted it all out.

I didn't want to pressurize her to explain further how it had felt, but she continued of her own accord to explain how her teacher at that time had continually encouraged her to 'play out', to 'loosen up', and 'let her emotions flow'.

> But I thought that by *not* playing out I could deny that there was any aggressive side to me. Above all, I didn't want to let it show.

This emotional straitjacket into which Tina laced herself proved quite detrimental both to her playing and to her self for a number of years. In his essay on *Psychological Types* Jung was perhaps the first to point out that forcibly changing a 'natural' disposition into an unnatural mould was harmful to the individual and had to be rectified. Although he was concerned here with inimical *parental* influences, whereas in Tina's case it was she who 'violated' herself, I believe that the outcome is similar.

Jung says:

> Ultimately it must be the individual disposition which decides whether a child will belong to this or that type despite the constancy of external conditions. Naturally I am thinking only of normal cases. Under abnormal conditions, i.e. when the mother's own attitude is extreme, a similar attitude can be forced on the children too, thus violating their individual disposition, which might have opted for another type if no abnormal external conditions had intervened. As a rule, whenever such falsification of type takes place as a result of parental influence the individual becomes neurotic later, and can be cured only by developing the attitude consonant with nature.[4]

This process of reacceptance of herself took time and was complicated by the fact that when she was 12½ her sister became and remained anorexic for about a year and a half. During that time the chief focus of attention inevitably shifted to Joanna and Tina was left feeling very much in the background, yet paradoxically having to take over in many practical ways the role of older sister which her sister could no longer perform.

When Tina transferred at 13 to this school as a boarder, she did not find it easy to fit in at first.

> I had lost all my self-confidence. There were people around me with something really special and I felt inadequate. I just couldn't believe in myself.

These feelings of inadequacy continued for two years, during which time Tina became progressively withdrawn, until depression was diagnosed.

> Part of me wanted to prove that I was intelligent but I hated the academic pressure – I felt *measured* by the O-levels. I didn't want to take them. Being quiet and aloof was tied up with that. I loved being mysterious. I felt wonderful when people said how introverted I had become!

In fact being aloof enhanced her sense of being beautiful – like her sister – and at the same time she at last began to receive the same sort of attention as her sister had previously. Both her parents were by now aware of the effect which her sister's anorexia must have had on her, and, consequently, at this time of incipient crisis they decided to go, as a whole family, to a family therapist. Over a period of six months he was able to help them sufficiently to enable Tina to take her O-levels. This 'proof' of her family's concern for her greatly helped Tina, even though she still felt very uncertain about the future – whether to continue with the violin – at this stage.

These doubts were only finally dispelled halfway through her A-level course, after a seminal experience on a trip to Germany with the school orchestra. During this she was inspired not only by the technical expertise of the Germans but also by the personal compliments she received for her playing as part of a sextet. This was perhaps the first time she had been able to 'hear' praise.

> That was when I suddenly realized that I wanted to make music my life and that I no longer had to prove anything by going to university.

One could surmise that perhaps she needed to be away from her normal environment in order to dare to open her eyes to her own talent. However, I also believe that it was significant that she was playing in a chamber group, which was praised as a *whole*. Being a part of this integrated organism may have encouraged Tina to re-own some of her split-off parts and come to accept that, even while flawed, she did possess that 'something special'. Or, to borrow Kleinian terminology, I believe it was an important move for her from the 'paranoid-schizoid' position to the 'depressive' position.

However, although this 'revelation' unblocked her in a certain way, allowing her to move forward more freely in her chosen direction, Tina is still plagued by doubts about her worth as a musician despite the mounting evidence to the contrary. I was taken aback by the alacrity with which she replied when I asked her if she had ever felt especially talented. Her wide grey eyes looked at me almost as if I had uttered a blasphemy: 'No – never!' This was no false modesty, but a genuinely held belief, although by the end of our third session together she was able to modify it slightly. To begin with, she said that she hated receiving compliments,

> but since Germany I have received a lot of recognition as a player by my peers, and I have also had a lot of support from Mr J [musical director]. It is essential to have someone like that behind me.

Then she paused and looked at me shyly before adding:

> It is a wonderful feeling, when I'm on my own, to be told I am good! But I know that I can be very moody and still reject what people say; it is easier to be harsh on myself. Generally when I receive a compliment I put it in a store at the back of my head and keep it there as a sort of confidence booster.

The proviso of 'when I am on my own', I feel points to Tina's need still to hold her belief in check: just as she repressed her aggression against her mother and her only partially admitted envy of her sister, her own objective success still feels too potentially threatening to 'rejoice in' openly.

When I asked her how she felt about competitiveness, both her own and that of others, she hesitated before answering:

> I hate competitiveness! I think it shouldn't be necessary. I don't like the feeling of being judged against other people, which happens here. . . .

Then she paused again before continuing:

> In fact I always thought I wasn't until a few week ago Mrs S [a member of staff whom she likes and respects] confronted me with it and said she thought that I *was*. I was completely taken aback! I've thought about it a lot since then and I think that maybe it is true that I am competitive – although I wish I wasn't!

That was a painful admission for her and her distress and confusion were very evident. However, it was a move away from her initial statement, towards the start of our first session together, that she didn't feel at all competitive towards her brother and sister. From this new position she was able to make the step towards recognizing the fact that other people might also feel envious of her:

> My success must affect others, because I remember how I was affected earlier by having to witness the success of my friends – I suppose it is something to do with the feeling of *not being recognized.*

Interestingly, when we came to talk about anxiety, Tina twice went off at a lengthy tangent and it was only when I gently pointed out that it seemed to be a very difficult subject to look at that she could bring herself to admit that until very recently she had been anxious before every single lesson with her teacher (a different one now from her original one when she first came to the school). When I asked her what she felt caused this tremendous anxiety she immediately said:

> Because I *mind* what she thinks and what she will say. I don't want to let her down and also I don't want to let *myself* down. I get anxious about not having done everything [in practice] and not being able to play something well.

Her present teacher is an extremely talented and much respected woman, who now no longer performs publicly herself, and Tina went on to explain that she feels guilty because she can perform and her teacher cannot. She even went so far as to say that, if it could do any good, she would willingly give her her youth. To begin with this feeling of guilt, coupled with a desire for reparation towards a very important parent figure, was more of an inhibiting factor in Tina's playing, because it was still tinged with a certain degree of fear of retribution, but within the last year the situation has been changing:

> I respect her enormously and her frailty is an added reason for me for wanting to do well, but of course I daren't tell her that – I can't be as open with her as I would like to be. So I can only show her through the music and we have a much better understanding now on a musical level.

Another modification which is taking place in Tina is that of the power of her highly developed superego, further evidence of which she had shown previously when she said:

> I can't really judge when I've played musically. In fact I have *never* felt that I've played really well.

However, again within the last year or so, she has been able to use her conscious 'adult' part of herself – to use a transactional analysis term – to help her out of the 'helpless child/disapproving parent' bind.

> I just *decided* that it was silly to go on like this. I realize that it doesn't really matter not being perfect every time. Now I am beginning to *allow* myself not to do everything perfectly.

Although arrived at from a very different route, this discovery echoes closely Patrick's realization that in his striving for ever-greater mastery 'I need to allow myself to play a passage wrong'.

Tom

Tom is 18 and, like Patrick and Tina, came to the school late – that is, at the age of 14. Unlike them, neither of his parents play an instrument, although they enjoy music and have encouraged him a lot; however, this may have led to the fact that Tom began playing the piano late. He started experimenting on the piano at the age of 6, but it was not until he was 13 that his talent seriously began to be recognized.

Tom talks very fast and almost incoherently at times, exuding nervous energy. During the course of our conversations his body was constantly on the move and his fingers hardly stopped flexing or tapping on the table.

When I began by asking him if he felt especially talented he unhesitatingly replied:

> Yes. I *know* I am good. I can't help knowing it, in myself and when my teacher and other people tell me so. There is no point in denying it.

This was said totally openly and although there was more than a hint of arrogance he was at pains to explain that he did not want to be perceived as arrogant – a conflict which he has not yet fully resolved. He appears to have a strong sense of his own worth and the inner fire is constantly bubbling over, like a volcano sending out sparks and streams of molten heat.

He went on eagerly:

> I think I have a good understanding of music and I am able to get the feel of it emotionally. It is the main thing in my life – it is more than just a job, more a way of living.

When I suggested that the word 'vocation' might fit he agreed, saying: 'Yes, it is a whole commitment.'

Interestingly, he attributes his tremendous vitality in his music to the very fact that he came to it late:

> I think that perhaps if I had come here at the age of 10, for example, I might not have had the same amount of determination. Being at my previous school [also a music school] for a year, where everybody was so much better than me, gave me a *burning incentive* [he stressed these two words] to improve. Already, there, although I could hardly play, people were aware that I had a 'special quality' and I felt their jealousy. But then when I came here I had to start from scratch learning technique – I really had to fight to master it.

As with Tina, the transition to this school was not an easy one for Tom, although for very different reasons. At his previous school he had very quickly learnt that:

> I had to 'muck around' in order to survive and be popular. When I came here I still felt very unsettled, and I did all sorts of stupid things. I felt very unsure of myself, mixed-up and not happy. I was a 'bit crazy' really. . . . Then at the end of my first year here I won a big competition and that in a way boosted my self-confidence. But I know that it made me unpopular.

In fact, at that time, although it did confirm his position musically speaking, he was perceived by many people – both students and staff – as being very difficult, volatile, and arrogant. Yet it seems to me that this arrogance and 'crazy', attention-seeking behaviour was a necessary compensation for his inner feelings of inferiority, especially *vis-à-vis* peers who had been steeped in a musical background practically from the cradle. And as Tom's self-confidence has grown, so his outward arrogance is beginning to lessen, although it is still liable to reassert itself at moments of stress, such as competitions.

Not surprisingly, when I asked him how he felt about these, he immediately admitted to being competitive, speaking about this with an ingenuous mixture of realism and idealism:

> Being king of the heap is a nice feeling! But I also need or *want* to have

> people to look up to; being with lots of good players you lose none of your own talent but gain from the communal glow. I think competitions should be a celebration of excellence – in that way there would be no real envy or destructiveness around.

Although showing many 'manic' tendencies, Tom says that he very rarely feels depressed. However, his need for a compensatory function in the form of a quiet, sure 'centre' is manifested by a profound and very private spiritual life. He spoke about this very hesitatingly and shyly at first, testing the water cautiously:

> It is not something I can talk about to people – most people would just laugh or be sceptical. . . . Although on the surface I know I am outward-going, a great actor, *deep* down I am inward-turned. . . . I turn to God [he looked at me almost fearfully to see how I would react to that statement] . . . I talk to Him often and He has helped me through many bad patches. I really believe in the power of prayer.

He then told me that his mother is religious, but, although he thought that this could have influenced him subtly since he admires his mother, he felt that his religious convictions had come to him more as a result of his own difficulties and needs, dimly at first, at his previous school, but growing ever more real. 'It is an integral part of my music although I couldn't say which is the more important.'

However, he feels that music only becomes emotionally moving, at an indefinable level, when it contains a 'spiritual quality'. But he was emphatic that this does not mean that the performer should be overtly moved as he plays:

> In fact, if I get very worked up and emotional in a concert, it generally ruins the effect of the piece. And even in practice, if I work too emotionally at seven o'clock in the morning, then I'm exhausted for the rest of the day. Inside I must be on fire, but outside stay quite cool.

The tremendous concentration required to remain in control of the sound, coupled with the relaxation needed to allow the inner fire to flow through, is perhaps one of the most difficult tasks of the musician. Either one without the other produces a performance which is unbalanced and therefore slightly less-than-satisfying, however technically brilliant.

Part of the spiritual quality of music also depends on the power of the musician to communicate it. For Tom this urgent desire to 'get across' to an audience is a significant motivating factor.

> When I am on stage the expectancy of the audience really keys me up. I want to *give*. I want to establish a rapport with them.

One of the things he finds helpful is his capacity to give free rein to his imagination in his playing and he continued with enthusiasm:

> For me, sitting at an open Steinway is like painting from the piano. I am creating different layers of sound in order to build up 'atmosphere'.

These childlike qualities of freshness and openness are those that Winnicott talks about:

> Creativity, then, is the retention throughout life of something that belongs properly to infant experience: the ability to create the world. . . . By creative living I mean . . . seeing everything afresh all the time.[5]

In our conversation Tom then paused for a moment before continuing:

> But I feel that giving a recital is like dropping a pebble in the water: it produces ripples and then it's gone. If a performance becomes really magical one can't necessarily recapture it.

So although magical moments can have long-lasting repercussions – one can feel 'changed' by them – one also needs the courage and the humility to let them go, not to attempt to hold on to them, but, instead, have sufficient trust and spontaneity to allow opportunities for further creativity.

I feel that there are links here both with a child's approach to life and with Maslow's description of 'peak-experiences'. Of its nature a peak-experience cannot be forced:

> People during and after peak-experiences characteristically feel lucky, fortunate, graced. A not uncommon reaction is 'I don't deserve this'. Peaks are not planned or brought about by design; they happen. We are 'surprised by joy' [a reference to C. S. Lewis's book of this title]. The reactions of surprise, of unexpectedness, of the 'sweet shock of recognition' are very frequent.[6]

Typical of a peak-experience are feelings of unity, rightness, exhilaration, specialness, richness, transcendence. But what is particularly important to recognize is that, although such an experience may occur infrequently, it is not the prerogative of a chosen few, but can happen to anyone at any time; it performs a fulfilling, integrating function in the development of the individual personality. It is a stepping-stone of wholeness along the path towards fuller individuation – or 'self-actualization', as Maslow calls it.

Intuitively, and yet by means of very hard work, Tom and the other students seem to me to be able to accept and profit by the many different experiences that result from their musical talent.

I would like to end this section with another quotation from Maslow:

> We may define [self-actualization] as an episode, or a spurt in which the powers of the person come together in a particularly efficient and

> intensely enjoyable way, and in which he is more integrated and less split, more open for experience, more idiosyncratic, more perfectly expressive or spontaneous, or fully-functioning, more creative, more humorous, more ego-transcending, more independent of his lower needs, etc. He becomes in these episodes more truly himself, more perfectly actualizing his potentialities, closer to the core of his Being, more fully human.[7]

THE ROLE OF CHAMBER MUSIC IN FACILITATING THE DEVELOPMENT OF THE YOUNG MUSICIAN

In this concluding section I would like to draw upon some of the things that each of the five students said about chamber music and to voice my own feelings about its value. During our conversations together I was struck by the fact that a chamber group provides an exceptional opportunity for its members to grow both as individuals and as members of an organic whole. This, of course, can be viewed from several different angles, but my overwhelming impression, from the manner in which they talked, coupled with my own experience as audience, was that Jungian concepts of the interplay between the conscious and the unconscious were being activated – both intuitively and cognitively. In other words, I feel that they are required to tackle the twin processes of differentiation and integration, for which Jung coined the term 'individuation'.

Jung very firmly states this to be a task of the second half of life, the first half being taken up by the ego-centred process of discovering and asserting one's position in the world.

> As soon as we speak of the collective unconscious we find ourselves in a sphere, and concerned with a problem, which is altogether precluded in the practical analysis of young people or of those who have remained infantile too long.[8]

However, I believe that, because of the specific demands and rewards of their musical talent, these students have already started to tread this path in a variety of ways, albeit not through in-depth analysis.

With all five of them, two factors were particularly striking: namely, the tremendous enthusiasm with which, eyes glowing, they spoke about playing chamber music and, paradoxically, the difficulty, almost incoherence, with which they attempted to explain their understanding of what actually happens when everything 'clicks', transforming a good performance into a uniquely memorable one. These two characteristics seem to me to be similar to those displayed by someone who has had a very powerful mystical experience, or someone who has experienced a moment of profound enlightenment during the course of analysis. In each case the experience is 'beyond words'.

Thus Tina said of her chamber group:

> When the chemistry works it is unspoken. Music is a way of expressing something you can't say.

And Robert, a pianist, said:

> I enjoy chamber music immensely! I find it more relaxing than solo playing and I love communicating with the other players. . . .

Those were relatively 'mundane' reasons, but then he continued in a different tone:

> I can't describe it, but for me, playing in a quartet, for example, is 'pure' music. It is different from anything else. Perhaps it is something to do with the feeling of togetherness, belonging; after all, that is what the word 'ensemble' means.

In this way he tried to explain the inexplicable, very conscious of the fact that it was impossible! However, the feeling of partaking in something of a higher order than normal day-to-day activities was inextricably bound up not only with his love of the music itself but also the sense of belonging to something greater than himself.

One could point out that this can be achieved by taking part in many different groups or team activities – and of course it can, playing an important role in our lives as social beings. However, I cannot get away from my sense that chamber music touches upon something even deeper. The sheer potency of music – both for player and audience – as a means of communication with others and revelation to oneself seems to lie in the very fact that it is 'beyond words'. Music has the power to bypass the conscious mind and appeal directly to emotions which may, until then, have been unconscious; furthermore, I believe that it goes beyond the merely personal to that which is universal.

Patrick, as mentioned earlier, had talked of the excitement of the collective enthusiasm and of the complexities of blending one's individuality with the whole. This point was elaborated on by Tom. He, like Robert, also began by saying 'I enormously enjoy chamber music' and linking this to the fact that, as a pianist, his life tends to be more lonely than that of other instrumentalists, who have more opportunity for orchestral work. (However, this is not necessarily a point of view shared by all pianists, some of whom find chamber groups very threatening.) Tom then tried to analyse what happened when all was *not* going well in a chamber group; for example, when there was a disagreement between members on a point of phrasing or interpretation:

> It is essential that there is give and take between the players. It can be *hard* to say something critical, because we are all equal. But you must have the courage of your convictions and yet be 'discreet' also. It is terribly important to *listen* – to be sensitive to sounds. When there is a

disagreement we try it both ways and the best way generally emerges. In a way you can never express in words exactly what you want in the music, but it emerges in the playing.

This conviction that 'things emerge in the playing' was held by all of them, although it is hardly a 'scientific' resolution! Yet it echoes interestingly what Norbert Brainin, leader of the Amadeus Quartet, had said to Bernard Levin in a BBC2 interview in 1981. When asked by Levin if he ever arbitrated in a disagreement he answered:

> Definitely not! It is a process of discussion whereby something new and *better* comes out of the original two points of view. One must remain *open* and be prepared to be persuaded and yet at the same time try one's best to persuade the others of one's own point of view. Out of this apparent contradiction comes, not a compromise – that is, not a compromise *down* but a compromise *up*.

Later on in the same interview Peter Schidlof said:

> Truth [he hesitated before finding this word] comes out of disagreement through discussion. . . . Sometimes a point of disagreement is left without apparent solution right until the concert itself, when it 'miraculously' seems to solve itself.

This faith in the process, in the work of the spirit in creativity, again has strong links with the faith demanded in the religious sphere – the 'waiting on God' – and also with that needed in analysis or therapy, whereby unconscious processes are awakened and set in motion long before being understood.

It is this interplay between the conscious and the unconscious, between the control which is needed and not-needed, which I also feel has a great deal to do with the fulfilment experienced by chamber group players, and also, by extension, by the audiences.

> By identifying ourselves, however fleetingly, with the creator, we can participate in the integrating process which he has carried out for himself.[9]

The integrating process is no mean task, for it comprises many intertwining layers: for example, first, that of the conscious individual personality with that of the conscious collective whole of the chamber group; second, the dialogue between the personal conscious and the personal unconscious of each player, and, third, the most complex of all, the interaction between each personal unconscious with the collective unconscious of the whole organism. Small wonder then that what happens is extremely difficult to express in words, let alone analyse! However, I would like to reflect a little upon each of these levels in turn.

The need to integrate one's individuality consciously with a greater whole is a rewarding challenge, but it can also feel like a threat or a responsibility. It was this last factor that prompted Elizabeth, who is a cellist, to say that, although she loved chamber music:

> I am much more nervous in quartets than for solo work because I am always afraid of letting the others down.

And Tina voiced another reservation:

> It is super *if it is working*. But otherwise it can be very difficult. Ideally, one must try to get rid of 'personalities'; but if, for example, I am playing first violin, I don't want to have to give in all the time in disagreements. So I *will* assert myself. One can reach a situation of deadlock.

She then cited an example when the chemistry hadn't worked, saying:

> It was utterly exhausting. I came away completely cold, as if I hadn't really played.

The opposite of this draining experience is what Hester Norton describes in her book *The Art of String Quartet Playing*:

> The first requisite for a good ensemble is that each player should have a *sense of the whole* [author's italics]. This he can only feel by *listening to the others* [author's italics]. . . . If he listens well and feels the whole, he will know in his own mind *the meaning of his part* [my italics]; then he will listen to himself more critically to be sure the meaning is clear to the listener. His own playing will ripen with this experience.[10]

Thus, this sensitivity both to his own role and to that of the others is one of the factors which enables a player to change and therefore develop.

However, in order to achieve this personal sense of well-being or strength, each individual needs to be in constant touch with the unconscious part of himself. This, of course, is one of the tasks of analysis, but it can also be achieved by other means. All the students I talked with showed a considerable awareness of the 'otherness' inherent in themselves and in life in general, whether they described it in visual or in spiritual terms. That is, they had all felt the pull of their unconscious and instinctively recognized its importance in their playing.

Robert made the point that one of the most difficult things to express in music is:

> Simplicity. Because the moment you start trying to play 'simply' it isn't simple any more!

In order to get round this he allows visual images to 'flow to the surface'. He stressed the importance of drawing on all human emotions, however long-forgotten:

> I think I am very lucky. I have already had a lot of different experiences – I've seen quite a lot of life. I feel I have it 'in' me to express, for example, *pain* in my music.

And after the hard, conscious effort of practising and working on a piece had been accomplished, when the time comes for performance, he said:

> I always go into another gear. I have two souls: with one I remain cool, but with the other I abandon myself to the music.

Jung has written extensively about the relationship between the conscious and unconscious aspects of the mind, both of which, he says, are equally important and need to be 'heard'.

> Conscious and unconscious do not make a whole when one of them is suppressed or ignored by the other. . . . Both are aspects of life. . . . This means open conflict and open collaboration at once. That, evidently, is the way human life should be. It is the old game of hammer and anvil: between them the patient iron is forged into an indestructible whole, an 'individual'.[11]

In his book *Music and Communication* Terence McLaughlin explores in a variety of interesting ways some of the physical bases for the patterns of tension and resolution which contribute to giving meaning to music. He also examines why we should find so satisfying the fact that music has the power to express several different things at once:

> The reason lies in the ability of music, and the other arts, to appeal simultaneously to different *levels* of our personality, so that we are made aware, at one and the same time, of intellectual, emotional and bodily patterns. . . . Not all of the patterns will be associated with conscious experiences: there will also be the analogues of unconscious and forgotten events, and the restatement of these, in synthesis with the conscious ones, can account for the 'mysterious' moving quality of music, and the difficulty that many people find in putting the experience of music into words.[12]

I think it is possible to differentiate the unconscious events into two types – those belonging purely to the personal and others which belong to the deeper layers of common human experience which Jung called the 'collective unconscious'.

This is the third dimension which it seems to me is present when a chamber group is 'at one' with itself and which communicates itself through their playing to the audience. It is almost impossible to describe in concrete terms because, of its essence, it springs from the spiritual, non-concrete, indefinable part of our being. How can one 'explain' the touching and awakening, for however brief a moment, of one person's unconscious, let alone his transitory, but deeply moving, understanding of a greater collective unconscious? Even Jung, who wrote so much on this subject, found it difficult to be precise and, indeed, has often been criticized for this.

However, it was this quality of emotional and mental contact that Robert was talking about when he said:

> If I manage to communicate with even one person in the audience for only ten seconds it is all worth it!

And Hester Norton uses an expressive analogy when she is giving practical advice on the art of quartet playing:

> Think of the forward motion of music as of a river. Tempo, as we shall see, is the current. Each player should feel his voice a tributary stream winding in and out again, part of a greater whole. He must *enter without beginning* and *cease without stopping*. He should feel as though the whole were emanating *from his own mind*, only his fingers being limited to his particular instrument [author's italics].[13]

The idea of entering without beginning and ceasing without stopping echoes for me the knowledge that my roots, both physical and psychic, are inextricably embedded in the past and, as such, affect me in the present; and, similarly, that my 'being' now will form part of the matrix for generations in the future. That this is obvious on a physical level is generally acknowledged, but not everybody would accept in on a psychological or spiritual level. The greater part of our lives is spent in fairly mundane, conscious activities, so that the occurrence of 'magical' moments which transcend the everyday are all the more to be treasured, and, if possible, used for further growth.

All my five students had, as part of a chamber group, once or twice experienced this momentous feeling of wholeness, recognizing its value, but also accepting the fact that it does not happen often. However, I would like to conclude with the thought that the living 'mandala symbol', which a chamber group can become, is one in which they are fortunate to be able to participate again and again, thereby enhancing their awareness of themselves and of others and enabling them to grow both as musicians and as individuals.

NOTES

1 R. Shuter-Dyson, 'Musical giftedness', in J. Freeman (ed.), *The Psychology of Gifted Children* (London: Wiley, 1985).
2 For convenience in this chapter I use the masculine pronoun to refer to both male and female musicians.
3 D. W. Winnicott, *Playing and Reality* (Harmondsworth: Penguin, 1974).

4 C. G. Jung, *Collected Works*, vol. 6 (London: Routledge & Kegan Paul, 1984), p. 332.
5 D. W. Winnicott, *Home is Where We Start From* (Harmondsworth: Pelican, 1986), pp. 40–1.
6 A. H. Maslow, *Toward a Psychology of Being* (New York: Van Nostrand, 1968), p. 113.
7 Ibid., p. 97.
8 C. G. Jung, 'The Psychology of the Unconscious' *Collected Works*, vol. 7 (London: Routledge & Kegan Paul, 1953), pp. 72–3.
9 A. Storr, *The Dynamics of Creation* (Harmondsworth: Pelican, 1986), p. 291.
10 H. Norton, *The Art of String Quartet Playing* (London: Gollancz, 1963), pp. 22–4.
11 C. G. Jung, 'Archetypes and the collective unconscious', *Collected Works*, vol. 9 (London: Routledge & Kegan Paul, 1975), p. 288.
12 T. McLaughlin, *Music and Communication* (London: Faber, 1970), p. 103.
13 H. Norton, op. cit., p. 23.

BIBLIOGRAPHY

Blos, P. (1962) *On Adolescence*, New York: Free Press.

Buckroyd, J. (1987) 'Why do dancers dance?', *Dancing Times.*

Butler, C. (1986) *Exploring Anxiety in the Musician & Performing Anxiety in the Music Student*, dissertation submitted for the Certificate in Student Counselling, University of London, Department of Extra-Mural Studies.

Freeman, J. (ed.)(1985) *The Psychology of Gifted Children*, London: Wiley.

Jung, C.G. (1953) *Two Essays on Analytical Psychology, Collected Works*, vol. 7, London: Routledge & Kegan Paul.

—— (1959) *The Archetypes and the Collective Unconscious, Collected Works*, vol. 9, part 1, London: Routledge & Kegan Paul.

—— (1971) *Psychological Types, Collected Works*, vol. 6, London: Routledge & Kegan Paul.

McLaughin, T. (1970) *Music and Communication*, London: Faber.

Maslow, A.H. (1968) *Toward a Psychology of Being*, New York: Van Nostrand.

Menuhin, Y. (1977) *Unfinished Journey*, London: Macdonald & Jane's.

Noonan, E. (1983) *Counselling Young People*, London: Methuen.

Norton, H. (1963) *The Art of String Quartet Playing*, London: Gollancz.

Storr, A. (1963) *The Integrity of the Personality*, Harmondsworth: Pelican.

—— (1986) *The Dynamics of Creation*, Harmondsworth: Pelican.

Winnicott, D.W. (1970) *The Child, the Family and the Outside World*, Harmondsworth: Pelican.

—— (1986) *Home is Where We Start From*, Harmondsworth: Pelican.

Chapter 9

Mirrors on girls and maths

Ena Blyth

It is not for everyone, said Freud,[1] to be continuously investigating the dark ravines of the unconscious, with only an occasional glance at the light of day. Nor is it for everyone to move in the world of mathematics with pleasure or understanding. The look of panic on a child's face during a maths lesson hints at a terror more in keeping with Freud's dark ravines than with a modern classroom. There are people who retain a lasting horror of mathematics. And yet there are others who take pleasure in its challenges.

In the classroom, a child may sit silent and withdrawn. She may look frightened. She may say she is bored. She may, if she finds courage, attempt to disrupt the class. Only the most sophisticated children will find it possible to say, with surprising vehemence, that they hate maths, that they loathe it. A teacher, who is not a mathematician, describes maths panic vividly:

> It's just like being lost. There's nobody you recognize. You don't know where you're going, you don't know where you've been. There's nothing on that page that you can actually relate to. Nothing at all.

Something about the language of mathematics can induce this feeling of loss of self. It takes children back to the black and white world of very early childhood, Melanie Klein's paranoid-schizoid position. Maths often seems a black and white subject. It is either right or wrong. This sense of absoluteness, implying the possibility of absolute failure if absolute success is not achieved, links it unconsciously to very primitive states.

A degree in mathematics does not by any means give immunity from maths panic. In spite of their skills, maths teachers may experience at times that sense of terror. But for the most part we have learnt to handle it. We have made a successful relationship with mathematics, within which we can tolerate the frustration of feeling lost at times. It is that capacity, to make a relationship with mathematics, that seems to distinguish those who are able to pursue it with understanding and enjoyment from those who cannot.

This paper looks at the emotional response to mathematics of girls and women who have successfully made that relationship. As opposed to Laurie Buxton's study,[2] which looked at negative feelings, the aim of this study is to explore positive feelings towards mathematics. I have based my study on interviews and discussions both with teachers in the maths department of a girls' school and with a group of sixth-form pupils, most of whom were in the first year of an A-level maths course.

My interviews were unstructured. In them I tried to find out what mathematically able girls and women felt about the subject. I wondered why they had chosen to study mathematics, and what early memories they could recall which might have led to their choice. I wondered too what encouragement or support, if any, they had received from their parents, their families, or their primary schools.

The two writers on psychoanalysis who speak to me most strongly are Winnicott and Kohut. In this study I have looked at the material through the mirror of my ideas about their work. But I have tried to follow where the teachers and girls have led. After a case history and some thoughts about creativity, I look at family relationships, then at school experiences, and then in greater detail at the reasons why the women I spoke to chose careers in mathematics. The emphasis of the whole study is on feelings, and I finish with an account of feelings towards numbers themselves, the building blocks of mathematics.

By way of a preface, I begin with an account of responses to the idea of infinity. It reflects my own feelings about the infinite nature of the subject of this paper.

INFINITY

Infinity is implicit in mathematics. Mathematics is based on numbers, and numbers go on for ever.

A teacher recalls her feelings about infinity:

> It was all part of this idea that the whole subject of mathematics was huge in various senses. It was huge because it dealt with some huge numbers. It was part of the mysteriousness. You couldn't say what infinity was. I liked it. It still does fascinate me.

But not everyone is fascinated by infinity, particularly as a child. Another teacher, who later made a very creative relationship with mathematics, remembers her first feelings about infinity:

> When I first thought about infinity it meant something just going on for ever. At the time, I perceived it in terms of the universe just going on for ever. It really used to worry me, it used to frighten me, the thought of this universe never ending. I just could not perceive it. I realized the limitation on our minds. I remember lying awake at night just worrying about that. And I linked that to death. I was quite young then. I remember it was something that worried me as much as realizing my parents' mortality, that they were going to die. I felt the same way about the infinity of space. I suppose they were the two things that were outside my own experience.

And a sixth-form A-level student writes about what she feels about infinity now:

> I find it impossible to accept the concept of infinity. How can something go on for ever? I find the hardest concept to grasp is that the universe has no boundary. It is not possible for me to imagine anything so massive and completely impossible to measure.

Infinity implies boundlessness. And loss of boundaries can be very frightening. It may also put people in touch with unconscious feeling states which are very primitive. Matte Blanco[3] has used the mathematical logic of infinite sets to explain the logic of the unconscious. He describes the infinite feeling states of very early childhood. Omnipotence, total helplessness, terror, idealization, grief, these are all primitive feelings in which there are no boundaries. The implicit infinity of mathematics may put some people powerfully in touch with those parts of themselves they find too threatening. Maths panic, itself an infinite state, may be a response to this.

On the other hand, all creative work occurs on or beyond the boundary. Creativity is a breaking of boundaries in order to establish new forms, new boundaries. The history of mathematics itself shows how each great mathematician has broken with the boundaries of his predecessor and created a new mathematical world. Pythagoras himself believed infinity was part of the original act of creation. The first unit, the heaven, took in the infinite, and produced the universe. It is this capacity to use boundaries, and to free oneself from them, that distinguishes the creative mind. Newton paid tribute to the boundaries of others. 'If I have seen further it is by standing on ye sholders of Giants'.[4]

Infinity is therefore implicit in creativity. If boundaries can be broken, infinite possibilities present themselves. I believe infinity is a key to creativity. Creative people have a capacity to remain in touch with the primitive black and white world of early childhood, and its infinite feeling states, and to integrate these with the world of boundaries. I see creativity as the imagination, oscillating between the finite and the infinite, in an attempt to find form. And for some people mathematics can provide this.

Sixteen-year-old girls who have made a creative link with mathematics describe their feelings about infinity.

> I think of infinity as endless waves resulting from a stone thrown into water. The ripples carry on and on.

> I have some idea of infinity being like obscurity, of not having control of it, of being frightened. It's like history. There's so much before us, so much will come after.

> Even though I don't think of infinity as a number, I do think of it as even.

> I can imagine space growing infinitely big, but not at any one instant

being so. I once wrote a story about a man walking round a circular corridor, shaped like a ring. It was a nightmare for him when he realized.

Infinity is a useful name people give to things they don't understand, or can't explain. It's like qualities in people that never stop. Not like a machine which breaks down. Energy in your body is infinite. I feel I can never get physically exhausted. I eat, and energy is restored. I carry on and on.

Infinity is an endless source. It is something going outwards. It is something getting smaller and smaller. It is impossible to imagine.

I remember sitting in the back of the car, and sometimes if I could count to three in a special mood it worked really strangely, and had to do with infinity. We don't know anything about comparative size. Our solar system, or galaxy, could be a tiny bit of dust in another world.

It's like the chicken and the egg, which came first? Imagination is infinite.

I think of infinity in the form of a circle. I think of it as a ring that you can follow round without beginning or end.

I can believe in infinity when I am standing between two opposite mirrors and I see my reflection repeated as far as I can define it.

A CASE HISTORY

Anna is in her middle twenties. She has a maths degree, and began teaching soon after leaving university. She is a spontaneous and original teacher, who very much enjoys maths. She finds maths 'so exciting and beautiful' that she feels frustrated when she cannot share it with her boyfriend. He is not a mathematician.

Anna's earliest memory is of always being put second to a boy in primary school. They sat in rows, in order of ability, and, however hard she tried, the teacher always put the boy first and Anna second. She felt it to be a great injustice because she believed she was cleverer than he was. It was the first thing she recalled when she talked about her childhood.

Later, in her last year in the junior school, when the children were being given different assignments, another boy was given more challenging and more interesting work than she was.

> He was treated quite specially. And that used to rile me. I was never given the sort of thing that he was given in the first place. Nobody gave me a chance. The teacher would give him some quite advanced stuff, not straightforward, and yet I wasn't given a chance. I resented that.

The problem disappeared when she went to secondary school, because she was then with girls only. They were clever girls. It was in the days of the 11-plus, and the school was the top school in the area. Anna recognized that some girls were more able than she was, but the feeling of resentment and the sense of competition stopped. She felt she was being treated more fairly.

At this stage she did not think of herself as particularly good at maths, though she was in the top division. In the third year of secondary school she began to worry about some exams.

> There were things I didn't understand. My father had always been very keen on maths. In fact quite a lot of the time before that he'd been trying to encourage me with it, and saying what a good subject it was. And I was arguing with him, and saying that French was actually more interesting. He definitely loved maths. He always used to help me anyway, and was willing to spend time doing maths with me.
>
> I remember before this particular set of exams he sat down with me, and he spent a long time going over everything. I did the exams feeling more confident. And it turned out I came first or second in the whole class. And this quite surprised me. And I can remember being quite shocked when the teacher took me aside afterwards to say that. I couldn't believe it really. And I thought, perhaps Dad's right, perhaps I am good at it.

Later still, after a move to a different school, where the standard was generally lower, another teacher recognized her talent.

> I found myself excelling more in things that I hadn't felt I was particularly good at. And the teacher noticed very early on.

She thought at the time that it was because she was among less able girls.

> I was quite surprised still, which is funny because all the time I must have been given a lot of encouragement, and been told that I was pretty good. But I didn't really believe it until this happened, and I was getting 95 per cent on O-level papers.

Then Anna said

> I'm sure that if I hadn't had all that feedback I wouldn't necessarily have gone in for it. It was definitely in my case an example of all the positive feedback giving me more confidence and more pleasure in it, because I knew it was something I could succeed at, and I could do well at.

Anna spoke about her father's strong influence. He had loved mathematical problems of all sorts. He used to give her problems to solve, even those he could not do himself. She remembered being on a family holiday, and sitting with him on the beach, trying to work out some mathematical puzzles. She was the eldest of three children, and the only child who shared his interest.

> There was an awful lot of time we spent together, doing things like that.

There was quite a close bond between us, the fact that we both liked doing maths.

In adolescence she had argued with him about her preference for French. Because of the closeness of the bond between them, arguing with him was one way of asserting her independence.

What finally drew her to maths was not just her father but also the encouragement from school. It gave her confidence, and became a challenge. So she went to university to read mathematics, the first member of her family to go to university.

My dream would be to be a good mathematician doing research, but I know I'm not that good. I'm not good enough for that.

This dream was with her all through her university career. She felt that to be good at maths was intellectually rewarding, but that it also gave her status. Other people would admire her. It was unusual for a girl to study maths.

At the end of her first year at university, she met and fell in love with a man in the third year who was generally regarded to be a maths genius. He achieved firsts, in spite of not working hard.

He was really clever. And I admired him so much. That was exactly what I would have liked to have been. I wanted to be like him, so I started adopting his approach to it. I desperately wanted to be like him.

After he had taken his degree he moved to another university to do his PhD. Anna wanted so much to be associated with someone who was doing a PhD in maths that she interrupted her course, and resumed it at his new university in order to be with him.

It was just too much. It was wonderful, the thought of getting some kind of appreciation from him as well. He would be there to praise me if I could do things and understood. And I would listen to what he was learning about and try and get involved with it. It was all again to raise my self-esteem and the esteem of others.

But she did not in fact work very hard, and she did not get a first-class degree. Before the end of her course she and the gifted mathematician split up.

During the last six months of her course she nevertheless became very involved in her dissertation. She enjoyed working on it, and thought it might be good. But she was scared when she finally handed it in. Some of the proofs were her own. She had not been able to find any in the literature. She feared that her work might be trivial, too basic. But it was commended. A lecturer took her aside afterwards, and told her that she had done a really original piece of work. She was very excited.

When he said that to me it was just wonderful, because it made me feel

> that what I had felt about it was right. I felt I really got something out of doing it, my own piece of work, and I did do bits of original maths in it.

Anna became more confident of her ability after this experience. She had used maths creatively. She is now taking it even further by taking an MSc in the subject.

Anna's story illustrates two needs of a talented child. One is to be recognized and the other is to find someone with the same talent to idealize. When these needs were not met, she felt angry and frustrated. But when she found them, in her father, and in her boyfriend, she shared in their skills in order to develop her own.

CREATIVITY

Anna's search, both for someone to recognize her and for someone to idealize, suggests a link with the work of Kohut[5] on the development of the self.

Kohut shows that a small child needs two different types of relationship in order to develop a sense of himself as a person, a sense of his own individuality. These are relationships, in Kohut's terminology, to self-objects. A child needs a mirroring self-object, and he needs an idealized self-object.

At the early stages of development, the mirroring self-object is likely to be an empathic mother who understands her baby's feelings. If she is able to contain them, and reflect them back to him, she gives them meaning for him. He learns through her to make sense of his feeling world.

Kohut's mirroring self-object has much in common with the later stages of Winnicott's[6] good-enough mother. At first, the good-enough mother provides an environment for her baby that protects him from too much disruption. He needs to be allowed to be, simply to exist. Any impingement, of hunger or of pain, for example, interrupts this continuity, and he is forced to react to the stimulus. If his mother can keep the impingements to a level the baby can tolerate, he learns, by repeatedly surviving the interruptions, that he has continuity, and that he exists. And so a sense of himself as separate from his environment begins to develop. At this stage mirroring begins. He begins an emotional dialogue between himself and the world. In her mirroring response, the good-enough mother makes sense of his feelings for him. The emphasis at the earliest stage is on the mother's face. This is a move away from the breast, central to the work of Melanie Klein.

Kohut shows that the need for mirroring continues well after the first few months. In order to create himself a small child needs reflection from an empathic parent. Part of mirroring is recognition. The mirror needs both to recognize and to reflect back.

In addition to the mirror, a child also needs someone he can idealize. To begin with he feels merged with this person, and shares in his power. This is the stage of omnipotence, the stage of Kohut's grandiose self. Later, as he becomes more aware of separation, he wants to be like his ideal, to identify with him. And he needs recognition from his ideal for his own talents and skills.

Both parents may at any time take either role. But both types of relationship are necessary for a child to establish a sturdy sense of self-esteem, to create himself. If he does so, he has made the first and most important step towards a creative life. 'Kohut's baby is born strong, not weak.'[7]

Kohut[8] describes the rage and frustration that follow when the self-objects fail and there is narcissistic injury. Anna's resentment when her primary school teacher failed to recognize her has echoes of this early anger. Kohut describes too how patients whose needs have not been adequately met as children become more creative as they work through these needs in analysis.

As the child develops, he needs both objects in order to be creative. He needs to make creative links with the ideal for the growth of his own individuality. But he still needs the mirror to record and reflect back to him each creative new move between himself and his ideal. A simple image would be of a small child, needing his mother to smile while his father is helping him to walk.

I see the triangle between the small child, his mirror, and his ideal, as creative space. In that space the child at first creates himself. Later, when the first self-objects have become internalized, the space remains for other creative activity. But the need for recognition and for an ideal remains. The need is strong through all the learning processes, and is important, I believe, in education. Later it exists in a modified form in adult life. Friends, colleagues, partners become mirrors. A career or leisure activity may become an ideal.

I believe too that the first triangle is also the source of envy. My experience does not suggest, as Melanie Klein[9] does, that envy is basically innate. I see it occurring when there is a failure in the creative relationship between a child and his ideal. If a child feels his own talent remains unrecognized and his creativity is frustrated, he will use his energy to create an envied object instead. Envy breeds where creativity has failed.

It may be useful to look at the development of mathematical ability as part of the creative activity within the triangle. If the talent for maths is not recognized early enough or if there is nobody with the talent for the child to idealize, the talent may simply die. Or it may lie so securely hidden that it remains undiscovered.

Research in America in 1964 showed that a group of boys whose fathers had been absent during their early childhood were later less mathematically able than other boys of their age.[10] It would suggest that part of the triangle was missing for them at an important stage.

The anger that mathematics often stirs up may be related to what Kohut describes as narcissistic rage following a failure by the self-objects. If the talent cannot be used creatively, it becomes a source of envy, and later of self-envy, which leads to spoiling and self-denigration. The complacency with which women sometimes say how hopeless they are at maths hints at a strong drive to disowning whatever ability they may have.

FAMILY RELATIONSHIPS

The first creative triangle occurs in the family. Before children meet teachers, they meet parents. And their first mathematical experiences will be at home and not at school. For this reason I was interested in what girls felt about their families.

The girls' parents were predominantly middle class and in professional careers. In several cases both parents had professional jobs. They attended regularly at parents' evenings at the school, and they showed interest and involvement in their daughters' work. One girl was the daughter of two doctors, another of two actors. The parents of a third were both philosophers. Among the other parents were more doctors, an architect, an accountant, an artist, a businessman, and an English teacher.

What came across very strongly in the interviews was the warmth of feeling expressed by the girls towards their parents. It surprised me. I had expected among the group to find some signs of irritation, to find some girls who were more rebellious.

The girls spoke of having discussed their choices of A-level subjects with their parents, and of being encouraged in their work, without, it seemed, being under undue pressure from home to achieve.

One girl spoke with great pleasure of being able to share her maths with her mother, who had been re-training to be a maths teacher. There seemed to be a strong bond between them. She denied that her mother had had any influence on her choice of A-level subjects. But when I said that maths, Greek, physics, and art were an unusual combination, she said with warmth that her mother thought the subjects were all pure,

> all clear, all very logical and clear, and they come together in this purity. My Mum always insists that it has to have some point where it all meets; they're very pure subjects.

This girl is the elder of two daughters. At primary school she always identified with the boys, and all her friends were boys. During her interview with me she made a point of telling me that her interest in maths probably stemmed from her friendships with boys at that time.

But relationships with fathers seemed important in more cases. Maths seemed to provide a bond between father and daughter. Anna's strong attachment to her father has already been described. Another teacher thought she might have studied maths partly because of her father. He was more interested in maths than her mother.

> I was always closer to my Dad anyway, always wanting to get his approval, as well as Mum's, but to a greater extent with Dad, whether or not that affected me, in the sense he could do maths, and so I felt I ought to be able to do maths.

She remembered a time when he had helped her, early in the morning while he was shaving, because she was worried about some homework. Ironically, she said, he had got the answers wrong, but she did not mind because she had got her work done on time. She admitted too to having been very competitive with her older brother, who was not good at figures and had a block about arithmetic.

The choice of maths for one girl in the group seemed linked to her need to surprise and impress her parents. She was the eldest of five children, and had always been very competitive with a brother who was a year younger than she was. She spoke with delight of the attention she was given in the family for being the mathematical one while her brother had settled for the arts.

> Whereas a boy should be good at science and maths, and the girls should be good at arts, it's the other way round in our family. It's like an achievement really. My father and my uncles are proud of my interest in maths. And my parents are always boasting in front of friends that I like maths.

Another girl spoke of her father helping her with her homework, even though her mother was good at maths.

> I find I'm turning more and more to my Dad as it goes on. If I'm not quite sure of something he can explain it to me. He understands better, and he's more patient than Mum is.

She said her father enjoyed helping her.

> He wants me to understand it, and he can shout his head off, but I don't let that worry me. The other day, on the way here, he parked the car in the road for twenty minutes while he was explaining this question on the way to school. I do like learning from him.

Another girl who also seemed to have a close bond with her father spoke of being encouraged to do science by him because of his interest. He was a doctor. She said she had at first liked her father's encouragement, but then became annoyed because she feared he was pushing her.

> I was a bit afraid I would do something because someone else wanted me to do it rather than that I wanted to do it.

She admitted to 'being scared' that she would not be independent. In fact, though she insisted to her father that she was not going to be a doctor, she is doing maths, physics, and chemistry in the sixth form. What came across as she spoke was a strong affection for her father, within which she was trying, and succeeding, to establish her own identity. And she felt pride in her growing independence.

To be 'the bright one' in the family was a theme in another girl's feelings about herself and her parents. 'My parents thought I was the intelligent one, and they encouraged me.' No one in her family was mathematical. An older brother and sister had not distinguished themselves academically. She seemed to respond to her parents' expectations and enjoy them.

When I looked at the girls' and teachers' positions in their families, I was struck by some curious facts. Of eleven bright A-level students, seven were the eldest children in their families. Of five maths teachers, four were the eldest children in their families. Of a total of sixteen mathematically able girls and women, eleven were first-born children. There were no only children at all. Two girls were the eldest of five, two girls and one teacher were the eldest of four, and one teacher was the eldest of three children.

Several questions remain with me. A first-born child is the child on whom parents learn. How much do the impingements of this particular experience lead to precocious and abstract intellectual development as a defensive measure?[11] First-born children often have difficult births. Is this experience, again, an incentive to abstract thinking? First-born children will identify more strongly with their parents, and later with adults, than others. What effect does this have? Does the trauma for first-born children of the subsequent births of their younger brothers and sisters, particularly in large families, lead to a need to abstract and order this experience; and is mathematical thinking one way of doing this? Addition, for first-born children, can be a real and painful experience. An image from one of the teachers seems to illustrate this. She was a member of a family of five. Her association to the numeral five was that it was a frustrating, pregnant woman.

Finally, how much does the eldest girl in the family need to find common links with her father that exclude both her mother and her brothers and sisters? Mathematics, still regarded as an unusual skill for a girl, may be a way of doing this. She may be responding too to what her father is seeking in his first-born child, a reflection of his own mathematical ability.

PRIMARY SCHOOL EXPERIENCES

The girls' memories of primary school showed evidence of early positive mirroring.

> Maths was really good fun. Half the point was impressing the teacher. I used to love getting the work back, that's the whole pleasure. I think it's partly because you want to impress someone. I wanted to know I was good at something.
>
> I had a really good teacher. We had maths every morning, an hour of it, and she wanted us to do it. She was very serious about it. It was an important subject to us. I enjoyed it because I could do it.

One girl said that in her primary school class everyone had been enthusiastic about maths straightaway. They had had a good teacher. She could remember doing fractions and really enjoying them. 'I used to look forward to the lessons because I could actually do the work.' Another said that all she could remember about primary school was that she had been good at long division.

One of the teachers recalled during her interview with me that she had not learnt from her mother until much later that her junior school teacher had always believed that she would one day do a maths degree. She herself had not thought of herself as being very good at maths. But she did in fact go on to take a maths degree. So some early recognition, perhaps not adequately mirrored back to her at the time, had sown seeds which led back to maths later.

A mother's mirroring role, supporting work at school, came up in the following memory:

> In Infants I used to come home if we'd done something new, and I would think a bit further ahead, and I'd say 'We've done this, Mum, but can you show me how you do it a bit further on'. That meant that when we did it at school I'd already done it because I was interested.

It may also be possible to use a friend as a mirror. Two girls from the same primary school recalled enjoying doing things together, without any element of competition.

> We always went really fast. It was the one lesson that we really worked in, We always went as fast as we could.

Most vivid of all was a girl who said, with great animation,

> I remember in primary school enjoying maths. I remember beginning to enjoy it because I was good at it. I remember a teacher told me 'Oh, you're good at maths', and then suddenly I really loved it. I think I only decided I liked it because I was told I was good at it.

What comes across so strikingly in this last account is the power of the mirror to recognize, to reflect, and then to give back something that was not consciously there before.

The particular mathematical topics and insights that the girls remembered most clearly showed their pleasure in puzzling over relationships, and their delight when they made sense of them.

> I was amazed that if you did two times six, then six times two, it came to the same thing. I remember that really amazing me.

Another early memory was of learning to add. After talking quite vividly about the satisfaction of seeing how things fitted, seeing the relationships between things, a girl said,

> I've always been able to do it. Even when you're learning to add. You've got two numbers, and you make them into special little columns, and you have your units and you have your tens, and you bring things down in something that does not seem to be related, and you get an answer that is related to the first two numbers.

The way she described this memory suggested a strong emotional content. I wondered whether she was recalling an early unconscious experience of relating maths to relationships at home. For her, addition seemed to symbolize the relationship between her parents, and her own arrival in the family.

Another girl, talking about fractions, said she remembered thinking '*How* do I do those?' But she had had a teacher who

> made us understand everything, and we could apply them, add them and subtract them, and divide them, whatever, and generally manipulate them. It's the achievement factor again. It's encouraging.

Fractions came up as a good memory for another girl too.

> I loved it when I understood fractions, because they did seem difficult. And now it turns out that a lot of people find fractions difficult.

She then went on to describe, with animation, why she thought they were difficult.

> You know when you're taught it, and they give you a big circle, and quarters, and eighths, and sixteenths, they're all fine. It's the other ones, the thirds, and the fifths, there's no way you can actually draw them and you get really frightened about them.

I wondered whether at an unconscious level she may have seen the circle as the family, and subsequent divisions were a symbolic way of looking at creation, and of generations reproducing themselves.

It is perhaps this ability to use maths symbolically to puzzle over family relationships, and to explain them, that distinguishes some of those who achieve in the subject from those who do not. At an early unconscious level some relationship between the family puzzle and the maths puzzle seems to be necessary.

SIXTH-FORM EXPERIENCES

No single clear theme emerged when the girls talked about their feelings about maths in the sixth form. They seemed to enjoy its structure, they enjoyed understanding how things fitted – a development, it seemed, from the interest in relationships in primary school – and they enjoyed manipulating, which seemed a sophisticated way of describing play. Perhaps most strongly of all, they enjoyed finding answers.

Most of the girls in the group had chosen maths as one of their A-level subjects because they enjoyed it. One girl said:

> I like it, and I think I'm quite good at it, and anything you enjoy and feel you're secure at you should continue.

Another girl, describing particular aspects of mathematics, said she liked what was abstract. She enjoyed manipulating and solving, 'tidying things up, working with shapes, with circles and triangles, particularly with circles.'

A pleasure in manipulating was shared by several girls. They spoke particularly of their pleasure in algebra.

> I've never thought of maths as related. That's why I like algebra better than geometry.

Another said:

> I like the way things work out. I like playing with numbers, I like shifting things around.

She added that it 'felt so good' when she had solved a difficult problem. Another girl enjoyed being able to resolve things, 'seeing how things work, all the theories work in with each other'.

A girl who had chosen to do maths because it was her favourite subject – and easier than Greek and physics, her other academic subjects – said:

> One thing that's nice is that you know what you've got to do and where you're going. It's got a structure in a way. It's also nice the way it's all so formal and it all fits together. I don't like it for any useful reason. It just appeals to me.

This girl, and several others, said they enjoyed the abstractness of maths. They preferred maths to physics for this reason. One girl said:

> I find it's less to do with anything, it's a bit more detached than physics. It's more relaxing.

But she admitted that she sometimes found maths hard. And then, when she was stuck with a problem, the detachment was irritating.

> You can't relate any of the figures to anything, you can't see any point to anything, and that's a bit annoying. I think it just depends on the sort of mood I'm in.

Another girl said she liked maths because she could do it without getting too involved, as she did in English or music.

> I can do it, and I can get it out of the way. I can never do that with English.

This girl, whose other A-level subjects were English, physics, and music, spoke imaginatively about the links between problem-solving in maths and getting at the meaning of a poem in English. A poem was

> like a problem, and you're piecing bits together. If you read a poem, there's some kind of core meaning you've got to grasp, and the rest is like a muff around it. You've got to get through to the core.

Her enjoyment came from finding out what the core was. This pleasure she described as

> always looking at what people are really meaning, in any situation, and what they're really saying, forget all the fluff.

Perhaps this is the great satisfaction many people find in mathematics. There is no fluff. It speaks simply and clearly to those who understand its language. This same girl related this pleasure to music too, which she found very mathematical in its structure.

> Even a Mozart string quartet, it's so balanced, and each little bit coming and doing its little part, and it sort of fits together. Like a puzzle that fits into place.

But some girls said they were frustrated when they had difficulties with their work.

> I get depressed. I hate it. It's really frustrating. It makes me feel thick at times.

> I just get very annoyed when I keep on getting the wrong answer. It's very nice when I eventually get the right answer.

> There are times in maths when you *want* to be told the right answer.

This last girl said that maths lost the quality of play for her when she did not get the answer for a long time. Then she got angry with herself. But another girl said firmly that she did not get frustrated if she had difficulty. Her satisfaction came both from struggling to achieve the right answer, and from getting it.

> It depends what kind of a person you are, if you're quite a secure person. A lot of people can't cope with not being able to get things right.

It was clear from all the interviews that getting things right did add greatly to the girls' pleasure in the subject.

> One of the nice things about maths is that you get an answer in the end. In some things you don't.

> It's just really good fun. You can actually get answers to hard questions.

> It's just nice when you finally do understand something, to be able to apply it, and see it come out right. Because you know you've got it right, which is something you're never quite sure with things like essay writing. You're never quite sure how well you're doing.

> In English there's no right and wrong. In maths it's got to be right, it's got to fit together in a special structure in order for it to work. I love that.

It seemed from what they said that maths had itself become a mirror for most of them, in which they were able to see their own success. A maths problem gives back an answer. If the answer is right, it mirrors back a smiling face. Each success reflected back to them their own ability.

TEACHERS

My interviews with the teachers revealed complex reasons for their choice of careers in mathematics.

Anna's pursuit of mathematics, which I have already described, has been a search for the development of a creative talent, in order to establish a stronger sense of her own identity.

Another teacher, Sally, has had a more complex and frustrating relationship with mathematics. She seems to have made it an idealized object, with which she has had some difficulty in establishing a satisfying creative link. But her persistence comes over strongly none the less.

Sally has been teaching maths for several years. She has a degree in mathematics and philosophy, and, like Anna, she is doing a further degree in mathematical education. She was a clever girl at school. Being good at exams gave her status. As a younger child she had always found maths easy. She said she could do it 'curled up in an armchair, without great mental preparation'. She wondered whether she had liked it because she was lazy. In the sixth form she had found applied maths hard, and though she had achieved – with luck, she thought – a good grade at A-level, she later wondered whether it would have been better if she had failed then, and not attempted to read it at university. But she admitted to being more concerned with status than she realized. And she saw maths as a status subject:

> It produces a strong reaction in other people. It makes you feel you've got something special. There's something about wanting to be a bit special, a bit different, that's part of doing it.

She sometimes regretted her decision to read this subject while she was at university.

> It was just too hard. And then it began to frighten me, really. I'd embarked on this thing that I'd got to pretend I was some sort of expert in. Now there were people who were heaps better, and just had an instinctive talent and gift that I couldn't hope to emulate at all.

Sally herself feels she has not got the gift. She sees it in other people, even in some – her husband, for example – who are not mathematicians. She recalled during her discussion with me several humiliating experiences, at school, at university, and at teacher-training college, where maths had made her feel inadequate. She said, 'I think I remember more the times that show me that I wasn't in the first flight'.

She saw maths as a huge subject. It fascinated her, but she thought she could enjoy it better as a sort of spectator. She would be happy being a member of the audience, being a layman in it. 'Whereas because of what I've done, I have to pretend to be a mathematician.' And yet Sally teaches maths – with great sensitivity – and is putting herself under strain in her attempt to achieve a further qualification in it. Her sense of inadequacy and frustration have still not prevented her from trying to make a creative link with her ideal.

At the end of her discussion with me she spoke with great feeling about what maths meant to her. What she said underlined the powerful need, in any creative learning experience, to make a strong link with an ideal. Kohut's strong child, in search of himself, and having difficulty with his idealized object, might have spoken with the same feeling.

> Maths is a subject you can't let go, in some way. It's sort of got me. I'm hooked and fascinated, even though in lots of ways it's given me experiences I haven't cared for, because it's made me feel a failure, and I don't enjoy that. Yet still I can't relinquish it.

The two youngest teachers, Mary, a student teacher, and Catherine, in her first year of teaching, both spoke with mixed feelings about their reasons for having chosen maths as a career.

Mary had always wanted to be a vet. But she had not been clever enough at school to pursue so competitive a career, and this had been a great disappointment to her. She had always been fairly good at maths, and so she went to university and took a maths degree. What she enjoyed about maths, she said, was its logic. She put great stress on this.

> I find I use logic all the time. When I'm having political or religious

discussions, I'm always coming out with 'Yes, but logically. . . .' It really frustrates me when friends and relations come out with silly illogical statements that don't follow. I think that's why I like maths. If you can think mathematically then there'd be a lot more logic.

During her interview with me, Mary spoke with some irritation and embarrassment about her father. She called him eccentric. He had been a brilliant scientist, after reading maths and physics at university. But when she was ten years old he had had a breakdown. He now worked in a factory. He had tried to discourage her from taking A-levels and going on to further education. He believed everybody should work in a factory.

I felt her passionate attachment to the logic of maths was a longing for some logic from her father. It is likely that she had had early positive maths experiences with him as a small child. His breakdown, and subsequent change of interest, must have been disturbing and disillusioning for her. It seemed that she was using maths as a defence both against her disappointment with her father and against her disappointment about her failure to become a vet. Some sense of this came over when she owned to having a bad memory. She thought this was one of the reasons she enjoyed maths. 'It doesn't require a memory. I do it from basic principles most of the time.'

Catherine, in her first year of teaching, had a different, much closer relationship with her parents. It was they who had encouraged her in an academic career and had advised her into teaching. She recalled how keen her parents were that she should do well in exams. She used to do multiplication tables in the garden with her mother. She got tremendous satisfaction from tables.

Just learning a bulk of knowledge you thought important, or other people thought important.

Later she said:

I was very frightened of letting Mum and Dad down, but the failure as it related to my self-concept – that didn't affect me. It was more how Mum and Dad's reaction would relate to me.

She added that she wanted to go to university because her parents had wanted her to go. Her parents had high hopes of the children. They had not been to university themselves. And it was her parents who had always thought teaching was a nice occupation for a woman.

Her mixed feelings revealed themselves when she said she had really wanted to be an art teacher. Her regret was that by teaching maths she might be losing something of her creative side. Because of her parents, she had concentrated on academic subjects at school, and so she was not qualified to teach art.

Her own reason for going into teaching was because she enjoyed activities with children. She loved teaching pupils who were interested. It upset her when the children she taught were not. She had gone into teaching 'to have fun with kids'; when she and the children did not have fun with maths, she said, they got fed up with each other, and with maths.

She admitted that she got on better with children than with adults. She felt she had the same sense of fun as they did. What came across as she spoke was her sensitivity to their needs.

Maths teaching for Catherine seemed to be a means of pleasing her parents. Behind this there were wistful echoes of a different Catherine, who seemed to find herself in the children she taught.

My own experience shows ambivalence too. My path to maths teaching was not straightforward. At school I had been expected to read classics when I went to university. But in the sixth form I retreated with relief into the ordered, black and white world of mathematics when the symbolic freedom of classics became too threatening. I needed the structure of the clear right and wrong of mathematics to hold my adolescent turbulence. Changing subjects in this way was partly defensive, and I studied maths at university with little deep inner satisfaction. Though I achieved a good degree, I was glad to leave mathematics behind when I left university. It was not until nearly twenty years later that I picked up a maths book again, and went with pleasure into maths teaching.

My experience, and possibly also the experience of Mary and Catherine, suggests that maths used partially as a defence is a way of ensuring an ordered world, where things can be right. And the need to get things right is very strong in those cases where a relatively insecure ego is protected by a false self built on compliance. Where a relationship has been made with numbers, and the necessary skill has been achieved, mathematics offers an excellent way of ensuring the approval of the environment. The answer will be right. Creative spontaneity has been lost, but the true self can retreat from the complexity of the emotional world of words, and hide behind the certainties of numbers. As with Hudson's convergers, the true self retreats to a haven 'from embarrassment, from criticism, and from emotions which are disruptive and inexplicable'.[12]

It may be that mathematicians who have used maths as a defensive strategy in this way in childhood or adolescence enjoy teaching because it offers them an outlet for a more creative use of their skills. In their relationships with children, they may be seeking those parts of themselves that retreated early from the too heavy demands of their parents. Among the teachers I spoke to, those most sensitive to the needs of their pupils are those most in touch with that part of themselves that was left behind.

It is as though the creative triangle, which partially failed these mathematicians as children, can be reached a second time when, as adults, they are trying to pass on their skills to their pupils.

NUMBERS

This paper has shown the complexity of feelings towards so rational a subject as mathematics. Even the rational alphabet of mathematics, numbers themselves, can carry a strong emotional content. One of the girls disliked numbers because, unlike words, they were too definite. But for many people, associations to numbers, whether conscious or not, are far from definite. So I also looked at emotional responses to numbers themselves.

Numbers are symbols. And symbols are associated, consciously or unconsciously, with feelings. We symbolize in order to make sense of the world, and our feelings about the world.

Pythagoras believed the number three represented perfect harmony. He interpreted the world through numbers. One represented unity, or deity, and two represented diversity, or strife and evil. The sum of one and two, therefore, represented the integration of unity with diversity, or the integration of good and evil. (In Kleinian terms, I suppose, he might be interpreted as saying that one and two were elements of the paranoid-schizoid position, and three showed that the depressive position had been reached.)

Three was an important magical number in the ancient world. Greek gods were invoked in threes, the dead were invoked three times. The Etruscans, and later the Romans, also grouped their gods in threes. And this triad later became incorporated into the Christian symbolism of the Trinity.

In *The Interpretation of Dreams*, Freud[13] refers to the number three as a symbol of the male genitals. A more feminist view might be that its shape was more likely to represent the female breasts than male genitals. For one teacher, the number three represented a child, 'quite young, a bit aloof'.

Hanna Segal[14] has described the process of unconscious symbol formation using Melanie Klein's work on object relations. Before the depressive position is reached, symbols are used primitively and are felt to represent the object itself. According to Hanna Segal, they are 'symbolic equations'. This leads to concrete, rather than to abstract, thinking, and there may be a clue here to the difficulty some children have in relating to numbers at all. If numbers for them have become associated at a primitive level with bad objects, they become terrifying and must be destroyed. But by the time the depressive position is reached, and good and bad objects have been integrated, a child's growing sense of reality leads to an inhibition of his instinctual aims. This becomes a powerful incentive for him to form symbols of a different kind. A child now creates symbols to engage with them creatively. And numbers will one day be symbols for him, both at a conscious and unconscious level.

Because of this I wondered what girls and women who were good at maths actually felt about numbers. The most vivid account came from a teacher.

I make numbers into personalities.

Number one goes into everything, either he's nosey, or he's friendly. My feelings go more towards the masculine/feminine thing.

Two is obviously curved. I feel a bit doubtful about number two, he's not too friendly. It sounds ridiculous. I tend to do that with most objects. I put a personality into them. I get vibes from things. They have personalities, traits, friendliness, unfriendliness, masculinity, femininity. Different ideas present themselves to me.

Number seven, as you'd expect, is a fairly angular character, rather aloof. If he were a person he'd probably be a salesman, a spivvy type, with a little moustache and a little trilby.

Number five is a rather ponderous type, a woman, a pregnant woman, because of the shape. Rather thick as well, a bit frustrating.

Number four is quite pleasing. I think masculine, but very sensible.

Eight is a nice number. Eight is feminine.

When I asked her about nought, she said 'I didn't really come into contact with nought. It's not part of my nice little family of numbers'.

This teacher has clearly articulated a process of giving numbers personalities, in order to relate to them. Though numbers are conscious symbols they may have unconscious symbolic associations. For this teacher her associations were more conscious than most. She needed them in order to relate to numbers.

When I asked the girls about their feelings about numbers, several said they did not have any. But I then asked them to write down some thoughts about particular numbers. Their feelings about nought and one I found especially vivid.

Nought is like the middle of a balance. There's nothing added on either side. And the system is at rest. But it's also a starting point – like a clean slate.

Nought is really an abstract number, more abstract than any other. You can't ever say that you have scaled down to nought. There can always be a tiny division on a scale that we can't see, that means nought is not actually there.

I don't like this idea. It's as if there will always be this secret, whether there's actually nothing or not.

Nought is nothing, empty, round, fat, straight, even black, beginning.

I think of nought as darkness. It's empty, quiet.

I think of nought as a middle. Either exact middle, or very beginning.

I don't think of nought as a number, but as an association, such as people with no clothes, or an empty basket.

You can see through it, put your hand through the middle of it, if it were actual.

Lots of noughts going off into the paper into the distance, so the one you see is the head, like a curly dragon. There seems to be lots you can pull out of it. If you grab this nought and take it away, there'll always be another in its place. It's always there.

The number nought seems real, round, solid. Not nothing, but something.

I kind of feel a nought on its own is more a picture and less of a functional figure.

Nought is a negative sounding word, but I think it's got quite positive associations for me. I think it is probably a bit difficult to grasp that it's not really an end or a beginning, and so sort of suspends. It's stationary. Other numbers can move, be negative or positive, but nought is always reliably, but somehow illusively, still.

In noughts and crosses I always want to be crosses.

A cross is a more definite sign. It doesn't have the mysticism that nought does.

We use a circle as our mathematical symbol for nought. If a child draws a circle during a therapy session, a Kleinian therapist might interpret it as a breast. A therapist using the work of Winnicott might interpret it as a face or a representation of the self. My own associations to the circle are of symbiosis, of union with another. It represents being contained, belonging. I see a mother and new-born baby, enclosed in the same skin, sharing the same world inside the circle of Winnicott's primary maternal preoccupation.

The associations of the girls seem to make a link between the idea of nothingness, which nought symbolizes, and the circular symbol we use for it. The unconscious link may lie in a return to the womb. The girls' associations give a sense of being at rest, of being free from strong feelings, of darkness and of mystery. Nought stands for the time before birth. It stands for pre-existence, as well as for non-existence, negation.

The girl who sees it as 'either exact middle, or very beginning' may have been voicing an unconscious association with her own beginning inside her mother. One of the difficulties many people experience with negative numbers may be associated with difficulties, at a primitive level, of understanding the time before birth. An interview in Laurie Buxton's[15] book suggests just that.

Though a return to the womb represents at one level a return to the garden of Eden, at another level it implies the loss of the hard-won sense of identity which follows separation from mother. The symbol for nought, the circle, may therefore stir up very strong conflicting feelings. It is perhaps not surprising that the imaginative teacher had no room for it in her family of numbers.

Some associations to the number one, like the teacher's description 'he goes into everything, either he's friendly or he's nosey', seemed quite strongly phallic.

> Even though it's more than nought, it's substantial, there's less to say.
>
> It's interesting as it has a little cap, a kink, and a long body. Perhaps it's secure, as it has a base. I feel pretty secure with it. It's what you strive for when you're going through all the fractions.
>
> Start, positive, countdown, red, not much to say.
>
> Jerky, opposite to nought. It disrupts, it's rigid, both in shape and what it means.
>
> One is the beginning of something. One is a tally, the beginning of hangman.
>
> An easy number, simple. I like finding ones in maths.
>
> I do see one as rather powerful, as if it was always carved out of stone. I remember in history once drawing a pyramid to represent the king at the top, the ministers in the middle and the slaves at the bottom. And the top of the pyramid is how I see one, as the leader, with others coming from it. Also a bit like the original amoeba, always dividing.

My own feeling about the number one is the link with identity, of the successful outcome of the struggle to separate from nought. And the symbol itself is the same as our symbol for our own identity. The link between the girls' associations and my own may be that the number one represents Winnicott's 'doing', the masculine element, and nought represents 'being', the feminine element.[16] Their integration is necessary for true identity.

It intrigues me that the symbol we use to describe our number base, ten, is a combination of these two powerful symbols, nought and one. I wonder how many primary school teachers, introducing the idea of tens and units for the first time, are aware of the symbolic hornets' nests they may be stirring up in the unconscious of their pupils.

Winnicott[17] made a direct link between the number one, personal development, and the start of mathematical understanding.

> Education in terms of the teaching of arithmetic has to wait for that degree of personal integration in the infant that makes the concept of *one* meaningful, and also the idea contained in the first pronoun singular. The child who knows the I AM feeling, and who can carry it, knows

about one, and then immediately wants to be taught addition, subtraction and multiplication.

In its simplicity this is a tempting key to mathematical ability. Taken with recent work on women's dependency needs and their low self-esteem, it has much to offer. Eichenbaum and Orbach's[18] sensitive work, pursued at the Women's Therapy Centre, has suggested that women's traditional role has made it difficult for them to develop a truly firm sense of self. In their view, the structure of society has led to a psychology in both men and women that makes it impossible for either parent to be truly good enough for little girls. Society has distorted their creative triangle.

The development of mathematical ability may indeed be linked to this. Several of the girls and teachers I spoke to felt mathematical ability to be a male attribute, and that it gave them special status. Their interest in maths was linked to identification with their fathers, or with other boys, and with rivalry with brothers. This suggests that, where both parents can make a more equal contribution, where both father and mother are truly good enough for healthy self-development, then good-enough teachers may more successfully recognize and foster creative mathematical ability in girls.

NOTES

1 O. Rank, *The Trauma of Birth* (New York: Harper & Row, 1973), p. 184.
2 L. Buxton, *Do You Panic About Maths?* (London: Heinemann Educational, 1981).
3 I. Matte Blanco, *The Unconscious as Infinite Sets* (London: Duckworth, 1975).
4 H. W. Turnbull (ed.), *The Correspondence of Isaac Newton*, vol. 1 (Cambridge: Cambridge University Press, 1959), p. 416.
5 H. Kohut, *The Restoration of the Self* (New York: International Universities Press, 1977) and *The Search for the Self*, vol. 2 (New York; International Universities Press, 1978).
6 D. W. Winnicott, *The Maturational Processes and the Facilitating Environment* (London: Hogarth Press, 1965).
7 M. Pines, 'Reflections on mirroring', *International Review of Psycho-Analysis* (1984) 11: 28.
8 H. Kohut, 1978, op. cit., pp. 615–58.
9 M. Klein, *Envy and Gratitude* (London: Tavistock, 1957).
10 L. Hudson, *Frames of Mind* (London: Methuen, 1968), p. 21.
11 D. W. Winnicott, *Through Paediatrics to Psycho-Analysis* (London: Hogarth Press, 1982), p. 185.
12 L. Hudson, *Contrary Imaginations* (London: Methuen, 1966), p. 134.
13 S. Freud, *The Interpretation of Dreams* (Harmondsworth: Penguin, 1976), p. 476.
14 H. Segal, 'Notes on symbol formation', *International Journal of Psycho-Analysis* (1957) 11: 391–97.
15 L. Buxton, op. cit., p. 132.
16 H. Guntrip, *Schizoid Phenomena, Object Relations and the Self* (London: Hogarth Press, 1983), p. 249.
17 D. W. Winnicott, 1965, op. cit., p. 100.

18 L. Eichenbaum and S. Orbach, *Outside In . . . Inside Out* (Harmondsworth: Penguin, 1982).

BIBLIOGRAPHY

Balint, M. (1968) *The Basic Fault*, London: Tavistock, 1979.
Buxton, L. (1981) *Do You Panic About Maths?*, London: Heinemann Educational.
Eichenbaum, L. and Orbach, S. (1982) *Outside In . . . Inside Out*, Harmondsworth: Penguin.
Fairbairn, W. R. D. (1952) *Psychoanalytic Studies of the Personality*, London: Tavistock.
Freud, S. (1900) *The Interpretation of Dreams*, Harmondsworth: Penguin, 1976.
Guntrip, H. (1965) *Schizoid Phenomena, Object Relations and the Self*. London: Hogarth Press, 1983.
Hudson, L. (1966) *Contrary Imaginations*, London: Methuen.
—— (1968) *Frames of Mind*, London: Methuen.
Klein, M. (1957) *Envy and Gratitude*, London: Tavistock.
—— (1963) *Our Adult World and Other Essays*, London: Heinemann Medical.
Kohut, H. (1977) *The Restoration of the Self*, New York: International Universities Press.
—— (1978) *The Search for the Self*, vol. 2, New York: International Universities Press.
Matte Blanco, I. (1975) *The Unconscious as Infinite Sets*, London: Duckworth.
Newton, I. (1675/6) *The Correspondence of Isaac Newton*, vol. 1, H. W. Turnbull (ed)., Cambridge: Cambridge University Press, 1959.
Pines, M. (1984) 'Reflections on mirroring', *International Review of Psycho-Analysis* 11: 27–42.
Rank, O. (1929) *The Trauma of Birth*, New York: Harper & Row, 1973.
Segal, H. (1957) 'Notes on symbol formation', *International Journal of Psycho-Analysis* 30: 391–7.
Storr, A. (1972) *The Dynamics of Creation*, London: Secker.
Winnicott, D. W. (1958) *Through Paediatrics to Psycho-Analysis*, London: Hogarth Press, 1982.
—— (1965) *The Maturational Processes and the Facilitating Environment*, London: Hogarth Press.

Chapter 10

Poor orphan child

An exploration of sibling rivalry

Diana Bass

My feet they are sore, and my limbs they are weary;
Long is the way, and the mountains are wild;
Soon will the twilight close moonless and dreary
Over the path of the poor orphan child.

Charlotte Brontë, *Jane Eyre*

The theme of sibling rivalry is an ancient one that echoes down through the ages, its power made manifest in myth, allegory, and fairy tale. Its roots are complex and tangled, finding sustenance deep in the primal conflicts of early infancy.

There is a wealth of information about this subject in psychoanalytic literature, and many theories have been advanced regarding both its aetiology and its consequences for the individual. There is little doubt that intense and unresolved sibling rivalry can have a major influence on the individual's adaptation to both inner and outer reality, with resulting social and political implications.

Freud's understanding of sibling rivalry was derived from his theory of the Oedipus complex, which he described as 'the nucleus of the neuroses'. He felt that it is this situation 'which gives grounds for receiving the new brothers or sisters with repugnance and for unhesitatingly getting rid of them with a wish'.[1] His observations led him to conclude that it is easier for the child to give vent to its feelings of hate and rivalry for a sibling than to acknowledge their source in feelings about parental figures. He describes how the child who has been displaced by subsequent siblings can become greatly embittered by this and can become permanently 'isolated and estranged from his mother's affections'. Freud sees this scenario being enacted in terms of infantile sexuality, and that the consequences of this displacement can be traced through the developing libido of the individual, affecting all later relationships. Freud believed that the child's position in the family birth order is a factor of extreme importance in determining the shape of its later life, and 'should deserve consideration in every life history'.[2]

Following on from Freud, Melanie Klein's revolutionary work in the field of child analysis led her to the conclusion that the starting point for neurotic or psychotic illness lies in the earliest months of the infant's life – much earlier than had been previously believed. For Klein, envious and destructive feelings, and the infant's ability to counteract them with those of a loving and reparative nature, are largely dependent on innate characteristics.

Unlike Freud, Klein postulated that the ego existed in rudimentary form from the beginning of post-natal life. The 'primordial anxiety'[3] for Klein was fear of annihilation, and the chief function of the early ego is to mediate in the struggle between the life instinct and the death instinct. She saw the tendency of the ego at this stage to split itself and its objects – which is the opposite of its integrative function – partly as a defence against the 'primordial anxiety' of annihilation and death and partly due to the fragility of this early ego.

The splitting of the object into good and bad is one of the defences of the paranoid-schizoid position, operating over the first three or four months of life. Klein saw this splitting into good and bad as necessary for the infant's emotional stability. The good object, preserved from contamination by the bad, can be integrated, but only if the inborn capacity for love is sufficient. If excessive envy, which Klein saw as coexisting with the destructive impulses, builds up, the internalization of the good object is impaired and the next stage, the depressive position, cannot be satisfactorily worked through. The first object of envy is the breast, because, according to Klein, this possesses everything that the infant desires, and is seen as having an unlimited supply of milk and love. When the infant feels frustrated it perceives the breast as holding back the things it desires and keeping them for itself.

Klein believed that the infant's relationship with the mother is disturbed if the feelings which frustration gives rise to are excessively strong. In this case, a good internal object is not satisfactorily achieved and this later affects the individual's ability to form satisfactory relationships. In children with a strong capacity for love the relationship to the good object is fundamentally strong and can withstand temporary states of hatred and envy without being destroyed. In the individual in later life, 'a deep and sharp division'[4] between loved and hated objects means that this early paranoid-schizoid position has not been satisfactorily worked through and envious and strongly persecutory feelings are present.

This situation seems important in the understanding of sibling rivalry, because it is in this early mother/child relationship that the seeds of later irresolvable destructive relationships are sown. Klein also discusses idealization which is very relevant to some of the issues discussed in this paper. Idealization is considered to be 'a corollary of persecutory anxiety'. It is a defence against the attacked and therefore retaliatory breast – if the object is idealized to the extent of placing it above comparison, then envy is counteracted. The object does not become fully integrated in the ego because its idealization results from predominantly persecutory feelings.

Klein emphasizes the importance of triumph in these early defences. This, I feel, is significant in any discussion of sibling rivalry:

> triumph is closely bound up with contempt and omnipotence. . . . We know the part rivalry plays in the child's burning desire to equal the achievement of the grown ups. . . . Some people are obliged to remain unsuccessful, because success always implies to them the humiliation or even the damage of somebody else, in the first place the triumph over parents, brothers and sisters.[5]

Klein's theories place the origins of sibling rivalry within the early conflicts of the paranoid-schizoid and depressive positions, with the amount of envy and hatred being mobilized as largely due to innate factors.

Donald Winnicott adhered to Klein's theories in terms of the stages of development of the infant. He concurred that the way the individual relates to the self and to the external world has its origins in those early stages. However, Winnicott believed it is the presence of a 'good-enough' mother in a 'facilitating environment' which is the crucial factor in the infant's healthy psychological development. Winnicott believed that, in the first few months of life, the infant feels that the mother is not a separate being but part of itself. As the baby slowly separates, the mother, by her sensitivity to the baby's needs, allows this to happen; otherwise, the infant may be filled with persecutory feelings. Winnicott, unlike Melanie Klein, believed that the source of the paranoid-schizoid position lies in some failure in the mother's 'maternal preoccupation'[6] with the infant.

The mother's inability to hold the child physically and psychologically, or to adapt to its needs, is, in Winnicott's view, the mainspring of the child's later difficulties in relating to and using those around him or her in a satisfactory and creative way. These factors are obviously greatly relevant to the way in which the child responds to subsequent pregnancies and births, and the developing relationships with siblings.

This paper is an exploration, in the light of these theories, of some of the issues of sibling rivalry and its consequences. The evidence of the universality of the theme can be found throughout literature. I have chosen to analyse the Victorian classic *Jane Eyre* from this perspective, linking it with some relevant case material. My choice was influenced by that fact that I perceived *Jane Eyre* to share characteristics with the 'Cinderella' group of fairy tales as discussed by Bruno Bettelheim in *The Uses of Enchantment.* The narrative has a similar power and complexity and can be read at many levels. *Jane Eyre* evokes the classic scenario of the 'outsider' or rejected sibling who rises from humble beginnings, survives rejection and despair eventually to triumph over her detractors and persecutors, both real and imagined.

Jane Eyre is a penniless orphan and at the beginning of the novel we find her living at Gateshead, the family home of her aunt and cousins. Jane's parents had both died in her infancy. Her father was a poor but 'virtuous' clergyman who had died within a few weeks of Jane's mother who, in marrying him, had apparently 'married beneath her'.

Jane was left in the care of her mother's brother 'Uncle Reed' who unfortunately fell ill and died soon after Jane's arrival at Gateshead. Mr Reed 'required a promise' of his wife when he was on his deathbed that she would rear Jane as one of her own children. This promise was to prove impossible for Mrs Reed to keep. It would seem, from the information we have been given thus far, that Jane has already experienced being trebly 'abandoned'. The chance seems remote at this stage that Jane has enough experience of a 'facilitating environment' to enable her to deal with future difficulties in an integrated way.

The first chapter opens with a classical evocation of the miseries of sibling rivalry:

> She [Mrs Reed] lay reclining on a sofa by the fire-side and with her darlings about her (for the time neither quarrelling nor crying) looking perfectly happy. Me, she had dispensed from joining the group; saying, 'she regretted to be under the necessity of keeping me at a distance; but that until she heard from Bessie . . . that I was endeavouring in good earnest to acquire a more sociable and child-like disposition . . . she really must exclude me from privileges intended only for contented, happy little children.'

Bettelheim's view of sibling rivalry is that, despite its name 'this miserable passion has only incidentally to do with a child's actual brothers and sisters'. The real source is the child's feelings about his (or her) parents.[7] It would appear that the situation Jane finds herself in – the feeling of being the outsider, not 'good enough' to receive love – has reverberations right back through biblical times and beyond. In the stories of Cain and Abel, Jacob and Esau, Joseph and his brothers, we have the same sense of the child who is excluded, who looks on while another or others get the attention that he or she secretly craves. The pain of this rejection is so great and the feelings stirred up so powerful, that the murderous consequences in fact and fantasy are well documented.

There is a powerful image in the *Book of Genesis*: 'The voice of thy brother's blood crieth unto me from the ground.'[8] This has as much meaning today when attempting to understand the agonizing forces of envy and hatred which can be unleashed in the psyche of the displaced child. More recently, the story of Cinderella dramatizes the same conflict. Bettelheim mentions that there are many different versions of the same fairy tale dating back to a story told in China in the ninth century AD and possibly pre-dating this. He describes how the German phrase 'to dwell among the ashes' was a symbol not only of degradation but of sibling rivalry, and of the sibling who finally surpassed the sibling or siblings who have debased him or her. The story of Cinderella replaced sibling relationships with those between step-siblings, perhaps in order to make acceptable an animosity which one wishes did not exist between true siblings. I find this interesting in thinking about Jane's relationship to her cousins and to her aunt, who is not a blood relation.

In dwelling on the negative aspects of sibling rivalry, it is perhaps necessary to mention Bettelheim's assertion that being a sibling generates as much positive as negative feeling between siblings.[9]

Banished from the family idyll, Jane nurses her injured feelings. Her mind is haunted by dark shapes and threatening figures. The pictures in the book she is reading, a book about wildfowl and their habitat, conjure up frightening and oppressive images:

> The broken boat stranded on a desolate coast . . . the cold and ghastly moon glancing through bars of cloud at a wreck just sinking. . . . The two ships becalmed on a torpid sea, I believed to be marine phantoms. The fiend pinning down the thief's pack behind him, I passed over quickly; it was an object of terror. So was the black, horned thing seated aloof on a rock, surveying a distant crowd surrounding a gallows.[10]

Jane's anxious imaginings can perhaps be understood at this point in terms of feelings of persecution arising from the split-off and hostile elements in her psyche. External objects become sinister and dangerous as Jane projects her rage outwards and she unconsciously expects and perhaps provokes retribution. Her older cousin John Reed finds her hiding place. Jane is in a state of terror:

> every nerve I had feared him, and every morsel of flesh on my bones shrank when he came near. . . . I knew he would soon strike, and while dreading the blow, I mused on the disgusting and ugly appearance of him who would presently deal it. . . . I really saw in him a tyrant: a murderer.[11]

As in 'Cinderella', Jane's persecutor is seen as ugly, beneath contempt, and this can perhaps be seen as an omnipotent defence against envious rage and unconscious guilt. Why should I envy or feel guilty about hating or attacking anyone who is so contemptible, so morally and physically undeserving?

Jane's altercation with John leads to her being locked up in the 'red room'. The words 'chill . . . silent . . . solemn' associated with the 'red room' are evocative of death and indeed it was in this room that Mr Reed had 'breathed his last'. The juxtaposition of life and death, the question of who dies, and who survives, is a fairly common theme in this novel. I wonder if the 'red room' with its womb-like but also tomb-like atmosphere is an unconscious reminder for Jane of her mother, who was alive to give birth to her (the flesh and blood colours of the room's interior) but who is now dead, cold, and silent.

It is interesting to note here Donald Winnicott's discussion on the fear of death in his paper 'Fear of breakdown'. He suggests that it is the death that has happened but that was not experienced that is sought. It is likely that the loss of her mother in Jane's infancy caused the death of part of her psyche. Jane was not mature enough to experience this. To seek this death in the present in suicide or self-destructive behaviour is the way to bring meaning to something which cannot be understood. This primary experience of hopelessness and emptiness is perhaps what drives Jane when she wishes 'to achieve escape from insupportable oppression – as running away, or, if that could not be effected, never eating or drinking more, and letting myself die'.[12] In Jane's experiences with death and catastrophe throughout this novel, it is perhaps feasible to consider that she has a 'a compulsion to look for death'[13] as a way of reaching for some understanding of her own history. The catastrophe in Jane's unconscious – the loss of her mother – in Winnicott's terms has not yet happened because she 'was not there for it to happen to'. The individual has a need to 'remember' but it is not possible to remember something that has not yet happened.

Jane is despairing about ever winning love or approval:

> Why was I always suffering, always brow-beaten, always accused, forever condemned? Why could I never please? Why was it useless to try to win anyone's favour? Eliza, who was headstrong and selfish, was respected. Georgina, who had a spoiled temper . . . was universally indulged. . . . John, no one thwarted, much less punished; though he twisted the necks of the pigeons.[14]

Bettelheim suggests that the child fears 'that in comparison to them he cannot win his parents' love and esteem' and it is this that 'inflames sibling rivalry'.[15] Jane feels unloved and unloveable, but also contemptuous of her persecutors . . . yet at the same time 'in contempt of their judgement'. Some of the appeal of *Jane Eyre* lies in the identification with Jane as a poor, misunderstood but virtuous victim. The message given and received early in the narrative is that she will (perhaps responding to most children's fantasies) eventually triumph over the wicked, cruel oppressors on whom she is dependent.

Melanie Klein's understanding of the defences of childhood and infancy, as described in 'Mourning and manic-depressive states', would seem to parallel Jane's struggle with her experiences. Klein emphasizes 'the importance of *triumph*, closely bound up with contempt and omnipotence, as an element of the manic position'.[16]

Jane's inner struggle is to reconcile her inner yearning to be loved and accepted with her envious need to deny that those around her could offer her anything that she could need or want. Klein talks of the unresolved guilt which results when the loved objects in the child's mind are the same as those over whom she wishes to triumph. This wish is projected into those around her and leads to feelings of persecution. Depression may follow, or 'an increase in manic defences and a more violent control of the objects' since she has failed to reconcile, restore, or improve them, and therefore feelings of being persecuted by them again have the upper hand. It is Klein's assertion that 'triumph impedes the work of early mourning'[17] which seems relevant to Jane's situation and responses.

Jane, having lacked Winnicott's 'facilitating environment' in the development of her sense of self, despairs of having her feelings understood by those around her. Her unconscious fear of being overwhelmed and of destroying others by the amount of rage she feels at being abandoned traps her, and she is unable to use the resources available to her. Her fear of being misunderstood may be rooted in her terror of her own destructiveness. In Kleinian terms, the fact that her primary objects did not survive, reinforces her unconscious belief that there is something inherently dangerous about her.

Jane leaves Gateshead to go to Lowood School. After an angry confrontation with Mrs Reed, it is decided that Jane should go away to school, her relationship with the Reed family unresolved. The night before her departure, sitting alone in her darkened room, Jane 'sought shelter from cold and darkness in my crib. To this crib I always took my doll: human beings must love something, and, in the dearth of worthier objects of affection, I contrived to find a pleasure in loving and cherishing a faded *graven image*, shabby as a miniature scarecrow'.[18] I am struck here by the juxtaposition of life and death images. Jane's strange description of her doll evokes the image of her comforting herself with what sounds like a death-like object, and this is startlingly repeated in her experience when her friend Helen Burns dies in her arms at Lowood School.

A mark of Jane's immersion in early conflict is the splitting of her objects, resulting in their idealization or denigration. Her description of her second encounter with Miss Temple, the superintendent of Lowood, is indicative of this: 'I suppose I have a considerable Organ of Veneration, for I retain yet the same sense of admiring awe with which my eyes tracked her steps'.[19] Jane's need to split her internal objects, to keep the good and the bad separate because of her unconscious anxiety about her destructive feelings, is manifest in the narrative. Feelings of persecution inevitably accompany idealization. The dreaded Mr Brocklehurst, the governor of Lowood, arrives: 'I had been looking out daily for the "Coming Man", whose information respecting my past life and conversation was to brand me as a bad child for ever'. She is seen as a vicious example who could 'contaminate their purity'.[20]

In Jane's perception Miss Temple is the obverse of Mr Brocklehurst. One is purity, goodness, and love, the other hatred, persecution, and oppression.

In projecting her vengeful frightening destructive feelings into Mr Brocklehurst, Miss Temple is kept safe from Jane's envious attack, as indeed, by association, is Helen Burns. Jane is struck with admiration as Helen converses intelligently with Miss Temple. On the strength of Jane's history this situation would appear to be fraught with anxiety and envious and jealous feelings. However, she watches the two 'with a controlling sense of awe', her 'Organ of Veneration expanding at every sounding line'. Jane expresses no resentment as Miss Temple embraces them but 'Helen she held a little longer than me: she let her go more reluctantly; it was Helen her eye followed to the door; it was for her she a second time breathed a sad sigh; for her she wiped a tear from her cheek'.[21]

At this point I would like to discuss some counselling work I did with a client whom I shall refer to as Susan. 'The tears that are for someone else' has been an unconscious theme throughout Susan's life and has been a factor in many of her past and present difficulties. It is something of which she only recently, very painfully, came to be aware.

Susan was referred to me because of her persistent depression. She was having great difficulty resolving her feelings following the death of her mother which had occurred two years previously. Susan joined a group which I had been running for a few months, but this came to an end after another three months for unforeseen departmental reasons, and our work continued in individual counselling. What was striking about Susan's behaviour in this female group was her need to dominate and to interact with the group leader to the exclusion of the other members. In one of the group meetings Susan revealed that she was, in fact, an adopted child, and that her mother had adopted her within a short time of losing her own baby daughter who had died at 8 days old. Susan said that she did not feel that this had caused any difficulty for her as she and her adoptive mother had an extremely close relationship. She did not want anything 'to spoil this relationship – I don't want anything to spoil my memory of my mother'. Another member of the group then talked of her experience of growing up overshadowed by an older brother who had died in infancy. This could perhaps have resulted in a bond forming between them but in subsequent meetings it became a pattern that either Susan or the other group member would not attend. This situation may have resulted from her perception of her unique experience of replacing a dead sibling being spoilt. I felt that Susan had a strong unconscious wish both to get rid of what she perceived as her rival and to preserve the idealized image of her dead adoptive mother and their relationship. I felt that the agenda was significant in terms of her unresolved mourning for her mother.

In individual counselling Susan talked of the difficulties arising from her husband's job – they had to move around a fair amount. She found it very difficult to make friends she could trust. She often felt like a 'square peg in a round hole'. This was a repetitive theme and also a very evocative phrase in terms of her life experience. I linked it to her feelings of being a replacement for her mother's first baby and also, in the transference, to me being the 'wrong' mother with perhaps what felt like the 'wrong' baby. Susan's ambivalence towards our work together, despite her assurances of how positive she felt about it, was brought into sessions by frequent lateness – she had 'too much to do'. Perhaps this was a reminder of the unfinished work of mourning which had placed such a load on her – both her mother's and her own. Susan used splitting and denial as a defence against her unconscious rage and pain at first being 'abandoned' by her birth mother and then having the burden of being a replacement child – her lifelong feeling of 'playing a part'. Her relationships were characterized by being 'wonderful' or 'terrible'. (Her marriage was in severe difficulties at this time.)

The first time she had really thought about the other baby was at her mother's funeral. Her mother had told her about Sally when she was young, but Susan said she had not thought about it again until her mother's death when she thought there should be 'something to acknowledge it'. When speaking about this at the end of the session she said softly, 'It's surprising how much grief feels like fear'. I saw this partly as a recognition of how much was at stake if she allowed herself to complete the mourning process, the inevitable pain and changes of perception resulting from emotional exploration and discovery about the true nature of her experience.

Susan had two children. She spoke of her fear during her pregnancies that 'something awful might happen'. Her first baby had nearly died at birth, and her second had a heart condition diagnosed at 8 days. This could suggest a strong unconscious identification with her adoptive mother complicated by her knowledge that her own mother had her adopted at birth. Susan could not understand, after having her own children, how her real mother had been able to 'give her up' after carrying her inside her body. I understood this to relate, in the transference, to the fact that we were reaching the end of our agreed time together and that this was re-awakening powerful feelings of abandonment and loss. In a sense she could never compete with her mother's first baby because Sally had shared the ultimate closeness with her mother that Susan had been denied, and perhaps was even now being re-united in death. I wondered if there were strong feelings of unconscious triumph and resultant guilt around the fact that the baby had to die in order that Susan might have this good mother. This feeling was strengthened because Susan had a miscarriage before her first baby and a termination before her second one. As for Jane Eyre, the themes of Susan's early life remained powerfully active. This is demonstrated during a session when Susan said she had been in a situation in which she had felt that what she had said had been misunderstood and misinterpreted. This had also occurred during the session and I suggested that this feeling had been around a lot in her life. She replied 'In all my relationships I find it hard to express myself, to find the right words, to make people understand what I really mean.'

DB: Perhaps there were things that could not be expressed for fear of being misunderstood. Perhaps things about your sister.

Susan: I don't understand what you mean.

DB: I'm talking about your mother's first child who died and it was not safe to really think or talk about it till she died.

Susan: It was at my mother's funeral that I started thinking about it – was there something to mark her grave. Shouldn't my mother be buried near her?

DB: So something that could not be talked about was very much alive in you even after all those years.

Susan: Yes, I remember asking my mother when I was about ten why I never saw her cry and she said 'I've cried all my tears'. Though I didn't want that, I wanted her to have some tears to cry for me, to cry for things about me. I was so glad she was with me when she died. I wanted to say so much to her but you can't say a lifetime's things in an hour.

DB: So there was a lifetime's things that it was never quite safe to say. Perhaps the way it feels here when it is so difficult to express yourself without fearing misunderstanding.

Like Jane, Susan feels at a deep level that she is an outsider, and has unconscious, denied rivalrous and envious feelings for those she perceives as having the special attention and affection she craves.

As Neville Symington observes in *The Analytic Experience*, 'There is no conscious guilt when hatred and love are split from each other and projected outwards towards different part objects which are not seen as being connected'.[22] Jane has placed Helen beyond reach of her envy and anger by idealizing her. It would seem that something must happen to avoid the inevitable disillusionment that this must lead to. As Jane is enjoying the beautiful spring at Lowood, wandering freely through the woods, Helen Burns is dying of consumption in a 'room upstairs'. It would seem that Helen has been invested with so much unsullied goodness that she cannot survive; perhaps to live would mean to become contaminated, to fall from the pedestal on which Jane has placed her. Jane climbs into 'the little crib' beside Helen. Helen comforts Jane, whispering that, when Jane dies, they will be reunited as Jane will 'be received by the same mighty, universal Parent'.[23] Jane sleeps and Helen dies in her arms, echoing the scene of Jane sleeping with the 'graven image' clasped in her arms. Whatever she loves is somehow dead or damaged in some way.

Jane and Susan both deny any angry, ambivalent, and jealous feelings they may harbour towards their maternal figures and sibling rivals. Jane idealizes Miss Temple (the name itself, Maria Temple, is highly symbolic) and Helen Burns – they are almost sacred in the way they are protected from Jane's potential attack. Susan is similarly extremely protective of her 'wonderful' relationship with her mother – she does not want it 'spoilt' in any way. Her mother's lost child, Sally, is attacked by denying her importance and continuing influence in both Susan and her mother's lives. Susan was caught in the debilitating scenario of sibling rivalry, when the other sibling is absent through family break-up or death. There is none of the reality-testing that is the day-to-day experience of siblings living in the same family. However rejected or inadequate the child may feel, there is always the hope that things can change, that it will feel different soon, the balance may shift. The unfortunate child who has to compete with a dead or absent sibling never feels that relief. The 'other' is always there, unchangeable, and the vacuum of the absence is filled with phantasy and projections which cannot be resolved in any realistic way. Perhaps this was true for both Susan and Jane, the losses of infancy impeding their potential to resolve their sibling and oedipal rivalries in a creative and life-affirming way.

Jane, on leaving school, moves to Thornfield, where she becomes governess to Adele, ward of Mr Rochester. Mr Rochester, a severe and forbidding figure, seeks out her company being 'not fond of the prattle of children'.[24] He sees her as 'cast in a different mould to the majority' and Jane's deep need to be special to someone, to be set apart as different and desirable, is met by his interest in her. However, it would seem that Jane is aware at some level that all her relationships are fraught with difficulties and loss and she warns Rochester, 'It will sting – it will taste bitter, sir'. Rochester idealizes her, he admires her, 'so fair a guest' who has 'put on the robes of an angel of light'. Jane is uncomfortable and frightened and warns him off: 'Distrust it, sir; it is not a true angel'. Nevertheless Jane thrives under his interest and solicitude – 'the blanks of existence were filled up; my bodily health improved; I gathered flesh and strength'. Jane finds in him, as in Miss Temple, the good-enough mothering that she yearns for. There is the intimation of a parent-like figure in Rochester, perhaps also an oedipal father. He is significantly older than Jane and has a child whom he rejects in favour of Jane's company. Jane's 'plain Quaker form' is contrasted with Adele's 'coquetry'. Like Bettelheim's Cinderella, 'her innocence is stressed, her virtue is perfect'. Bettelheim suggests that in earlier versions of the story, the picture of sibling rivalry is complicated by oedipal considerations. This may well be the case in Jane's relationship with Rochester.

> The many stories in which innocent Cinderella is claimed by her father as his marital partner, a fate from which she can save herself only through flight, could be interpreted as conforming to and expressing universal fantasies in which a girl wishes her father would marry her and then, out of guilt because of these fantasies, denies doing anything to arouse this

> parental desire. But deep down a child who knows that she does want her father to prefer her to her mother feels she deserves to be punished for it – thus her flight or banishment, and degradation to a Cinderella existence.[25]

Jane, having nothing to fear from a childish rival, has to deal with one who is far more threatening. It is interesting that it is immediately after Jane recognizes and acknowledges her tender and loving feelings for Rochester – 'his face the object I best liked to see; his presence in a room was more cheering than the brightest fire'[26] – that catastrophe, in the form of deranged wife, strikes. Jane is awoken by a mad demoniac laugh and discovers Rochester's bed ablaze. The fire is quenched with water by Jane, but in psychoanalytic terms the incident can be seen as very revealing. If we consider the unconscious weight of Jane's experiences, the loss of her parents in infancy, rejection at Gateshead, the privations and losses of Lowood School, it would be strange if she could survive this without massive defence organization. Jane's difficulties with the containment of her angry and destructive feelings are not surprising, given her primary experience of tremendous emotional deprivation. Jane has been deprived of the opportunity to learn that her objects can survive destruction. In the absence of an experience of 'holding' in Winnicott's 'facilitating environment' there can be no integration. Jane is not able to integrate the destructive parts of her own personality; she is forced to repudiate them, because they can be owned only if there is an experience of survival. If we consider this narrative, at one level, to be an elucidation of Jane's unconscious world, then perhaps the image of the 'madwoman in the attic' could be understood as the projection, a split-off part of Jane's psyche. At the very point of acknowledgement that Rochester can give her good things ('so happy, so gratified did I become with this new interest added to life, that I ceased to pine after kindred'), the envious destructive element is aroused to attack and destroy the 'good breast' that Rochester represents.

The 'madwoman in the attic' could also be understood in terms of the Jungian 'shadow' which, as the disowned part of the self, can often erupt in dreams as a threatening murderous presence. Jung observed that:

> Everyone carries a shadow, and the less it is embodied in the individual's conscious life, the blacker and denser it is. If an inferiority is conscious, one always has a chance to correct it. Furthermore, it is constantly in contact with other interests, so that it is continually subjected to modifications. But if it is repressed and isolated from consciousness, it never gets corrected, and is liable to burst forth suddenly in a moment of unawareness. At all events, it forms an unconscious snag, blocking the most well-meant attempts.[27]

Jane disavows any rivalrous feelings. Blanche Ingram, an erstwhile rival for

Rochester's attentions, is dismissed: 'Miss Ingram was a mark beneath jealousy: she was too inferior to excite the feeling'. Jane pays a return visit to Gateshead, the scene of her childhood. Mrs Reed is dying and wishes to see her. Jane sees that her old adversaries Georgina and Eliza are not worthy of her rivalry – one is 'intolerably acrid' and the other 'despicably savourless'. In a way Jane's victory is complete: her old persecutors are either dead (John has killed himself) or no longer enviable.

Jane returns from Gateshead to marry Rochester only to have the marriage ceremony disrupted by the revelation about his locked-away wife. Jane flees from Thornfield – 'Gentle reader, may you never feel what I then felt . . . for never may you, like me, dread to be the instrument of evil to what you wholly love'.[28] This recalls Jane's earlier warning to Rochester: 'It will sting – it will taste bitter, sir'.

Jane's headlong flight from Rochester results in a harrowing, desolate journey during which she suffers 'moral degradation, blent with the physical suffering'.[29] She has to beg for food and shelter. It would seem that this journey could be seen as one of oedipal punishment – is the cause of her grief and humiliation the dream of winning father from mother?

Jane, nearly dead from grief and starvation, is rescued and taken in by two fair sisters and a brother (a mirror image of the Reed family of the early chapters). They are kind and loving towards her, and treat her like one of the family. St. John Rivers is a clergyman, again an echo of the past. Jane becomes the schoolmistress of the local schoolhouse, and thus independent and self-sufficient, although she feels 'degraded. . . dismayed at the ignorance, the poverty, the coarseness of all I heard and saw around me'.[30]

Shortly after this Jane discovers that she has been left £20,000 by a rich uncle in Madeira. Through this will, Jane and the Rivers family discover, to their mutual delight, that they are first cousins. St. John Rivers wishes to marry Jane, spurning the attentions of a rich heiress, Rosalind Oliver. Rosalind is very beautiful but St. John prefers Jane even though she is 'not one tenth so handsome'.

Jane refuses his offer of marriage and returns to Thornfield. She is horrified to find it a blackened ruin. Her frantic enquiries reveal that there had been a catastrophic fire the year before, started in Jane's old room in the bed she had slept in by Rochester's mad wife, who had then leapt from the battlements to her death. Rochester, while ensuring that all the occupants got out safely, was blinded and crippled, losing a hand.

Jane seeks Rochester out where he lives in lonely isolation in the middle of a forest, with a servant for company. Rochester is now broken and dependent and Jane loves him more: 'The powerlessness of the strong man touched my heart to the quick.' He is 'a sightless Samson', someone whose power has been shorn by a jealous, vengeful woman. Jane has no need to fear his masculine power over her, his independence, his ability to exploit or abandon her. She is now the one he needs, he cannot manage without her . . . 'just as if a royal eagle, chained to a perch, should be forced to entreat a sparrow to become its purveyor'.[31] Jane marries him.

The conclusion is in stark contrast with, but yet forms a calm resolution to, the turbulent and desolate emotions of the beginning. Jane has been happily married for ten years to Rochester, who has partially recovered his sight. They have a son who has inherited Rochester's 'own eyes'. Jane's cousins are happy and contented – Diana and Mary married to good men and St. John, a 'high master-spirit', unmarried but fulfilled. This contrasts strongly with the unhappy fate of Jane's cousins from the Gateshead days. Bettelheim observes that 'in the best fairy-tale tradition, the anxiety Cinderella's pitiful existence evokes in the hearer is soon relieved by the happy ending'.[32] It would seem that in *Jane Eyre* the same forces are at work; however, no happy ending is truly complete 'without the punishment of the antagonists'.[33] With this thesis in mind, Rochester's blindness is perhaps a symbolic representation of his oedipal blindness in seeking to marry Jane, a 'child-like figure' when he already has a existing wife, possibly representing the bad/mad mother whom Jane wishes to replace.

By the end of the novel, Jane's objects are restored, they have survived envious and destructive rage and attack, and the rejecting and cruel family of the first pages has been transformed into a warm supportive one, in which Jane holds a central place. Like 'Cinderella', *Jane Eyre* charts the child's 'greatest disappointments' – 'oedipal disillusionment, castration anxiety, low opinion of himself because of the imagined [and real] low opinion of others'.[34] These have been overcome by growing autonomy, maturity, and the ability to perceive that she can have, and create, good things too. Cinderella, at the story's end, is indeed ready for a happy marriage, as is Jane. In her immortal words 'Reader, I married him.'

I have attempted to link together, in a meaningful and accessible way, the strands of some ideas about sibling rivalry. Reading, researching, and writing the theory, literature, and some case material have been extremely valuable in my work, greatly increasing my understanding of the forces of envy and rivalry. It has also given me some fresh insight into the often precarious balance within the individual between the urge to create and the urge to destroy.

My enjoyment of this project – perhaps a reflection of my interest in both literature and psychodynamic understanding as a way of understanding human experience – was fuelled by my perception that at times these interests have been competitive. My first weeks on the counselling diploma course were marked by my anxiety about having chosen the 'right' course. I had had difficulty in turning down the offer of a place on a postgraduate English literature degree course. Perhaps there is a need in me at some level to resolve this 'sibling rivalry' by marrying my two 'favourite children' to each other! In considering the positive and creative aspects of sibling rivalry there is a hope that they could both gain a understanding of what they can offer each other, as well as a broadening and enriching of the other's experience by access to different, but equally valuable, resources and qualities.

It is from this perspective that I feel a thoughtful understanding of sibling rivalry and its origins is immensely important in the counselling relationship. The acknowledgement of the possibility of envious and rivalrous feelings in both counsellor and client, as well as in the material that the client brings, is essential in ensuring that the relationship is creative and therapeutic. The issue of the client feeling out of control or powerless in relation to the counsellor must be considered and explored, because this can affect the client's ability to 'use' what is on offer in the session, without being driven enviously to attack or destroy that which they cannot control. On reading over some of the case material, I found that there was much in both my own and my client's contributions that I had not previously understood. This reflects both the challenge and the satisfaction of this work, that often, at the very moment of understanding, there is a sudden awareness of unexplored depths of meaning still to be reached.

> Yet distant and soft the night-breeze is blowing,
> Clouds there are none, and clear stars beam mild;
> God, in His mercy, protection is showing,
> Comfort and hope to the poor orphan child.
>
> Charlotte Brontë, *Jane Eyre*

NOTES

1 S. Freud, *Introductory Lectures on Psychoanalysis*, ed. James Strachey and Angela Richards, *The Pelican Freud Library*, vol.1 (Harmondsworth: Penguin, 1976), p. 377.
2 Ibid.,p. 377.
3 J. Mitchell (ed.), *The Selected Melanie Klein* (Harmondsworth: Penguin, 1986), p. 3.
4 Ibid., p. 217.
5 Ibid., p. 218.
6 D. W. Winnicott, *Playing and Reality* (Harmondsworth: Penguin, 1988), p. 12.
7 B. Bettelheim, *The Uses of Enchantment* (Harmondworth: Penguin, 1986), p. 238.
8 *Genesis*, Chapter 4, v.9.
9 B. Bettelheim, op. cit., p. 237.
10 Charlotte Brontë, *Jane Eyre* (Oxford: Oxford University Press, 1991), p. 9.
11 Ibid., pp. 10–11.
12 Ibid., p. 15.
13 D. W. Winnicott, 'Fear of breakdown', in *The Independent Tradition*, ed. G. Kohon (London: Free Association Books, 1988), p. 179.
14 C. Brontë, op. cit., p. 15.
15 B. Bettelheim, op. cit., p. 238.

16 J. Mitchell, op. cit., p. 154.
17 Ibid., p. 154.
18 C. Brontë, op. cit., p. 28.
19 Ibid., p. 47.
20 Ibid., pp. 62, 67.
21 Ibid., p. 74.
22 N. Symington, *The Analytic Experience* (London: Free Association Books, 1986), p. 268.
23 C. Brontë, op. cit., p. 82.
24 Ibid., p. 130.
25 B. Bettelheim, op. cit., p. 246.
26 C. Brontë, op. cit., pp. 147–8.
27 A. Storr (ed.), *Jung: Selected Writings* (London: Fontana, 1983), p. 88.
28 C. Brontë, op. cit., p. 326.
29 Ibid., p. 333.
30 Ibid., p. 345.
31 Ibid., p. 444.
32 B. Bettelheim, op. cit., p. 249.
33 B. Bettelheim, op. cit., p. 273.
34 Ibid., p. 276.

BIBLIOGRAPHY

Balint, M. (1988) *The Basic Fault*, London: Tavistock.
Bettelheim, B. (1976) *The Uses of Enchantment*, London: Penguin, 1986.
Brontë, C. (1847) *Jane Eyre*, Oxford: Oxford University Press, 1991.
Freud, S. (1916–17) *Introductory Lectures on Psychoanalysis*, Harmondsworth: Penguin, 1976.
Kohon, G. (ed.) (1986) *The British School of Psychoanalysis: The Independent Tradition*, London: Free Association Books.
Kubler-Ross, E. (1970) *On Death and Dying*, London: Tavistock.
Mitchell, J. (ed.) (1986) *The Selected Melanie Klein*, Harmondsworth: Penguin.
Murray, C. M. (1972) *Bereavement*, Harmondsworth: Penguin, second edition 1986.
Noonan, E. (1983) *Counselling Young People*, London: Methuen.
Pincus, L. and Dare, C. (1978) *Secrets in the Family*, London: Faber.
Storr, A. (ed.) (1983) *Jung: Selected Writings*, London: Fontana.
Symington, N. (1986) *The Analytic Experience*, London: Free Association Books.
Winnicott, D. W. (1964) *The Child, the Family and the Outside World*, Harmondsworth: Penguin, 1976.
—— (1971) *Playing and Reality*, London: Tavistock; Harmondsworth: Penguin, 1988.
—— (1977) *The Piggle*, London: Hogarth Press; Harmondsworth: Penguin, 1989.
Yalom, I. D. (1985) *The Theory and Practice of Group Psychotherapy*, New York: Basic Books.

Chapter 11

James

Working with a stammerer

Barbara Rickinson

INTRODUCTION

This case study, taken from my case load as a university student counsellor, illustrates counselling processes based on psychodynamic principles.

Psychodynamic counselling aims to establish a relationship of unconditional care and acceptance. This relationship provides the security in which defences can be relaxed and underlying feelings faced and experienced. The balance between security and frustration is crucial. The student's capacity to bear the anxiety and pain of his true feelings must be assessed and monitored throughout the process, so that he can be put in touch with as much of his true feelings as he can accept.

David Malan[1] has described how 'changes in the level of rapport' are a barometer for estimating how appropriate a counsellor's intervention is at any given time.

In order to reach the true or 'hidden feelings' it is necessary to penetrate the 'defence' and the 'anxiety'. To understand the feelings exposed they must be traced back to their origin in the past, usually in the relation with parents.

Two triangles are used by Malan to represent the basic principles of psychodynamic therapy or counselling.

> The first may be called the triangle of conflict and consists of Defence, Anxiety and Hidden feeling. This is related to the second triangle by the fact that the hidden feeling is directed towards one or more categories of the triangle of person, namely Other, Transference, and Parent, represented by O, T and P respectively.

The aim of counselling 'is to reach the lower apex of the triangle of conflict, i.e. the hidden feelings, in relation to the lower apex of the triangle of person, i.e. parents, but for the most part the only route by which this can be reached effectively is via the transference and the T/P link'.[2]

I would like to present the case session by session, and then conclude by analysing how, in this particular case, the aim was achieved despite the difficulties experienced in establishing and maintaining the balance between security and frustration.

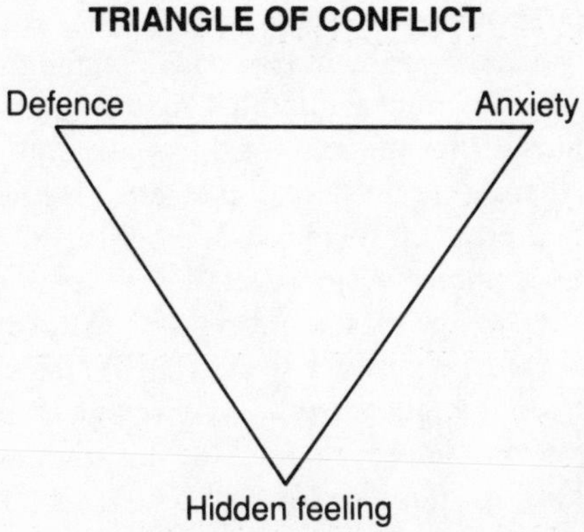

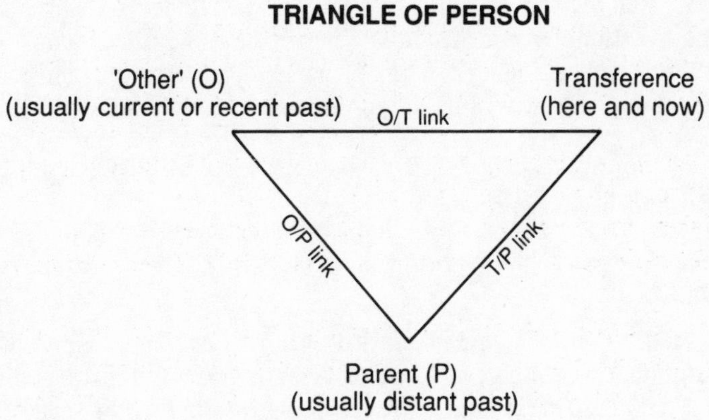

I would like to acknowledge James, colleagues in my case study group, and particularly my case study supervisor.

CASE STUDY

James, a fourth-year medical student, was referred by his tutor because of a long-standing stammer which was interfering with progress in medical school. James had four 'A's at A-level, and his exceptional academic ability was recognized by the school. He had been rejected at interview by two other medical schools before being accepted here, and he was very concerned about the possibility of his stammer hampering his qualification and future medical career.

His family history revealed that his mother lived alone following the death of his father, aged 47, when James was 14. His sister, two years his junior, was a student in fashion design. Father died of Hodgkin's disease.

James is a good-looking, well-built young man. He claimed to enjoy a social life, having friends who understood his stammer. He met his girl friend, an older woman and a qualified doctor, during his first year at university. He claimed that the relationship was good and volunteered the information that there were no sexual problems. He played rugby, and his stammer was only a problem socially when he was in a new situation.

The onset of his stammer occurred at age 6 when he was attempting to answer his name during the classroom register. Altogether he has received about eight years of treatment since then. This has included three courses of speech therapy, hypnosis, and various psychological techniques, but there was never any significant improvement. Now his stammer is most noticeable when he is speaking to more senior colleagues, and the more senior the worse the stammer. This affects performance on ward rounds and had reached crisis when his surgical viva had been abandoned because of uncontrollable stammering. James stated that he was 'fine when addressing patients', and the stammer was also less of a problem if he was in a position of responsibility such as being 'on take', particularly at night when few people were about. He was due to go on an intensive speech therapy programme soon.

I saw James for seventeen sessions, mostly once a week, but more frequently around his exam time.

First session

James presented a confident manner, with an air of eagerness and expectation. His stammer was slight, and he was keen to give a full history of the stammer and details of treatment with emphasis on the lack of success of previous treatment. I soon realized he was keen to give factual information but the moment I tried to shift the focus to emotional issues (Did you anticipate rejection at interview? how did you feel when you were rejected?, etc.), the stammer became much worse and communication was impossible.

I observed that the pattern of the stammer was a block to expressing feeling of any kind. When giving factual information James spoke in a clear, well-modulated voice.

The second and third interviews continued in a similar vein. James imparted the family and personal history listed above but stammered when I tried to elicit information concerning the nature, or quality, of relationships.

I observed during these two sessions that, though James was superficially cordial and co-operative, there was an intense underlying communication of anger and anxiety. I abandoned trying to reach him emotionally by verbal means and relied on non-verbal communication in an attempt to establish an atmosphere of trust and acceptance.

Fourth session

James's manner at the opening of this session displayed increased tension and suppressed anger.

I remarked that he appeared angry. He responded with a severe burst of stammering. He eventually recovered and said that he was angry with himself for wasting the time with me by stammering.

I said 'So you feel you have some control over whether you stammer or not?' He said that he had been given exercises and taught techniques but didn't practise them or use them. I asked why. He said that they didn't do any good. I asked whether he had sought speech therapy himself or whether his tutor had arranged it. He replied that it was his tutor, but he was glad that *they* were doing something about it. I said, 'They?', and remarked that he appeared to have taken a very passive attitude to treatment with his stammer and asked if he felt he had any power to help himself. In response he stammered badly and on recovery said he was pinning his hopes on the intensive speech therapy course in a few weeks' time. I explored the same theme with regard to counselling, and he said he was keen to have help. We made a contract to meet weekly during the term and review at the end of term.

Fifth session

I asked James how he felt. He replied that the stammer was no better. The pattern of the stammer, preventing emotional expression, continued during this session. At one of these breakdown points I gave him a paper and pencil and said 'Write down what the stammer is preventing you from saying'. We had been talking about his father's death and its effect on the family. James *wrote* with tense anger: 'when most boys are arguing/talking/playing with their father – I had little contact with him or other men and that is why it's worse with men. I have had my stammer since I was 6 and it has nothing to do with my father. My only problem is the stammer.'

As he wrote there was a strong communication of anger and grief, then an abrupt and complete 'switch off'. I was startled by the contrast between the intensity of the feelings one minute and the complete absence of all feeling the next. I felt James had employed a schizoid defence when faced with the threat of being overwhelmed by his feelings of anger and grief. He left with polite but vacant words.

In reviewing the session in my own mind I realized that I had confronted the defence before I had established a secure enough therapeutic alliance. I had reacted to my own frustration that it was going to be a long haul and we were making little progress, and to the external pressure from medical school requirements for James. I was conscious of my own inexperience in psychodynamic technique but felt that there had to be some dramatic intervention to shift James's entrenched position.

Presentation to case group

The discussion ranged around stammering and potency – the frustration/protection ambivalence of the stammer – the dangers of collusion with the defence if paper and pen were used routinely and, as had been experienced in this case, the importance of the therapeutic alliance.

The group supervisor reminded me that it was important, in every interpretation, to mention the protection afforded by the stammer as well as its frustration in regard to career prospects, i.e. his ambivalence about losing his stammer.

Sixth session

To my relief James arrived early for the next appointment. He talked about speech therapy and how he had been advised to stammer deliberately and observe other people's reaction – whether they were sympathetic, impatient, etc. He said his main fear was 'being laughed at' which reminded him of when he first stammered.

He then shared the full details of this early, painful experience. James, aged 6, was unable to say his name when the teacher called the register at school. His classmates laughed and pointed their fingers at him as he eventually stammered out his name. The teacher labelled him 'a stammerer' from that moment onwards.

I asked about his parents' reaction to the stammer. He said that his father wanted it cured and made him feel very guilty about it. His mother accepted it and protected him.

I took the opportunity to interpret the ambivalence in his desire to cure his stammer. James agreed.

I felt the relationship was more relaxed between us and that trust was being established at an underlying level. I was aware of the overwhelming quality of both his strength and his vulnerability.

I was also aware he was keeping control of the counselling sessions with his stammer and passivity. He kept the focus on the stammer at all times.

Seventh session

James arrived looking dishevelled, on crutches, with one leg heavily bandaged. His appearance and manner were in sharp contrast to his earlier carefully dressed, confident manner.

He told me the injury, which he described as very severe, was obtained playing rugby. I resisted his obvious plea for the 'sympathetic mother' response. He went on to say he hated rugby – the macho image – but felt it was what was expected by his peers.

He then talked about the intensive course which he had been on that weekend (as well as the rugby). He was very disappointed with it: 'It was to help people live with a stammer rather than cure it.'

He talked derisively about all the other stammerers and was frightened by the realization that he was a member of this group. He said that he experienced a feeling of 'weakness' when he had to speak aloud in the group.

I said that perhaps he was asking himself if *he* controlled the stammer or *it* controlled him.

He then talked about medicine and expressed ambivalent feeling about his desire to 'struggle on' – 'maybe he could sell antiques'. He also related an incident in which a fellow student had borrowed, and damaged, his car and then neglected to pay his fair share of the damage. James said he was very angry but described how he retaliated in an indirect way. As this student was also a tenant in James's flat he 'got his own back' by putting up the rent.

I said that I felt this incident illustrated the way he expressed his anger passively and it seemed this was the way he kept control in all areas of his life. His response was the usual stammer. I mentioned the ambivalence again in relation to the stammer.

Eighth session

James failed to come. I wrote my usual brief note acknowledging his absence and decided to check on his medical records (which I have access to as I am based in a health centre) in case there had been any complications with his leg injury. From these records I gained the following information:

1 James was adopted.
2 He had a history of recurrent illness of allergic nature, e.g. asthma in early childhood. The GP notes mentioned his weak, over-protective mother.
3 His current leg injury was not as serious as he had led me to believe.

The day before his next appointment James phoned and in response to my warm greeting stammered. I felt very helpless on the other end of the phone, unsure whether to speak or remain silent and wait. Eventually, after what seemed a long time, I said gently 'I hope to see you tomorrow.' I *think* he said 'yes' and then hung up.

Ninth session

James arrived like a small boy who had won a prize. He told me that he had done his presentation the previous afternoon, after grappling with the desire to get out of it, and felt very pleased with himself. He felt he had been in control of the stammer and it had not interfered as much as usual with his presentation; he felt he had gone up 'a whole level'. He then talked about how he really did want to do medicine very much, and it was only when he felt his stammer would make it impossible that he started thinking he might give it up.

I asked why he had not come to the previous session and he said he had 'forgotten it – I know it sounds silly but the truth is I can forget things'. I said, 'Yes, sometimes things are too painful to remember.'

He then spoke of an earlier occasion when he had been gardening at the local doctor's. His mother had come to collect him, and he overheard a conversation between her and the doctor concerning his father's illness and expected death. He remembered being shocked at this information and just 'forgot it'. After his father's death he remembered it again.

I was now confused because James, when relating family history, had said his father died suddenly with a heart attack; now he was talking about a chronic illness. I asked for clarification and was told that James had said that because it was 'easy'. People asked lots of questions in connection with his father and his stammer, and his father's death had nothing to do with the stammer. After all, he had had the stammer since the age of 6 – long before his father's death.

I asked what he remembered about family events around that time. Between stammering bursts he said he couldn't remember anything except what he had told me. He felt it was 'like a brick wall wrapped in tissue paper – I unwrap a bit of tissue and the brick wall remains – whatever people do'.

He said, 'Why don't you hypnotize me and find out what happened when I was 6? I don't know and can't remember. I want to know. Do you do hypnosis?'

I replied that I didn't, but I felt it was not just knowing the information that was important, but that he felt ready to face it. Perhaps what couldn't be faced at age 6 may not be so difficult now.

I asked about his sister and family matters – questions which would give him the opportunity to disclose his adoption if he knew about it. His replies indicated that he was oblivious of it.

There was a quality of suppressed anger throughout this session.

In reviewing the last few sessions I realised that what had been clearly illustrated had been James's anxiety about 'being out of control'. The only defence he knew against this was passive, negative control.

He wanted to do medicine very much but he wanted to do it on his own terms, without taking the risk of giving up his defence. Thus the resistance was very entrenched.

How could I help him to move from a passive negative position to an active positive one?

I didn't feel I had made much progress so far.

Presentation to case study group

The discussion centred on the following points:

1 The repetitive negative control, lack of concern for others, or any real relationship. The group felt that they had 'lost patience with him'.
2 The psychosomatic quality of his stammer.
3 The fact that he actually enjoyed a 'sick' identity.
4 The information concerning his adoption and what it might mean.

In digesting all this I felt that certainly the prognosis was poor, but having been with him I was aware of the vulnerability which lay below this negative defence pattern.

I decided that I must confront, and review where we were going, or I would be drawn into collusion with the negative defence and be of no use to James.

Tenth session

I greeted James with the suggestion that it was time for review – an assessment of progress, of what counselling could and could not offer, and what his expectations were.

He agreed, saying that he didn't feel we were getting anywhere. We were still no nearer to discovering what caused him to stammer or curing the stammer – it was no better.

I said I saw his stammer as a symptom but felt he saw it as his identity. I said there was no magic cure – I couldn't cure his stammer. I could offer him help for himself, to enable him not to need his stammer. I felt he had reached a crossroads and must make a choice. I was not interested in working with a symptom. If he could put his stammer aside, and separate from it, we could start work.

I felt the focus had to be not what had happened in the past, but what was happening now. Why did a good-looking, intelligent young man in his fourth year of medicine continue limiting his life in this way?

James was visibly stunned and said nothing, but he didn't switch off, nor did he show anger which I had expected.

I suggested that he think it over and we meet next week to decide about continuing counselling. I stressed that it was important that he come back and tell me his thoughts and feelings about what I had said.

James left abruptly, quiet and stunned. I was left with my feelings. I questioned what I had done, and the way I had done it, but it had seemed right at the time. I hoped my care for him was communicated with my confronting words.

Eleventh session

James arrived promptly for the next session and said that he had been shocked by what I had said and had spent some time feeling sorry for himself. However, he had then looked at his stammer in a new way. He felt that what I had said was true – he did have difficulty separating himself from his stammer and kept looking for a magic cure. He now realized that there was none. He felt it was like two pieces of wood stuck together and for the first time he was able to prise them apart, but the gap frightened him and made him feel very helpless.

He went on to talk about power. He said that he wanted to be powerful. He dreamt of being a famous surgeon or a powerful businessman, but he was afraid of being powerful also because he wanted to be liked. He related this to his medical experience. In the presence of people more powerful, especially consultants, he alternated between feeling very weak and helpless and sometimes very clever, cleverer than them but afraid to show it. He said that he hated being made to feel helpless, and would do anything to avoid that feeling. I said, 'So you use your power negatively to control people.' He said, 'Yes! That is the way my father controlled people – he used his illness to get attention . . . I didn't have much respect for him . . . he was weak. I now realize I am just the same. I thought my stammer was to blame for my weakness but now I feel it is the other way round.'

He was visibly upset and I shared his feelings non-verbally. I felt a close bond with him. He then said, 'I want it to be different, but I don't know where to start.'

I said gently that I felt he had started.

We then confirmed that we would continue the weekly sessions.

I felt it had been a good session and realized that it was the first session not disrupted by the stammer – in fact, James had not stammered once.

Twelfth session

James did not stammer in this session either but was very anxious. He talked in agitated terms about the forthcoming examinations and explained his anxiety in these terms. He had not suffered anxiety like this before previous exams. He usually took examinations in his stride, but he felt he didn't know enough, and so on. The level of his anxiety disturbed me, and I was not convinced that the examinations were the real cause. He had done exceptionally well in written examinations so far and his stammer should not be a problem here.

I concentrated on containing the anxiety and offered him an extra session later that week.

I was pleased to be able to present him to my case study group the next day as my anxiety level had risen.

Presentation to case study group

My concern at the level of anxiety was shared by the group and we discussed the possible roots.

The group was surprised by his reaction to my confrontation and the fact that he had stopped stammering, in the sessions at least. I was unsure, not having asked him, what was happening outside.

The group supervisor felt that the two pieces of wood had got put back differently and his anxiety was displaced on to exams. She also pointed out the omnipotence question – his feeling I must be the most powerful person he had met, and how helpless he must feel in the counselling situation.

I realized that in telling him I would continue counselling if he put his stammer aside I was not, as perceived, giving him unconditional care but placing a big fat condition on the care offered. We also discussed more appropriate ways of wording my challenge, to have the effect I desired.

I thought very deeply about perception and omnipotence after our discussion and feel the lesson will stay with me.

I realized I must address the issue, if possible, in the next counselling session and not only contain anxiety but explore the roots of it.

Thirteenth session

James arrived ten minutes late for his extra session. His manner was tense and resentful. He said, 'I haven't been stammering but I feel worse'. There was an underlying bitterness in his voice.

He went on to say that he was very angry about the pathology examination, which was to be faced the following Monday. He then launched into a long tirade against the medical school lecturers who were more interested in their own research than the students and 'expected too much'. Last year the questions on the pathology paper were outside anything they had covered in lectures and many people had failed. There wasn't time on a medical course to deal with all the input and to have something outside the lecture course was just unfair. It was more than they should be expected to cope with.

I asked how he had coped with the paper last year and he said he had done quite well – very well, in fact, but he didn't feel ready to face unfair demands at the moment. He was afraid he might fail, or worse, be borderline this year and then he would have to face an extra viva as well as the routine one he had to do.

He went on to say that the medical school lecturers 'made him sick'. They had no idea how difficult it was for students. They had the power, and you had to fulfil their requirements or you were 'out' and after all the effort 'you were still at the mercy of these consultants on the wards who hammered you every day and made you feel useless and inadequate'. There was an air of deep bitterness and resentment in his tone and manner, but the underlying vulnerability was there as well.

I said that, though there was some reality in his comments on the toughness of the medical course, I felt that he was displacing some of the bitterness he felt within the counselling relationship on to the examinations. I felt he was getting the test I had set him – to put aside his stammer – mixed up with his pathology exam. Perhaps he felt that I didn't understand how difficult it was for him to fulfil my requirements and that if he didn't he would be 'out' as far as I was concerned, and this made him feel angry and afraid.

He threw me a withering look of dismissal and said, 'I'm not afraid of *you.* You are just *trying* to do your job of curing the stammer which the medical school say I *have* to cure or I can't qualify, and I *want* to qualify as a doctor. I'm intelligent enough, but it takes all my energy to stop stammering. Who cares or understands how difficult it is?'

'James, I feel you are saying that in asking you to cope without your stammer I'm saying that I don't care about that part of you and that leaves you to face all the pain on your own.'

He replied, 'Yes! I want to stop stammering and you've shown me I can, but I'm finding it harder to keep control of myself so in fact I'm worse off. Sometimes *I wish I had never come near you.*'

The last sentence was uttered with such bitterness and hate that it took my breath away, and I registered shock I'm sure. There was a short silence and then, recovered, I said, 'Yes, I see you are very angry and I understand your feelings. However, I feel we must clarify a few things. I do care about all of you, but I was trying to make you realize that the stammer was getting in the way of communicating with you and hence we could make no progress. You have a lot to cope with at the moment in the form of exams but the written exams are an area that is unaffected by your stammer. You *mustn't* confuse the two.'

James became quiet and thoughtful and then said, 'Yes, I understand what you are saying. Last year I actually found the pathology exam a challenge and wasn't as affected by it as other people were.'

The session had run over time so I said 'good' and smiled, and James smiled back and seemed much more relaxed.

We then discussed a change of appointment for the next session because of his exam timetable.

Fourteenth session

James arrived and seemed calm and less bitter. I enquired how the pathology examination had gone that morning. He felt that though he may not have done as well as usual he had avoided the threat of a viva.

This focused on his main concern at the moment: the compulsory viva. He said thoughts of this were causing him to have nightmares from which he awoke in floods of tears.

I asked if he would like to talk about his dreams. He said that he didn't remember them all – they were very confused with people from his present life and people from his past, but he didn't want to talk or even think about them. He wanted to concentrate on his exams and preparing for his viva.

I respected his wishes and said nothing. I thought he was afraid of losing control and was not ready to face dreams or their associations at the moment.

The discussion continued with the focus on practical matters surrounding the viva. James explored his feelings about seeing his personal tutor, with whom he had an appointment the next day.

I asked him how he saw his relationship with his tutor. He said that his tutor had been very sympathetic and helped him all he could, but somehow he didn't want special help and would like to face up and do it himself. However, he was afraid that in fact he did need help and wasn't strong enough to cope on his own.

I asked if he thought his tutor was perhaps the sort of person who would understand his ambivalent feelings; it might help to talk to him, not asking for anything, but clarifying what the situation actually was regarding the viva.

James said he would do this and asked if he could have an appointment before his viva on Wednesday afternoon. We made an appointment for Wednesday morning.

Fifteenth session

James said he had talked at length to his tutor and found him very understanding and that he had remarked on the improvement in James's stammer. James had expressed his anxiety and ambivalence and felt understood.

The situation was that there were to be no special arrangements but the format of the viva was different to the previous year – only one person would do the initial viva and if things were okay that was it. If there were problems, a panel had to be faced.

James then told me a long story about going to the post office to get some stamps en route for his appointment with his tutor. He had to wait in a queue and was in a terrible hurry. He couldn't decide whether to abandon it, as he might be late for his tutor's appointment, or wait and post his mother's birthday card which would be late otherwise and upset her.

His frustration reached such a peak that when he got to the counter he couldn't speak and stammered uncontrollably at the girl behind the counter. She just stared at him but eventually asked if he wanted to post the letter in his hand. He felt like a baby but pleased she had worked out what he needed. So he posted the letter and ran all the way to his appointment.

Fortunately he found the tutor had also been delayed so he had time to collect himself. However, after that incident he felt unsure if he mightn't stammer in the viva; he felt it had put him back.

I realized there was much in the story but wasn't able to conceptualize and interpret it at that time. I was very aware also that the viva was looming.

I just said that I felt, even if he did stammer, he would be understood and, though I could feel he was afraid, I thought he could trust himself to contain his anxiety and cope. I wished him luck and said I would be keen to hear how he got on.

He phoned later that afternoon to say it was OK – he had stammered slightly initially but had settled down. He knew the area that he had been examined on well and so was very happy with the viva. He felt he had done better than ever before.

I shared his pleasure and congratulated him. He confirmed his appointment for the Friday.

Sixteenth session

James said that he felt very good after the viva but that night, after a few drinks, had gone to sleep and woken up in the early hours of the morning after a dream which had disturbed him ever since.

He hesitated, and I waited, hoping he would share his dream. He then said that he had been having lots of dreams about his father (stammering on the word father – as ever) mixed up with hospital consultants, and in the dream they were all pointing their fingers at him and laughing, saying that he was no good and he wouldn't make it in medicine. It was just like the class in primary school when he first stammered.

He then remembered having a conversation with his father when he was 6 in which his father told him he was adopted but then, frightened of what he had done, told him not to tell his mother because it would upset her and she couldn't cope.

He then woke up and was relieved. 'I remembered I am adopted and he is dead and it's all over – it doesn't matter – he is not my real father.'

I said, 'What is over?' He said, 'I don't have to keep the secret.' I said 'What secret?' He replied 'That I am adopted.' I asked who he had been keeping it secret from. 'Everyone!' he said.

I asked if he had known and thought about it himself or if it had been a secret from him also.

He said he thought he had known but had pushed it out of his thoughts. 'I've been afraid of it somehow. Why should I remember it now?'

I said gently, 'Perhaps you are ready to face your feelings about it now.'

He said sadly, 'I don't think I am.' He then broke down and wept with such grief I wanted to forget I was a counsellor and put my arms round him.

However, I shared his grief silently and he left when he had recovered.

Seventeenth session

James said that he felt better after the last session but was having trouble digesting all that was happening.

His manner was buoyant and confident. He had passed his exams including the viva and had no further problems.

He then told me the big news that he was to go on 'elective' to Australia, which, of course, meant it was 'all over' and he was sure to qualify. He said 'You are Australian, aren't you?' I confirmed that I was and then came a flood of excited questions about Australia.

I was afraid of being drawn into a personal discussion and asked when he was going on this 'elective'. When he told me the date I received a shock. I said I hadn't realized it was so soon, and we would have to look at the diary to see about counselling appointments.

We got the diary and realized that, with his being away and my Easter break, there was time for only one more appointment before he left.

I think at this point I was not in control of the session: I found myself in an ending I hadn't prepared for.

He became very upset at the idea that I wouldn't be there over Easter as he had arranged to work in the children's hospital and imagined I would be there for his appointments.

He then became very angry and said he didn't think it was worth coming for one appointment and stormed out.

I wrote a note saying what day I would be back in the health centre and sent it to his term-time address.

I didn't hear any more till the day before his departure for Australia. He phoned and said he was sorry for his behaviour and could he come back to counselling on his return from Australia?

We had a warm conversation and I wished him luck.

As these five sessions were so close together I have decided to review them together and make my conclusion following the final case presentation to my group.

Presentation to case study group

I shared my ambivalent feelings with the group. I was pleased that James had been enabled to reach a position in which he could express anger and grief. However, I was disappointed that the last session had been so confused and that we did not have the opportunity to work with the feelings surrounding his adoption and the end of our sessions.

I was pleased and relieved that he had qualified (or was sure to now) and was taking a risk on going such a long way away. I just wished the timing had been better.

The case group supervisor felt productive work had been done. She pointed out areas where I could have made useful interpretations and clarified the difficulties of the last session.

She felt James was looking for 'a home' and asking about Australia was asking 'Could he come into mine?' She suggested that this would be the possible focus of further work.

CONCLUSIONS

I'd like finally to refer back to the ideas presented at the beginning of the case study, to relate them specifically to the sessions with James.

The relationship

Establishing a good therapeutic relationship with James was difficult. He was used to eliciting the care and attention he desired by displaying a 'sick' identity. Thus he retained control and avoided the risk of being rejected and feeling helpless. Trust was a risk to his survival.

It was essential to resist his control and yet offer him the experience of unconditional love. As the sessions illustrate, maintaining the balance was a constant struggle.

In the end the relationship was good enough to withstand a negative transference, allowing him to face and express his true feelings.

The triangle of conflict

In the last five sessions the *'defence': stammer* was penetrated, exposing the *'anxiety': fear of losing control*, and the *'hidden feelings': anger, grief, and helplessness* were reached and expressed within the transference relationship.

The triangle of person

The confrontation in Session 10 paved the way for James's acknowledgement in Session 11 of his identification with his despised 'weak' father, which he had so far vehemently denied. This was all the more moving because it connected with his own ambivalence: his 'weakness' stood in the way of his own development, whereas before he had felt that others' inability to recognize the pain behind his stammer hindered his progress. Dreams confusing the past and present began then, culminating in the dream related in Session 16, when James associated his dream of the laughing and pointing hospital consultants with the class in his primary school when he first stammered. This led on to his linking his stammer with 'not being able to say his name' and his father telling him he was adopted. This was the critical Other–Parent link which released 'the secret'.

Meanwhile, by Session 13, his hurt, rage and hatred could no longer be contained, and it spilled out in relation to his lecturers. By making the Therapist–Other link, and bringing into our relationship his feelings about my 'unreasonable' demands and threat of rejection if he didn't meet them, we were able to experience and talk about them directly – and to survive them between us in all their intensity. The final Therapist–Parent link came in Session 16 when the anger, helplessness, and grief experienced in the transference relationship with me were derived from his relationship with his parents and the 'unthinkable' thoughts about his adoption. His desire for me to be his perfect, strong, non-rejecting parent was expressed in the last session but, unfortunately, not fully understood by me at the time. His expectation that I would be there for him, regardless of my needs, indicated the extent of his need and desire for constant care.

I failed him without having the opportunity to work through the failure with him. I hope we have the opportunity, on his return from Australia, to focus on this failure, link it with the past and thus understand it.

David Malan reminds us of Winnicott's phrase that

> the function of the therapist is not to succeed but to fail. Where a major part of the patient's problem consists of loss, deprivation, or unfulfilled love, it is the therapist's task not to try to make this up to the patient – which is impossible – but to enable him to experience his true feelings about it, and to pass through them and come out on the other side.[3]

I sincerely hope James will 'come out on the other side'. I feel that coming into 'my home' in Australia will help. This, of course, is *my* countertransference.

POSTSCRIPT

James has since graduated and is pursuing his medical career without the interference of his stammer.

NOTES

1 D. H. Malan, *Individual Psychotherapy and the Science of Psychodynamics* (London: Butterworths, 1979).
2 Ibid., p. 93.
3 Ibid., p. 193.

Chapter 12

The man no one wanted to see

Maya Jarrett

In the organization where I worked, my job as a counsellor involved seeing people who come to seek help because they couldn't manage on their own.

Psychodynamic counselling for me means to be aware of what each client brings in their unique and particular history to the session. No matter how bizarre this external reality may look, psychodynamically I have to be aware and to 'see' beyond this, which means working with the unconscious to get in touch with the inner feelings they bring to the session, to try to understand the best way I can how they may be feeling, and at the same time be able to maintain a distance. It also means that I don't reassure, give advice or have any physical contact, and I maintain boundaries.

For this present case study I will present my client Mr D, whom I saw under a new scheme that offered clients six months' short-term in-house counselling.

Mr D, a 56-year-old man, approached my agency after having been passed on from agency to agency where he had sought help. The last agency had told him after an assessment that he could not benefit from counselling and gave him our address as a last resort. He arranged an assessment after a phone call saying very little, apart from the fact that he needed some help.

H, the assessment officer, saw Mr D on one occasion for an hour. Mr D presented himself with a letter of introduction written by a woman friend of his which started: 'To whom it may concern, This case has been the sick helping the sick, D has an incurable neurological illness, hospital help is scarce and the breakdown he has been going through has gone unnoticed. His mother's death was a severe blow.' And at the end of the letter: 'I hope you will take care of him and help a forgotten member of our society.'

Mr D was a disturbing person to see. The way H described him to us later in the group was: 'He was all over the place with symptoms corresponding to his illness, "Giles Tourette Syndrome", which is a chemical deficiency in the brain that made him twitch and jerk out of control. He also swore, turning his head to the side and looking over his shoulder.'

In the assessment he explained that he wanted to go back to work. He had worked most of his life until his mother's death three years previously. He talked about his inability to communicate and make friends, leading a very isolated life, and feeling extremely angry about specific things such as black people, young people, and Greeks. He talked monosyllabically and H felt the same as the previous agencies, that Mr D wouldn't be a candidate for counselling.

Under this scheme our rules stated that, after an assessment, the notes taken would be brought to the counselling section group, so each of the members could come up with ideas and a conclusion for H to follow up in a second assessment of the client. In Mr D's case, however, no one knew where else to refer him. Some of us felt angry about this client being passed on like an object from place to place and wanted this to stop. Others felt we shouldn't 'touch' him as he seemed more suited for a long-term scheme, which was something we used to operate some time ago but were unable to continue because of lack of funds. As a result no decision was reached, and we left it for a second meeting.

During this time, Mr D constantly rang the office asking about the outcome of the assessment.

In our second meeting we took the fact that Mr D had rung up several times into consideration; I felt this was a sign of some ego strength in Mr D. H felt that we could focus on helping Mr D to return to work. No one wanted to see Mr D. All of us felt scared by this image of a very angry man with such a strange and awful illness. Impulsively I decided to volunteer because of the last lines in the letter of introduction. Once this decision had been made, my agency also decided that Mr D could benefit from its new development, of helping clients with counselling, housing, and employment problems altogether. In a way I was forced to accept that Mr D was also going to have another person to deal with, i.e., specific help from the employment officer.

According to our procedure, my office wrote a letter to Mr D offering him six months' counselling starting from the date of our first meeting and asking him to confirm this. As all of this was happening during the summer period, I had already booked two weeks' holiday that I was going to take after only three sessions with Mr D. I felt a lot of the pressure of having to accommodate these six months' counselling within the limited period I had before my redundancy (the project was closing because of lack of funds).

I had at my disposal a good counselling room and could be flexible with its use. It was a small room with an attractive arched window through which plenty of light came and in summer afternoons gave the room a warm glow. The two large black comfortable swivel chairs face one another and there was a small table in the corner. A clock on the wall was visible to both people. On the whole it was a very contained warm room. I particularly liked the swivel chairs that gave the clients the chance not to face the counsellor directly if they didn't feel they wanted to. This setting gave me a lot of confidence and security in working with clients.

The first day I was to meet Mr D, I felt very apprehensive and anxious, with lots of regrets about my impulsiveness in offering myself as the counsellor. I imagined Mr D to be some kind of a monster, an awful and aggressive man. I clung to the small hope that he might not turn up after all although he had confirmed that he was coming. I was due to see him at 4 p.m. and he arrived at 2.20 p.m. I received a call from reception, with the receptionist saying 'He's here, he's here!' I went out to greet him and the moment I saw him in a corner of our waiting area we made eye contact and I knew everything would be all right.

I think that Mr D must have felt similarly to how I was feeling before the meeting as, after this brief moment, we shook hands when I introduced myself, and my anxiety disappeared.

He was a sturdily built man with lovely green eyes that seemed warm and full of expectation, almost like a baby's eyes. I noticed how much effort he was making in trying to control the twitching and jerking by the way he held himself tightly, his arms close to his body. He was trying to keep eye contact even when he muttered to his side and over his shoulder.

I explained to him that our meeting was at 4 p.m. and that he could wait for me at the reception area or in the small corner area that we used as a waiting-room. He could also have some tea if he wished. He said he knew he was early but he didn't want to be late for our first meeting and he had brought a paper to read while he waited.

When we started the session I explained to him for how long we were going to meet, the two breaks that I was going to have, the first in three weeks' time and the second at Christmas time. He said he would like me to write all these dates for him as he might not remember them later on.

I felt perhaps I was overwhelming him with the strictness of my schedule due to my own pressures. In different circumstances I would not have started seeing a client only to have a break so near the start when it is crucial to establish a continuity and a good relationship.

During this time Mr D was gesticulating, winking, and sticking out his tongue; he continually kept rearranging the hair that covered some baldness at the front of his head. At times he jerked so much that the chair he was sitting on moved with him and I began to feel uneasy about the diminishing space between us. I felt I needed the space for me to maintain a distance that would allow me to work with Mr D.

From the assessment I knew that Mr D's mother had died three years ago, that his father had died thirteen years ago and that he had two brothers, an older brother living in the North and a younger brother with whom Mr D kept in regular contact. He also had a woman friend who helped him by writing his letter of introduction. The family were farmers.

When I asked how I could help Mr D, he answered saying that he was very lonely and 'very, very angry' and that his anxiety was so strong that it was like a bad pain in his stomach. I believe that the word 'anxiety' was being used by Mr D after his assessment at other agencies as I don't think he knew what it really meant. The important thing was that now he was able to put a name to the feeling in his stomach.

MJ: What do you feel angry at? [pause] Any ideas?
Mr D: Young people mostly, I hate them. . .I don't know why.
MJ: How were you as a young man?
Mr D: Ill most of the time [pause], I can't remember [long pause].
MJ: So you have a good reason to hate young people because when you were young, you were too ill to enjoy it.
Mr D: That's very true [looking at me, quite surprised]. I was very ill [pause]. No one knew what was wrong with me [this last sentence barely audible].

Little by little he told me about his illness, how he was in and out of hospitals between the ages of 3 and 20. At the age of 21 he left home. He was born in a small village and the 'stupid' doctors didn't know what was wrong with him. They gave the family different advice. One doctor told the family that he needed lots of looking after, love, toys, and the family did this for a time. Another doctor said that he needed a good lesson in learning to behave, and the family punished him and locked him in the chicken coop.

MJ: Who did this to you?
Mr D: My older brother, locked me inside for hours and hit me and poked me with a stick through the wire. I was the village idiot.
MJ: How did you feel when all of this was happening? [pause] How do you feel about your brother – the one that did all these things to you?
Mr D: Nothing really, I forgave them all.
MJ: How about the doctors?
Mr D: I was very angry with them [pause] I feel angry now, I feel very angry.
MJ: You have good reason to be angry.

He looked at me, surprised, and I felt that he understood[1] what I was trying to say. There was a long pause. I asked him if he could tell me a bit more about his childhood. He said that he remembered very little apart from the memories of his brother punishing him, and then he went on to describe the times he enjoyed best, when he was working, when he had 'mates and girlfriends' and had money to take girls out and buy them presents. I asked him what job he did and he answered 'driving heavy lorries with merchandise.' I was taken aback and I asked how he controlled his illness while he drove. He looked at me and smiled and said something like: 'You won't believe this but it doesn't happen when I'm driving.'

When his mother died three years ago he let the time pass by and didn't renew his driving licence but had done so since and wanted to get back to work. He had very high expectations about work. I explained that I would put him in contact with a colleague of mine who specifically dealt with employment. I also made a note to tell my colleague about these unrealistic expectations. We talked again about his loneliness, having no friends and not being able to communicate very easily. I said that maybe he was having the same problem in communicating with me.

Mr D: I have no problem speaking with you, I like it, I feel angry against young people.

I said that maybe he was angry with me as I was younger than him.

Mr D: No, I don't think so, I don't hate you. You will help me.

At the end of the hour he was very grateful and very keen to come back.

When I started writing my notes I felt extremely sad for Mr D and what he had told me, almost trying to forget the very angry man that he also was. I think this had to do with my feeling frightened about his anger and my reservations about my own capabilities for working with anger. My reservation about involving someone else from the office was that we were going to invite unnecessary splitting of the client's problems, and I decided to cope with it by having very close links with my colleague in the employment section. We arranged a system where, any time Mr D needed to see my colleague, she and I would have a talk first and clarify what was going to happen, what information was going to be given and to make sure my relationship with Mr D was formal and had boundaries different to the relationship he would have with the employment office.

I thought a lot about the attachment Mr D would form with me as he was a very lonely man. I felt a bit scared about this. The following week I felt even more concerned when Mr D arrived again fifty minutes early. He looked a different man. He was wearing a smart grey suit and strikingly noticeable socks which I thought were a bit young-looking for a man of his age. He had a smart haircut, kept in place with Brylcreme. I felt he had made all this effort for me. This transformation was both comic and tragic, simply in the way he had been deeply affected by just one meeting with someone.

Also there was the way he looked at me and told me that after our first meeting he felt 'so good' that he walked for an hour and a half on his way home. He stopped at a pub to have a drink and went home happily feeling he had had 'a full day.' I also realized that whatever we talked about in that first meeting had helped him in this change. I thought to myself, 'I hope we carry on like this', and almost immediately another thought overwhelmed me, 'this is a one-off situation and things will get worse.'

In the second session he told me about his friend A, the one who had written the letter of introduction, how she had urged him to seek help and had convinced him that all his problems could be solved if he could find someone to talk to, which made me think that he also had big expectations or unrealistic expectations of me, along the same lines as he did about finding a job.

He also talked about another girlfriend, B, and referred to her as 'a thorn in my flesh' and he said he loved her like a brother. She turned out to be a woman he met fourteen years ago when she approached him asking him for money near a tube station. She had a long-standing alcohol problem and Mr D 'adopted' her and has looked after her since then, giving her money, buying clothes for her, accepting her sudden disappearances and subsequent reappearances that usually occur at four or five in the morning after a weekend. This relationship caused Mr D to be taken to court by one landlord, with him finishing up in a bed and breakfast, as he used to give his key to B when he was away working. Eventually he was rehoused in a council flat.

When I asked why B couldn't go back to her own place I learnt that she lived in a hostel where she wasn't allowed in if drunk. B used Mr D and his place to sober up. Mr D used B as an excuse for not being able to work, saying something like: 'Where would I leave her the keys?' He also said: 'She is family, I cannot leave her now, I'll never leave her.' He described B in a very sensuous way, petite, fragile, pretty, thin, very different to his description of A, the other friend, as strong, big. I suppose this could also apply to the way he saw me during the months we worked together.

We arrived at the third session, the one before my two weeks' holiday and our first break. He arrived twenty minutes early and said he felt very low that morning when he woke up but had felt better later on remembering that he was to come to see me.

Mr D: Nothing much about this week, quiet and lonely, I called A and saw B, gave her £10, she needed food. [long silence]

I reminded him that we were going to have two weeks without a meeting and maybe that had something to do with feeling low in the morning and quite lonely already. There was a long silence. He talked about maybe going to visit his younger brother in Brentwood and although he was looking forward to this, as this brother had always been kind to him, he was apprehensive about the woman who lived with the brother. He said that the brother used to understand more about his illness and be more patient with him. I was thinking how this could be related to our break: not having me, he was going to find someone else who could listen to him and understand him, but there was also this woman who made him feel uneasy. However, I didn't have any space to say anything as he immediately continued saying:

Mr D: I want to talk about my anxiety, where does it come from? I felt angry last night against the people in the pub, they were all happy, all enjoying themselves, while I was miserable in a corner, why? why?

MJ: Perhaps you are trying to tell me how miserable you are because I'm going away for two weeks, that I will be happy and I'm leaving you in a corner. . .you are also telling me how angry you are with me. [He looked directly at me.]

Mr D: Sometimes I think the anger shows in my face very clearly and I even insult people under my breath, like 'stupid.' . . . Maybe that's why people attack me sometimes. . .like when I was 12, the teacher sent a letter to my parents telling them not to send me to school any more.

MJ: Why?

Mr D: Teachers felt the other kids were not learning, constant fights, they said I was distracting them, and they took the piss out of me constantly.

MJ: So you were punished, you needed more support but were sent away.

Mr D: Yes, but I taught myself to read and write and when I was 16 I used to take the family car without their knowledge and learned to drive. Now my brother has a new car and he allows me to drive it, you know what they called me in my job?. . .the Twitch, that hurt very much.

Mr D carried on, saying that two weeks seemed too long and things like, 'Look after yourself; when are you coming back? Write it down for me.' I wrote in my notes afterwards 'difficult goodbye.' This whole session reminded me of the writing of John Bowlby and the Robertsons, talking about protest – when the child does everything in his power not to be abandoned by the mother.

I felt that Mr D was experiencing this early separation in a very traumatic way; as well as his attachment to me there was the painful abandonment of the mother's death, the many times he must have been left in hospital.

I also felt extremely angry against my organization for putting me under pressure to accommodate such a client in a very tight time schedule, and it was very difficult to remember that I had volunteered to see him. The anger I was feeling was also the anger that Mr D had been feeling towards me for abandoning him. His anger was apparent in the session but also his worry that once I noticed his anger I would retaliate and attack him or, worse still, not ever come back to see him.

After our two weeks' break Mr D arrived, for the first time, five minutes late, saying that, although he had remembered first thing in the morning that he was coming back to see me today, it had taken him a long time to get ready and he had left his home much too late. (I'd like to explain here that Mr D made an hour's bus journey to come to see me. He used to leave his house three hours before our appointment.)

It was a very silent session. He talked monosyllabically, saying things like: 'Good time with my brother, four days there, happy to see me, common in law wasn't' (his word for the woman of the house).

He became a bit more lively at the end of the session when he talked about his wish to buy a car with some money that was left to him in a trust by his mother, and the younger brother was ready to help him. Although it sounded a good idea, I was left with the feeling that Mr D was saying, 'If only I could get a car, everything would be all right.' I also thought that having a car would mean that he would be in control and would possess something that wouldn't be abandoning him, unlike his experience of our break.

We started to work with his loss, talking about his mother's death, his father's death, and going into his own kind of death when he became ill and the many losses he experienced from then onwards, school, friends, etc.

We worked with his anger, most of the time finding clear reasons why he felt angry, like his anger towards young people, as I explained before, his anger towards black people (on a few occasions he had been attacked by some), but here also he started to realize that, in fact, it wasn't black people that he hated but young aggressive people. He was a church-going man, attending twice-weekly Bible readings where most of the other church-goers were black people but of a similar age to him and he never felt threatened by them. His specific hate of Greek people came from his rejection by them in their cafés on the road where he had tried to get a meal while working as a lorry driver; on a few occasions he had been shouted at in Greek. Hearing all this, I could also see how Mr D used to split his anger and project it onto specific areas which had good foundations, showing me how much anger he carried in himself and how scared he must have felt about it.

The changes that occurred in his life were very noticeable: first, he came to terms with his own limitations in respect of finding a job as a lorry driver. He bought and sold a car in the space of a weekend, saying that, while he was driving, he didn't enjoy it at all and it was nothing like what he remembered. He started considering voluntary work as a way of learning to communicate and talk to people. He started cooking his own meals for the first time in his life, and the major change was that in one of our sessions we talked about Christmas and he told me how lonely he felt, especially on Christmas day when everyone seemed to be involved in some kind of celebrations, and at this particular Christmas time he also had to cope with my second break. I told him how some boroughs organize Christmas lunch and that maybe he could look into it. Although this break we had was not just two weeks but four, due to my becoming ill, he coped with it and found a church where he spent Christmas day having drinks and food and, although he didn't communicate with people, he stayed with them.

When he first started to come to the office, he used almost to hide himself in a corner of our waiting-room or in the gentlemen's toilet, but gradually he started going into the reception area, talking with people and shaking hands with them, and he developed a good relationship with my colleague from the employment section.

He never once failed to come and I used to imagine that on Wednesday, the day we used to meet, his whole day was taken up by our appointment at 4 p.m. Although this had a lot to do with his lonely life, I also felt he took in a lot of what used to happen during our sessions. Some sessions were very quiet, when he was monosyllabic and used to say: 'I want to talk about my anxiety, I want to talk about my anger' and, no matter what I said he used to respond: 'That's it.'

I didn't really know how to interpret this except perhaps as a signal to me not to pressurize him into talking, into finding deeper levels of his anger. He used to recline happily in the chair and just be there.

Halfway through these six months I attended a lecture about his illness given by an American psychiatrist and, although the lecture was geared towards research into this illness in children, I understood Mr D's passion and commitment to his job, as in the lecture it was stated that people with this illness have to find something in life to hold onto. I also realized that Mr D was one of the lucky ones compared with how I used to see him before, as he had had that commitment and had found it by himself. Perhaps as a result of this lecture my work with Mr D changed, as I saw him as quite strong in his own way and I myself didn't feel so hopeless about what would happen to him when our sessions ended.

I will now describe our last session.

Mr D arrived only five minutes early, looking smartly dressed, with a good haircut, and I saw he had a box of chocolates under his arm.

Mr D: How are you? Our last week [silence]. I was nearly late today.

MJ: Why?

Mr D: Traffic. [pause]

MJ: I remember how in the beginning you used to be here at least an hour earlier.

Mr D: Yes [pause]. . .very difficult to come today.

MJ: Today is our last day.

Mr D: Yes [pause] sad, isn't it?

MJ: Yes. [long silence]

Mr D: What are you going to do?

MJ: You seem concerned about what I am going to do, but I think you are more preoccupied with what you are going to do.

Mr D: Yes, that's it [silence]. You'll be all right, won't you?

MJ: Yes, but what about you? Will you be all right? [pause]

Mr D: [looking at me intently] Mmm. . . . What do you think?

MJ: I think you'll be sad and also very angry.

Mr D: Yes, that's it, sad [pause] sad [pause]. Yes, that's it. . .the anger has changed, you know. . . it's nothing like before. It's not here any more [signalling his stomach]. I get angry sometimes, but it goes after a while.

MJ: We talked about your anger and your anxiety these past six months.

Mr D: The anxiety. . . Yes [pause] that has gone [pause]. . . . I've forgotten. . . . Why do you think it's gone?

MJ: Perhaps because we have talked about what made you anxious, like when you told me how anxious you felt with young people.

Mr D: Yes, that's it. Maybe now I know why I get angry, I don't feel anxious, well not as much.

MJ: [pause] I think now you are a bit anxious.

Mr D: [looking at me with a smile] Mmm. . . . [silence] It's sad, isn't it? Sad, no more money, all of this will disappear, no more.

MJ: I am the one disappearing [silence]. Maybe it feels like everything is disappearing because, although I know you need me, I am abandoning you.

Mr D: Yes, that's it, yes sad, six months, so quickly [looking at me intently] passed very quickly, hasn't it [pause]. . .feels like the time you got ill, remember? I didn't come here for how many weeks?

MJ: Four weeks.

Mr D: Yes, but it's not the same, is it?

MJ: Yes, at the time, you knew that I was coming back to see you again, now it's our final meeting.

Mr D: Yes [silence]. The anger is not the same. . . .

MJ: How is it now?

Mr D: Feeling sad [silence]. Do you think I've improved?

MJ: What do you think?

Mr D: Let's see, I cook now, found the church for the morning coffee, the Christmas lunch, I found that. . . . I went to my brother for the New Year.

MJ: Lots of changes.

Mr D: And I have come here every week, I haven't been ill.

MJ: I was the one failing to come to see you.

Mr D: Do you think I should go to the new place tomorrow?

MJ: What do you think?

Mr D: Maybe I'll go next week. I'll miss you [pause]. It will be different [pause][looking at the clock]. . .time has passed so quickly.

MJ: Yes, hardly any time to say goodbye.

Mr D: Yes, that's it.

MJ: You asked me earlier if I thought you had improved, I think you have. I'm seeing the change now, here. I also know that you are a very capable man. You have managed all these years with a difficult illness and I admire you for that [pause]. I will remember you.

Mr D: Will you?

MJ: Yes, I will remember you [long pause].

Mr D: It's nearly time. Do you like the chocolates?

MJ: Yes, thank you very much [pause]. It's time.
[We shook hands]

Mr D: Thank you, thank you, I'm going to reception to say goodbye to everybody.

Later on I found out that he also told my colleague in charge of employment to look after me.

This last session was just enough time for us to say goodbye. The previous week I had given Mr D the address of the place I was referring him to. When he asked me 'Do you think I should go to. . .', I felt like saying 'Yes go there immediately', but also thinking 'I hope he doesn't go yet'. I felt it was important for Mr D to have some experience of our final goodbye.

His sadness was clear in the session and different from the feelings he had about the previous separation due to my illness when he knew we were going to meet again, because this time it was final. He also talked about his anger and he felt it was a bit more manageable now. When he said: 'All of this will disappear', referring to my own disappearing, I thought that maybe he was imagining that the whole of the building was going to disappear. His loneliness and his insecurity about how he would feel after this final session was also clear when he asked me if I would be all right. At the same time he more or less enumerated the improvements of the last six months, clearly reminding me that I was the one that 'failed' in our contract when he said he hadn't been ill, and checking to see if I remembered exactly how many weeks I wasn't able to see him.

This short-term counselling period taught me a lot about working with a person to whom, at the beginning, you cannot see the point in offering counselling and whom you think could benefit only from long-term support. Although he did go from my agency to another agency, a day centre, this transition can be seen as a step forward for Mr D.

Many areas of Mr D's disturbances I didn't even approach, e.g. his problem with girlfriends, sexual problems, and deeper levels of his anger.

I can clearly divide my way of working with Mr D into two stages: the three months previous to the lecture and the three after. In this first three months I felt hopeless, feeling that I had very little time to do anything and that I couldn't manage the strong pressure that my colleague from employment was putting on me: she wanted me somehow to get the message to Mr D that his job expectations were too high, that I should suggest different jobs, voluntary work, for example. My attending the lecture changed this; it made me acknowledge that Mr D had managed, against all odds, to find something in life to hold onto, that he had had and maintained a job for most of his life, long before he met me, and once I acknowledged this I felt I had found some strength within myself, to work a bit better perhaps.

In the weeks previous to our finishing I worked hard to find a suitable agency that could accept Mr D. I think the urgency I felt was more to do with my own desperation, that I didn't want Mr D to be left with nothing afterwards. Maybe this was parallel to what I was facing myself, imminent redundancy, so for whom did I really do this referral? For Mr D's benefit or myself?

As a last point I want to say that Mr D's illness changed dramatically during the six months, but I can only refer to the hour-long sessions we had; I would like to imagine this change was happening outside but I can only speculate. From the jerking and restless person I met, there were times when he hardly moved at all, and if he did I didn't notice it, apart from the occasional times when he would quickly bend as if picking up something from the floor. The facial gesticulations were greatly reduced. The major change was in the shouts to the side which were simply not there at the end.

As a kind of conclusion, I'd like to add that as a beginner in this short-term counselling I learnt a very important point and that was not to be carried away with my own omnipotence as I was with this client, imagining that I was the only help he would ever find and almost forgetting that this 56-year-old man had lived those years without me.

The loneliness and isolation that Mr D brought to the sessions affected me in such a deep way until I started to separate what belonged to the client and what belonged to me, as I had experienced those feelings myself, being an immigrant in this country. Looking back, this is the most important point I learnt.

NOTES

1 What I mean is that I had been very concerned and influenced by what I had heard about Mr D not being a suitable candidate for counselling, but, when I responded to him with some kind of interpretation, I felt (putting it simply) that he understood the rules of the game, i.e. counselling.

Name index

Subject index